A Sharecropper's Daughter

A Sharecropper's Daughter

A Sharecropper's Daughter

Lenora McWilliams

Published by Cold Run Creek Media

A Sharecropper's Daughter

© 2019 Lenora McWilliams

ISBN 978-1-7333997-0-8

Photo page 68 by Lewis W. Hine, Yale University Art Gallery, public domain.
https://commons.wikimedia.org/w/index.php?curid=14573531
Photo page 118 by Lee, Russell, public domain, Library of Congress Catalog:
https://lccn.loc.gov/2017877606Image
All other photos property of the author.

Dedication and Memoirs

"To God be the glory. Great things He has done."

To my loving husband of sixty-six years, John L McWilliams (Sugar-Daddy) for his faithful support.

To our only daughter, Margie McWilliams Johnson, who lives the closest and graciously volunteered to type this book for me. She retired as a nursing home administrator and loves being a stay-at-home grandmother.

Our older son, John Daniel McWilliams, has been helpful building this book. He is a science professor at Oklahoma Baptist University, and has written a few books, also.

Gary Damon McWilliams, our younger son, lives in Caddo Gap, AR. He has been an avid supporter of this creation from the "git-go". He is known on YouTube and his website <u>farmhandscompanion.com</u> as Pa Mac. He has written many non-fiction books.

Finally, I say to my eleven grandchildren and thirteen great-grandchildren, thanks for sharing your parents with me.

1

Pleasant memories flooding my mind, bringing peace, joy, and life into a tired, aching body. I'm praying that God will see fit for me to always recall the happenings and sayings of yesteryear! I can easily bring the sound of my daddy's voice to mind as well as those of the five siblings that I knew. However, the voice of my mother is erased somehow. She spoke softly and infrequently I know…

I was the youngest of the eight children she bore. All were live births. The second baby, James Roy was born with a cleft palate, but no external deformity. He simply had no roof in his mouth. After two surgeries in Little Rock that were unsuccessful in correcting the problem, Mama and Daddy chose to bring him back home. He had been in a charity hospital for two months without family close by. The only communication with the doctors had been by letters, which were two weeks old when they arrived. U. S. mail was very slow, and there were no telephones in our world at that time. Roy didn't even recognize his own parents when they went to get him. How convenient are email and texting today!

Roy was the only baby born prematurely, weighing about two or three pounds. He was unable to nurse, so he was patiently fed with a medicine dropper until he was able to take food independently. He has reached the ripe old age of ninety-one and is heartily enjoying his meals at Hillcrest Nursing Home and snitching food from his tablemates' plates. He has had a speech impediment all his life which caused difficulties in school and work, but he has always been clearly understood by all of us.

Roy's nickname was Jack. When I visited him in the Alzheimer's unit at the nursing home yesterday, he recognized me immediately and hugged me. I said, "Who are you?" and he replied, "I'm Jack". I hadn't heard him say that in years and years. He was Mama's pet, and he returned her love many times over. After he got a job, he bought her a present every time he got paid. He liked for her to wear pink and bought her pretty dresses and gowns, bath powder, and such.

Mama's third child, Lois Marie died with symptoms of diphtheria at the age of two. She apparently choked from congestion in her throat. There was no official diagnosis, since doctors were scarce.

August 9, 1937 was a very important day in my life, and I can't seem to remember a thing that happened! I'm sure that my mama was still grieving over the loss of her seventh child, Charles Lee. He died in the same manner as Lois eleven years earlier. Like Lois, Charles was also two years old.

August 9 would have been Lois' eleventh birthday. God chose that I would be born on that day, perhaps to cheer up the family. I've been told by my oldest brother, John Milton that it seemed as if I always tried to keep everybody laughing. He turned fifteen in August of the year I was born. Milton often told me, "I'm the First and you are the Last! Alpha and Omega."

My birth took place at home on Highway 24 East, just south of Prescott, Arkansas. My older brothers said it was a typical "dog day of summer" that quickly turned into a more memorable day. They had all worked in the fields that day, harvesting late crops of watermelons, corn, okra, tomatoes, and cantaloupes.

It was a trait of my father, John Wesley Daniel to work long, hard hours to gratify his landlord, Louis Daniels, who just happened to be his half-brother (from another mother). Notice the "s" on the end of his name. He changed the spelling to distinguish his father, James C. Daniel's first four children (whose mother had died) from the last set of four children that he fathered with his second wife, Icy Monk. My daddy was the oldest of his family with Icy.

Daddy took pride in "going the extra mile" for whomever he worked for, whether it was plowin', plantin' or pickin'. That was the example he set for his boys who were literally walking in his plow tracks. There were few jobs to be had in those days outside of farming. Not many farmers owned their own land, so they did the hard, menial labor for the rich folks who usually owned hundreds of acres of land. The acreage was divided into row crops of cotton, corn, sorghum and many other vegetables. Fruit trees provided many a farm an income. They didn't have tree farms as we know today. They wanted wide open fields for growing anything that would provide labor for poor families as well as turn a good profit for the owner.

Uncle Louis was considered the rich farmer because when his father (my grandfather, James C. Daniel) died suddenly, the children from his first marriage acquired all the land. It was quite a lot. My daddy, his three siblings, and his mother were left with only the house, which eventually had to be sold to purchase the bare necessities. They were virtually penniless.

My father, John Wesley Daniel, shortly after the death of his parents.

Needless to say, John Wesley had very little formal education, yet in my eyes he was the smartest man that ever lived! He possessed all the good qualities with which God can provide a man, even if he didn't have a dime. Daddy was blessed with lots of wisdom, honesty, good looks (I know from his youthful photos), and the ability to work and work and work! He was the oldest child and shouldered the responsibility of his family's survival. It's hard to imagine the circumstances my father was faced with in our present day of welfare checks and fast-food factories. There are jobs to be found; money is made and money is wasted.

John Wesley truly graduated from the "school of hard knocks". He learned integrity at his mother's knee and helped others learn to do right rather than wrong. The first time I heard the phrase, "Honest John", I thought surely, they were speaking about my dad.

Daddy said he never thought about a family of his own until his precious mother passed from this earth. He then began a search for a wife and found the best, my mother, Priscilla Odessa Bradford. They were soon married. Their first child arrived fifteen months later—a bouncing baby boy, Milton.

I've been told a story of right before I was born. My mother was craving watermelon, and she knew my brothers had brought up a wagonload of them and piled them under a tree between our house and Uncle Louis'. She went out a good little piece through some weeds to get her a watermelon, so my brothers told me. Just as she was starting back to our porch with it, Uncle Louis' wife, who we called Aunt Bell, screamed at Mama to put that melon back where she got it. "Those melons are not to eat—they are to sell", she said.

3

My own family had planted, cultivated and harvested the crop, but weren't allowed much for our table. Uncle Louis was the rich farmer and we were the sharecroppers. The arrangement was that our family did all the hard labor and Uncle Louis and Aunt Bell got two-thirds of the harvest. A few hours after the watermelon incident, while the boys and my sister were still spitting seeds from the huge melon they stole from the pile for our mother, she went into labor.

Our sharecropper's shack didn't have enough room or privacy to accommodate giving birth amongst the children, so Daddy asked Aunt Bell if the other children could stay with her since night was falling. She wouldn't let them in her nice house, so they sat on her doorsteps throughout the event. Fortunately for them, Mama's eighth delivery went quickly and smoothly.

Daddy had taken the wagon and team to town for a doctor, but I made my appearance before he got back—all ten and one-half pounds of me! I've always been a little anxious and I guess I've always been a little fat too! They weighed me and all the other babies on the same scales that the cotton-pickers' sacks were weighed on.

My father and mother, John Wesley and
Priscilla Odessa Bradford Daniel.

If the landlord had to meet a deadline getting his cotton to the gin, he might hire extra help to pick the cotton Daddy had grown. They were paid by the pound for how much cotton they had picked that day. The sharecroppers' family of pickers worked just for one-third of the crop money that Daddy collected for the whole family's labor after all the crops were in. This was the time that sharecroppers made the difficult decision as to whether they would continue with the same landlord or find a more generous one. Sometimes they moved to a farm with more fertile soil or better fences. They were constantly in a survival mode and looking for a better deal, even if it meant packing up and moving, always hoping for a better house.

Families like ours didn't make many purchases at the store, therefore, we didn't accumulate piles of "stuff" to be moved when Daddy said to pack up. We only had plain beds, one homemade wooden eating table, three or four straight-back wooden chairs, and a wooden bench as long as the table that seated at least three children when we all came to breakfast, dinner and supper. We also had a big cook stove that required building a wood fire in its belly early every morning so we could cook some good smokehouse ham and eggs and lots off biscuits to fill our bellies.

What few clothes we had were used to cushion the breakable dishes when we packed. With all the family helping, we could pack up and be on the road again in about three hours. It was difficult trying to get a bunch of kids placed safely on the wagon. The big kids had to hold or watch us little ones. I was always sad to leave our old house, but it was exciting to get to a new place and explore the surroundings as quickly as we could. I remember looking for good spots to make a playhouse.

I was still a baby when Daddy decided he could make a better living for us on another farm. He had an agreement to make a crop for Mrs. Roxie Bolls, a widow who lived nearby. I don't remember that move, but Mama said that Uncle Louis held me in his arms, then stood me on a wagon wheel and gave me an Indian Head nickel. She said she wondered if he thought that paid for all the wrong he had done his half-brother.

I don't know how long we abode in that second home. It was a decent house, they say. I do remember that the CCC's (Civil Conservation Corps) camped near us in the woods. This was a government program to train and employ young men who couldn't find a job. They did conservation by planting trees and fighting forest fires. It ended in 1944. My brothers benefitted from them greatly. The men divided their meager rations and when the camp ended, we scavenged until we found many edible treats in cans and packages that were hidden or buried in the area. We had never seen such nice treats.

It was there in the Redland area, east of Prescott, that my brother, Clyde, who must have been eight or nine years old, began practice preaching. He made all of us kids sit on tree stumps in the woods while he stood in front of us and read the Bible. Afterwards, we all sang. One of the songs was "Kneel at the Cross" which I mistakenly heard as "Mule at the Trough".

One day, Bob and I walked to Mrs. Bolls' house to take her some sweet peppers that Mama wanted to share. As soon as we entered her back door, we could smell fresh ripe apples. She always kept her place clean and neat and the fragrance of the big basket of red fruit on her table just seemed like Heaven.

Mrs. Bolls was a good hostess. She laughed and talked and made us feel so welcome. And, of course, she gave us both one of those tempting fruits as we left. I've thought of Mrs. Roxie so often during my lifetime. When children come to visit me, I always try to make sure they have a little something to take home with them.

She was a wonderful landlord, but from what I understand now, she didn't have enough land to keep our whole family in work. When couples married back then, their desire usually was to have many children so as to have a good-sized work crew. All of Wesley Daniel's offspring were taught at an early age what an honest day's work was.

Daddy didn't often quote scripture to us, but he did teach us, "What the Book says in II Thessalonians 3:10... "This we commanded you, that if any wouldn't work, neither should he eat." I think that was appropriate in the 1940's and it still needs to be heeded today.

Northward bound, the wagon was loaded once more, moving our family to another house on another farm. This time the wagon had to make two trips. We were moving to the Boughton area, about five miles north of Prescott to a farm owned by Mr. and Mrs. Richie DeLaughter.

I was still pre-school age when my brother, Clyde, who was seven years older than me, and I were assigned to accompany our fortune from the recent summer crop to our new home. It was a load of unshucked, dry corn piled to the top of the sideboards on our wagon. I guess it was considered too valuable to be left behind a few hours, hence it was the first load moved. Maybe Clyde and I were considered to be too valuable to leave behind, too.

We sat on top of the loose ears of corn for approximately ten miles or so. It was entertaining to watch the acrobatics of the dozen scared chickens who were fastened up in a wire coop tied on the back of our wagon. The feet of the two mules that powered our loaded wagon on down the dusty dirt road pounded a pleasant lullaby.

Clyde told me that I slept in my bed of corn at least half the trip. He awakened me on arrival at another "new" home. We climbed up the rickety steps and jumped across holes where planks were missing in the porch floor. Inside the front room, Clyde showed me a large spatter of red on the plank floor and told me it must be where somebody was killed. Naturally, I thought I could smell blood and something rotten. I ran back outside to tell Daddy and caught a glimpse of him on the wagon going just over the first little incline back toward Redland for the remainder of our family and belongings. I later learned it was just spilled paint on the floor, but I still didn't want to go back inside that house without my daddy or mama.

Venturing around the yard in weeds almost as high as my head, I felt something sharp beneath my bare foot. Looking down I saw a piece of something very pretty, like a treasure I had never seen before. When I lifted it up, I was gazing at the face and part of the head of an old China doll.

I ran inside to show Clyde, but he was busy raking up trash to make room for the furniture coming on the next wagon load. He hardly noticed what I had in my hand. I closed my fist gently around her and hoped I could keep her.

The next day as soon as I awoke, I started blabbing to my whole family about my doll and Daddy said, "Whatever you dream on the first night in a new house will come true if you tell it before breakfast".

I said, "But Daddy, I didn't dream this!" Then I opened my hand and showed him my doll head. It was about the size of a hickory nut. He looked it over and remarked how pretty it was.

Later that same day the older boys were assigned the job of cleaning out an old shed behind the house so it could be used to store tools. As I was hanging around watching, I spied a little cloth tobacco sack that had been left behind by the former tenants. It had no monetary value, but it gave me a splendid idea. I searched for a stuffing for my bag. My family was surprised when I showed them my real "Dolly". I had poked some old cotton remnants in the tobacco sack and placed its drawstring around her neck and tied it. Now she really was a doll, the only one I ever had.

7

2

After our folks made a crop or two at this "house on the hill", our same landlord offered Daddy a house that was a little bigger and better just down our dirt road about a half a mile. Mama was always willing and ready to do whatever pleased the head of the house. She was pretty frail and sickly and unable to do much of the work in moving. Daddy worked fast, so moving became something we were all really good at with his direction.

There wasn't much visiting going on with the Daniel family until a preacher, John Baker, and his wife, Annie, moved nearby. They had raised seven daughters and the oldest six had married and moved out, leaving the youngest, Betty. After we were well acquainted, Betty used to beg our mama to let us spend the night with her. My sister, Mary and I were excited to the moon and back when we were told we could go, but we must come home early next morning to get all our chores done.

I remember once when Betty and Mary rubbed Vicks salve in their eyes so their mothers would think they had the pink-eye and wouldn't make them do any work. Mrs. Annie was shocked at first until she smelled the Vicks. Mary and Betty's stunt backfired on them because they had to do all their work with burning eyes!

Betty married Roy Gant Cagle from Redland and many years later our paths crossed again. She had become a school teacher, and in 1974 I was chosen by the school superintendent, Mr. Bill Shirron, to be her teacher's aide in seventh and eighth grade remedial reading classes. That was a blessing that I think we both enjoyed for seven years. It gave us lots of time to reminisce. We were close friends until her death a few years ago. When she was about eighty years old, she just didn't wake up on Thanksgiving morning. I don't think Betty ever did like to bake turkeys! I miss her!

The Adams family moved in the old house we vacated. Daddy had known them years before. Mr. Will and Mrs. Ada Adams had three children, Junior, Bonnie, and Adell. Mrs. Adams' mother, Mrs. Jacks, lived with them, also. She suffered terribly with asthma attacks, and they ordered something through the mail that she burned in a tin pie plate and inhaled it to help her breathe.

The next place we moved to was at the largest farming job we had ever undertaken. It truly was "early to bed and early to rise"! When planting time came, or cultivating, or harvesting, it was all-hands-on-deck, except Mama. I don't remember her ever going to the field, and I didn't go to real work until I was five.

At twenty, Milton married Bonnie Lou Smith, who lived on our dirt road, up close to Highway 67. We didn't have anything to measure miles then since cars were rarely seen, but it seemed about a mile. Mr. DeLaughter did have a nice car, and some of us were fortunate enough later to ride in it.

Milton and Bonnie lived with us for a while after they married. Bonnie started fixing our hair and making us some clothes. She was only sixteen and still enjoyed playing paper dolls with me. I learned a lot of life skills from her, like cooking and sewing. Most importantly, she taught me to take pride in the way I dressed and to do my best with whatever I tried to do. I fully understand now that the Lord sent her to join our family and help my sick mother. She fit right in and my whole family loved her.

When my time came to join the work force in the fields, I first served as a water girl. My job was to carry a metal water bucket up and down the long rows of cotton or corn to allow all the workers to take a drink, each person drinking from the same dipper. Much of the water splashed out on the ground as I struggled to carry something almost as heavy as I was. As I grew, I had to join the bigger kids and hoe my own row. That's where I learned who really loved me—when someone would slip over and hoe a big skip for me on my row. In our family we weren't in a habit of saying, "I love you", but we saw repeatedly in the actions of those around us that we were indeed loved.

Mama didn't allow us kids to drink coffee, even though it was a must for Daddy at breakfast every morning. He always said there were two things he couldn't do without, no matter how high the price went—that was coffee and snuff! He always poured his coffee from the cup to a saucer to cool a little. I sat next to him at the table and when Mama wasn't looking, he would slide his saucer toward me and let me have a sip. I still get teary-eyed just thinking how much he loved me. He didn't have to say it!

∽ô∂

I had my fifth birthday in 1942. It was a sad time for a lot of folks we knew. World War II was going full throttle. My family felt the brunt when Milton was drafted into the Army and had to leave his new bride. They were still living with us, so Bonnie was cared for and loved. I tried especially hard to cheer her up when she cried. We spent a lot of time walking on trails through the woods. I remember us climbing up in the barn loft where our recent crop of peanuts was drying. We picked some off the vines and parched them in the oven of our wood cook stove.

During this time of raging war, it seemed there was more gloom everywhere. I could always read my daddy's face and his actions, and know when he was worried. Problems that had plagued poor families for years seemed to be multiplied now. Besides worrying about loved ones who were gone to war, there was either too much or too little rain for the crops. Everyone now had to worry about rationing. Some of the vital items that couldn't be raised on a farm were usually purchased at a store, but now the government was limiting how much of certain things civilians could buy due to war needs. Things like rubber for tires and gasoline were rationed to the public simply to provide plenty for the war effort. Other items that were already scarce for civilians including guns, ammunition, tires, shoes, and many general household items were rationed. Daddy used his coffee very sparingly as it was one of the items that was limited.

The government issued each member of our family a packet of sticky stamps which we received by mail. These stamps were used like coupons when making a purchase at a store. The merchant would tear out the number of stamps needed and paste them in his book, identifying who used them. We had more stamps than we could possibly use. Our family had never owned an automobile and we certainly couldn't afford one now, thus no need for items such as tires or gasoline. We seldom used our stamps. Mama's relatives once tried to buy some of them, but Daddy said he didn't think that was right. He didn't trade them off either. Honest John! I loved him.

Shortly after I turned five, we all worked long, tiring days in the cotton and corn fields to get our crops in. All the families I knew did this in the fall. We were up by daylight every day, except Sunday. For breakfast Daddy usually fried ham or side meat he got from the smokehouse behind our house while Mama made biscuits.

We killed hogs and butchered them in the coldest part of winter so the meat wouldn't spoil. Everybody in the family had to pitch in and help as we did with most big family chores. I remember it being so cold. Daddy would shoot the hog right between the eyes with a 22 rifle. After the hog was dead, the men would dip him in a metal barrel of scalding water for a few minutes, then retrieve him. We all took sharp knives and scraped the short bristles off the carcass. The men did the butchering as Mary and I cut up the chunks of fat meat and threw them in a wash pot over a small fire. In a few hours, all the grease cooked out. This was called "rendering the fat". We poured the fat in metal buckets that we used year after year. The fat would become hardened and white just like Crisco. We had made lard!

The small bits of meat in the fat became shrunken and crispy. They were called cracklins. Our mouths watered just thinking about baking cornbread with fresh cracklins mixed in the batter. Often times, our supper consisted of fresh milk and cornbread (if Roy would milk the cows on time. He was a superb cow-milker). On cold days, Mama would allow us to take our cup of milk and bread to the front room and sit by the fire to eat it. It not only filled our bellies, but it filled our hearts with joy as well.

In early Autumn when the cotton bolls were ripe to harvest, the whole family, except Mama, was expected to be in the field before sunrise. We were reminded of the Bible verse, "The fields were white unto harvest, but the workers were few." At this time, we all hoped and prayed that rain would hold off until the last boll of cotton was picked.

Cotton bolls had sharp "fangs", and we were constantly bitten by them as we pulled the fluffy white fibers out.

11

Daddy was "picky" about his pickers. He taught us kids how to make one quick pluck at that boll and get all the cotton out of it the first grab. The hull that had secured the boll before it opened had sharp "fangs" and we were constantly bitten by them as we pulled the fluffy white fibers out. In the absence of gloves, we girls wore old socks on our hands with finger holes cut out to try and prevent our hands from being sore and bleeding.

Bonnie sewed the cotton sacks and made ready for the long haul before harvest began. They were made from strong duck cloth. (No animals were harmed in the process.) They had a strap to hang across our neck and shoulder the way a lady wears her crossbody purse securely. Each picker had a sack. Mine was child-sized, but I don't think it was ever fully packed. I had to quit picking frequently and make sure everybody got a drink of cool well water!

Several times a day Daddy would holler "weigh up", and he weighed each sack so he would have an idea about when he should go the cotton gin with a full bale, hopefully. I dreamed of packing my sack to the brim so Daddy would be surprised, but it never happened.

Occasionally when rain was eminent, the crop owner might hire neighboring hands to get the cotton picked before it got wet and was ruined. They were paid by the number of pounds they picked. Cotton scales were on a balance beam with a hook where they hung the sacksful of cotton and balanced it out with what was called a "pee". Sacks full of cotton were weighed and emptied into a side-boarded wagon until Daddy and his figures on paper determined a possible bale. Since I, being so small, wasn't worth much in the field, I usually got to ride on top of the soft fluffy cotton to the cotton gin in Boughton. It was a thriving small town at that time, surrounded by cotton farms. Unlike today, the little town boasted a busy mercantile, a hotel, doctor's office, church, school, and railroad. The merchants never got much of our hard-earned money. If we weren't finished with our cotton crop when school started, it was understood at Boughton School that children were automatically excused from absences until the family's crop was in. The gathering of that crop was completely dependent on the weather.

It's hard to describe the clean, awesome fragrance of fresh-picked cotton. I think that somewhere in my childish mind, I knew that it was the smell of prosperity to my daddy. When I rode to the gin, I wasn't anxious for the trip to end.

History class taught me that Eli Whitney invented the cotton gin to remove the seeds from cotton. These seeds were useful in manufacturing several types of oil, food for animals, soap, and even phonograph records. Farmers always saved enough seeds to plant their next crops. Cotton fiber had too many uses to mention, but we mainly think of clothing and some household goods. I still love to visit fabric stores. It seems I always migrate to the cotton sections of the fabrics and feel the bolts of cotton cloth. It's a pleasure to remember from whence that pretty material originated.

I often wondered whether Daddy's hard-working hands and body would hold out long enough to raise us kids. Most of his ancestors died young and suddenly. This caused me much worry, especially when he wore a frown too often. I am so thankful that as I grew, my faith grew also. I learned to pray more and worry less.

Our only payday came in the fall when all the crops were harvested. According to the pre-crop agreement between the owner and the farmer, a certain percentage of the cash received for the crops that sold went to the farmer. Mr. DeLaughter was a generous landlord. Besides cotton, we also harvested dry corn with some to be sold and some saved to feed our mules and chickens. The corn stalks, or fodder, were cut by hand with a butcher knife and saved for cow feed. Sometimes the corn fields were so large it took days and days for us to get it all cleared and the dirt turned under in preparation for another crop in the spring.

Autumn was also when we harvested our sorghum crop and made molasses for our own use and to sell. Daddy always knew when the stalks were to be cut to obtain the most delectable flavor. My four brothers cut the stalks and carried them to a borrowed sorghum mill. The mule provided the power to turn a grinder, which chewed the juice out of the stalks. Aww—such a sweet, tasty juice! We often chewed some of the stalks before they got to the mill.

When enough juice was extracted, we poured the sweet watery substance into a large copper pan where it began to slowly cook over a low fire. After running through two or three pans with varying degrees of heat, we girls canned the molasses in clean, sterilized glass gallon jugs. Whenever our chickens went on strike and didn't lay eggs, we still had the best breakfast of sorghum syrup, biscuits, and ham or sausage.

3

We were so blessed in all the houses we occupied near Boughton. There were always interesting water playgrounds where Bob and I discovered secret places. We could walk a short distance and find what he defined as "One of the World's Greatest Wonders". Brushy Creek was shallow and lazy most of the time, but our inquiring minds had to investigate the loud and boisterous stream that emerged after some spring storms had awakened it somewhere upstream. As we approached the little wooden bridge on a seldom-used dirt road, I yelled in amazement. I couldn't even see the rocky floor of the creek now. The muddy water was hurrying along faster than I had ever witnessed, right at the place where we usually slid off the bridge into water. It was usually so shallow and clear that I could count dozens of little bitty fish "in school".

Bob and I decided to take off our shoes and dangle our feet in the cold creek water that was rushing by. I had been taught, even though I was only five years old, to take care of my personal belongings. I tucked my well-worn socks inside my shoes and carefully set them at my side as I plopped my bottom on the cold, wet bridge. The rapid flow of the icy-cold water caused my legs to tingle.

I was laughing and having such a good time, when I saw a brightly colored box floating by. I stretched to grab it, thinking it probably had treasures inside. Unfortunately, I missed the box, and bumped my shoe. My heart sank as I saw one of my shoes floating right on down that swollen creek, alongside the box.

All I could do was watch as the shoe shrank into the distance. I thought I wouldn't breathe again! My daddy could only save enough money to afford one pair of shoes for each child in the fall when the crop money was divided. Now I had only one well-worn shoe and a very-worn pair handed down from Mary, whose feet were four years older than mine. God blessed us with an early spring, and what country girl needs shoes in warm weather!

On "Sharecropper's Road" there were many other sparkling streams where my siblings and I could take a quick dip as necessary to rid our body of red bugs, sometimes known as chiggers. We would have to find a sunny spot to swim to avoid the swarms of mosquitoes. They loved the water, also, and seemed to hang around it to multiply. Our favorite place to swim and play was the Little Missouri River, just a short dirt-road walk from all the different houses in which we lived. "Little Mo", as we called it, was *cold* even on the hottest summer days. A modern air conditioner cannot compare to the luxury of cooling off by swimming in that river after working in a cotton patch or peach orchard all day.

We never swam without adult supervision, and we certainly knew to stay away from Little Mo when heavy rains had caused her to roar like a lioness. On a typical hot summer afternoon when all our chores were done, Daddy would sometimes yell, "Who wants to go to the river?"

Most evenings she was just lazily rolling on down south, soft as a whisper. We floated on discarded inner tubes that the boys found along Highway 67. The tubes invariably spewed around the concocted patches that my brothers had applied. When the tube blew, I knew that even though I was "in over my head", I would be dragged safely to shore. Being the baby child of our large family, I always had several sets of eyes watching me and many hands ready to rescue me from my frequent mishaps.

Sundays after church and after lunch was the best time for swimming. Daddy was always with us, so we could usually stay in the river until our teeth would just about chatter themselves loose from the extremely cold water. We would laugh and tell Daddy, "This is a cold day in August, now what are some of the things you said you would do on a cold day in August?"

Our fingers turned blue and our skin shriveled. This kind of togetherness made us very happy. You can bet we were well-thawed by the time we walked home on that gravel road. Taking this same road in the opposite direction from our house was how we got to Boughton School during the winter months. I skipped happily along the road and across Cold Run Creek bridge in the mornings but coming home in the afternoon was a different story. One of my brothers usually took me piggy back. I never asked them if they loved me—I knew they did! On some of the warmer autumn days we would stop and wade in the shallow, clear-bubbling Cold Run Creek.

We were a fortunate bunch of kids in that our parents wanted us to go to school—after all the crops were gathered, that is. I had just turned five in August before I started trekking to school with my siblings. Nobody asked my age the first year. I had to repeat with the first group the next year when our teacher, Mrs. Nellie Clark, asked how old I was. I guess we, in our family, didn't think it mattered. I have always been grateful that I got to tag along with them my two years in first grade.

Boughton School had three or four groups of learners in one room. I don't believe our teacher called them grades then. Mary was in the same room, but in the fourth group. Sometimes Mrs. Clark would allow me to sit with an older group because I was "doing so well".

The second year in school, when the teacher asked my name, I told her, "Mary".

When she said, "I know your mother didn't name two girls Mary," I started crying and told Mrs. Clark that I wanted to change my name because nobody could spell Lenora. I told her when folks asked my sister her name, they seemed to always just write it down. When they asked for my name and I told them, they always asked, "How do you spell that?" She wrote "Lenora Daniel" on the chalk board and asked the whole class to spell it out.

I loved school, especially reading. I was the only avid reader in the family, and they couldn't understand why I liked to hide and read the books I borrowed from Mrs. Clark as often as I could. I hid because if anybody noticed me reading, they would tell Mama or Daddy I was lazy. *Then* they would find me another chore to do. Some of the borrowed books I read ten times or more.

I don't recall a lot about the red brick school building. (Although I do recall the outdoor toilet, which had two sides, one for boys and, of course, one for the girls.) After walking four miles in cold weather, we were glad to enter that cozy little building. Some neighborhood gentlemen took turns building a roaring fire in a big wood heater early each morning.

Our only recess was a long one at lunch time. All groups had to have lunch at the same time because each family's dinner was packed in one single container, usually a lard or molasses bucket. Mary wanted to carry our full lunch bucket to school because she helped pack it and didn't want our happy-go-lucky brothers to mess up the contents. She packed molasses or thicknin' gravy in the bottom of the clean bucket. She then turned a bowl bottom-side-up over this and carefully laid those good old homemade biscuits, ham, sausage, bacon or pork ribs on top of the bowl to keep them from getting soggy.

When the teacher picked up the small brass bell and shook it there was a smile on nearly every face. We knew that meant recess and eating time. Each family of children would gather under a shade tree and have a picnic-style feast. Everybody was really quiet until their bucket was empty. If they had any food left, there was lots of sharing and swapping with the other families until the last morsel disappeared.

Right after lunch at school, we played or watched a variety of creative games and activities. We didn't require bought equipment or athletic uniforms, etc. We had grass, sand, trees, tow-sack swings, and many other motivational tools that allowed our imagination to develop. We played games handed down from the generation before us like Red Rover Red Rover, Annie Over, Blind Man's Bluff, and Flying Dutchmen. Such great fellowship amongst the Boughton School young'uns during those times. So many lasting friendships were made there.

Walking to and from school, we had to cross US Highway 67, which was heavily trafficked at that time. There were no interstates in the 1940's. We saw many airplanes in the sky, but were told it was mostly military cargo planes, not for passengers. Much of the air traffic going eastbound or westbound across the southern U.S. came right over the farms we worked.

Even though this was a very rural area, there were two stores where our little dirt road crossed 67. Baker Britt's grocery store was on one corner and Harris Langley's Five-Way Market and filling station sat on the opposite side of the highway.

Mr. Britt liked to talk politics, not just on election year, but all the time. I don't know if he was a Democrat or not. Most folks around us were. He was very well-liked, so much so that every year on Halloween night, Mr. Britt's outhouse would end up in the middle of the highway. Each generation of Boughton youngsters kept the tradition going. He was a really good sport about it and was the only resident nearby who got a new toilet every year.

As we meandered past Harris and Estelle Langley's store, we often heard the rattle of bottles as milk trucks and soda pop trucks delivered their goods to sell. I wondered why folks bought milk instead of milking cows like we did.

Occasionally, the ice truck stopped at the store. We would race to pick up the small chips of ice that fell to the ground as he chipped off a fifty-pound chunk for the store. This was how they kept soda pops and dairy products cool. There were no freezers at that time, therefore, no ice cream at local stores.

Our family purchased very few items from the stores because we grew most of what we ate. Money was too scarce, and my daddy was very frugal. He was the one who made the decisions for the family's spending. Usually, when we asked for something from the store, he reminded us that he was desperately trying to save enough money to buy us a "forever home" so that we would never have to move again.

We always had a roof over our heads, though sometimes the roof leaked. In one house we lived in, Mary and I slept with a dishpan between us when it rained because the rain was slowly dripping right over our bed. It didn't take Daddy and the boys long to fix the roof.

No matter where our gravel road trudging took us, we were always glad to return to our "humble abode", knowing we would see Mama and Daddy there to welcome us home. We knew we were so blessed when our olfactory senses detected bacon and potatoes frying. The house was pleasantly filled with the fragrance of oak wood burning in the cook stove.

We always had supper after all of us were home. We had three meals a day. Sometimes the noon meal was carried to the field, usually by the youngest child. I think that was because the older siblings were more valuable in chopping or picking cotton. Whatever the reason, I was glad to help.

Food was plentiful, but we had to cook it. There were no quick stops to pick up prepared food. If we snacked, it might be a raw sweet potato or peanuts from the barn loft, or a raw turnip from the winter garden. We were always hungry at meal times. The whole family gathered around the homemade wooden table to eat together. When I close my eyes now and see this sweet group of my loved ones, my memories turn wet and roll down my cheeks.

Several tasks around our house were gender-assigned. Cooking, cleaning and the laundry were to be done by the only two female siblings, under Mama's supervision. Mama was sick most of the time after I was born, but we were so blessed that she was able to explain how to get the necessary jobs done. Before we sat down to eat, Mary or I had to fill our old black iron kettle with water from the well and set it on the stove. The waning coals would heat the water for washing dishes after we ate. We used two small pans to wash and rinse.

In the summers after evening chores were finished, we were turned loose to play in the yard. Mama and Daddy sat on the front porch in straight back wooden chairs to rest. Sometimes they shelled dry peas or beans for the next year's planting seeds, or to be soaked and boiled for our hungry mouths. When it was hot, I brought a pan of cool water from the well so Mama could soak her tired, swollen feet.

I often saw them chuckling at our spontaneous games, which could more accurately be described as capers. Creativity wasn't lacking among us kids. We dared not mention being bored to Daddy, lest he find us another chore. Once, they curled me (the last), into a fetal position and poked me into an old car tire (we called them caissons) and rolled me down a hill on a clay road that was seldom traveled. It didn't kill me, but it brought Mama to a standing position. I found out what it felt like to get drunk.

We saved twine strings from feed sacks, and wound them into a baseball, which we batted with a crudely carved stick. A lot of energy and sweat was expelled in our chinaberry fights. Our parents kept saying we were "gonna put somebody's eye out" with those berries, but we all grew up two-eyed.

I never heard about emergency rooms. I'm sure there were some, just not in Boughton. I was grounded once when I stepped on a board with a rusty nail sticking in it while I was walking barefoot. Their remedy for preventing lock-jaw was to have me dangle my foot over an old bucket, which contained slowly burning wool rags; that kept my foot in plenty of smoke. The pain was tolerable, but I surely did hate having to sit still.

As darkness approached, we would find an old jar with which to make lightning bug lanterns. The glimmering and glowing of their tiny lamps seemed to be sending out beacons of hope…hope that every day of the rest of my life would be just as good as these childhood days of mine.

19

4

As we moved from farm to farm, Daddy kept a sharp eye out each time to try and find a better house for his family to occupy. He particularly wanted a good water well on the premises. Sometimes that attempt was unsuccessful. Our house behind Buchanan Cemetery had a rusty old water pump that we had to prime by pouring a coffee can full of water into the top of it and pump the iron handle really fast to get a sufficient amount of water to flow before we could quench a bunch of thirsty mouths. Being the most eager, I was the first to drink. It didn't take a moment for me to spit, sputter and mutter! That was the worst tasting drink I had ever had. Daddy soon gave up on us drinking that water and found neighbors, Mr. Trosie and Mrs. Lily Formby, whose store was also located on Highway 67, north of Prescott. We carried our drinking water from there about one fourth of a mile in glass gallon jugs.

Our clothes and dishes could be washed in the iron water from that pump. Homemade lye soap was plentiful, but no matter how much we used, it never lathered because the water was so hard or "irony". All our white clothes took on a deep rust-colored hue. My brothers were ashamed of their white Sunday shirts. Mary and I still had to wash them on a rub board after we heated water in a wash pot situated over a bonfire in the back yard. Sunday clothes and school clothes had to be starched and ironed without electricity. We heated heavy "smoothing irons" on the stove to finish up the ironing. Mary and I often had to miss a day of school to get the jobs done.

All of us Daniel kids were somewhat unconsciously trained by Daddy to forage for food, when it wasn't growing season for veggies. The Buchanan Cemetery place had bountiful sources of berries and fruit such as huckleberries, dewberries, blackberries, plums, and persimmons. We were overjoyed when a dormant pear tree blossomed and bore an enormous supply of fruit for fresh eating, cooking, and canning--enough to last all year. The brothers helped us peel the pears, and with Mama's instruction, Mary and I got the jars and lids washed. Over a period of three or four weeks we filled almost a hundred jars!

Our fruit shelves were in a darker corner of the kitchen, and we made a curtain from feed sacks to hang from ceiling to floor. I remember idly walking by and pulling the curtain open quickly and thinking all those pears had smiley faces.

⤚⤙

On one of my excursions with Bob, we noticed there were nuts cracking under our feet as we walked. He picked some up to examine. Neither of us had ever seen nuts like those before. We hurried home to show what we'd found, afraid to taste them for fear they might be poison. Our siblings became wide-eyed when Bob held out his hand, holding a tree branch on which grew sharp, prickly leaves similar to holly foliage and a hairy looking bur. The bur had two nuts inside with a rare flat-on-one-side shape. Daddy mashed the nuts from the ugly bur and pronounced them to be chinquapins. We all got a tiny taste and smiled.

I'm so glad I had that experience because chinquapins, from the chestnut family, are said to be fairly extinct due to a virus that appeared from Japan. The trees were also over-harvested and cut because their strong, long-lasting wood was desired for railroad ties, telephone poles, and fence posts. Our recent searches for these trees have not been successful. I firmly believe if Bob and I could take another stroll, he would surely stumble upon a chinquapin tree!

5

We all knew my daddy was an expert at finding just the right vegetable garden spot at each new residence we moved to. It was always well-drained with not so many rocks and located in a place that could receive plenty of sunshine and rain. By the time we were finished covering the complete lot with barnyard dirt and manure, we ascertained the soil was rich in nutrients.

Another thing we were sure of was that it was always a family project. We saved seeds after every garden was finished in the fall, and seldom had to buy new ones to plant in the spring. All hands aboard for seed scattering until every vegetable we could think of had been hidden in our new dirt. Mama read the *Ladies Cordial Almanac* and kept us posted on when to plant what. She depended on the signs of the Zodiac for planting, so that when those seeds sprouted and matured enough to bear, they would supply quality and quantity sufficient to fill many empty bellies.

Milton was still serving in the military, and we still had the pleasure of his wife, Bonnie living with us. She was so much help and loved working outdoors anywhere she was needed. Soon, we had another little fellow around to play with, her firstborn son, Milton Dwayne.

When canning time came around again, Bonnie learned the process quickly and filled the void, teaching Mary and me, as Mama was beginning to get weaker and complain of pains in various places, including around her heart.

Daddy and my brothers had the cotton and corn crops laid by, meaning the plants were growing and free of weeds and grass. While they waited for the crops to produce something to sell, they helped us women can enough vegetables and fruits to last our big family through the next winter of non-producing months. The men also built fences, sheds, barns or whatever was needed on the farm during their wait for crops.

There was one summer when we lived on what was known as the old Highway 67 in the last house on the left going toward Little Missouri River, Daddy found what he thought was a perfect plot of dirt to plant a tobacco patch. It adjoined the barn lot and caught the manure drift, if you know what I mean. Oh boy! He was right! When those plants came up, they really started growing fast… Faster than any of the veggies in the garden. The rains and the sunshine blessed the tobacco field and brought about a bountiful harvest.

We picked the leaves when they were slightly turning brown and were about as big as an elephant ear leaf. Daddy tied several large leaves together around the stems and hung them on the rafters on the sunny side of the barn loft. It was an exciting event when the last leaves were gathered and hung. I checked the barn loft often. The fragrance of drying tobacco met me halfway up the ladder. I cannot fully describe the hearty, sweet smell that permeated the barn, which was ordinarily stinky. If I could have had a biscuit, I would have tried what smelled like fresh sorghum molasses.

Nobody in our family smoked, but Daddy and the boys sure found out how many friends they had when all that stuff was ready to smoke and chew. To prepare it to sell or give away, they stacked about half a dozen leaves, then rolled it and lastly, they made a twist or braid about eight or nine inches long and rehung them in the barn to await use.

Some of our relatives that we hadn't seen in forever showed up nearly every day to "taste" what they usually took home with them. We never knew how word got around so fast with no phones or automobiles. Daddy didn't switch to chewing or smoking. He just kept on dipping his snuff twice a day after breakfast and after supper.

6

I've enjoyed back yard gardening for a whole lot of years—too many to count. I can't truthfully say that I was exactly zealous when I was younger. I could hold the harness lines and plow stocks, and direct old Dan (our mule at the time) down a row without destroying too much beneficial growth. Some of my brothers taught me to plow, and it was fun to have them guiding me till I learned a little about it. They often made mistakes, too. It helped to have a slow, sure-footed hinny like Dan.

I loved dropping seeds with Daddy, or watering his newest transplants of cabbages, tomatoes, and other early growers. We were after dark some evenings getting in for supper. I would rather work in the garden with Daddy than help Mary cook supper, even with the knowledge that I would still have to dry the dishes after we ate. I had to dry them always; never got to wash them! Sister's demands were eagerly met by our parents since she was older than me.

One evening I was taken by surprise when I was going to the garden. Daddy and old Dan were breaking up new dirt beside our existing plot. He smiled at me and said, "This what ye wanted?" I had asked him nearly every spring if I could have my own garden, even though I knew he always seemed busy trying to keep a farm and household going for a sizeable clan but he found time to plow up a spot for me to practice the art of planting and growing so eventually I could be just like my daddy

Nevertheless, there it was right in plain view. It was at least 8x8 feet. I didn't measure, I just fell on my knees and kissed that dark, comely earth. I flung the dirt as my mind was whirling around what I would plant.

Eventually, my gardening efforts were very successful. I held my head high when I marched in the back-porch door holding up a ripe tomato, two sweet peppers, and three pods of butterbeans. It was a slow harvest for me, but tasty when added to all we derived from the big garden. The experience outweighed the produce by far!

Later in life I ran across a scripture in God's Holy Word (the Bible), that caused me to believe that Jesus was a horticulture enthusiast also. I would strive to be just like Him! He told a story once to his disciples, which was called a "parable" because it may not, but certainly could be, true. In the Gospel according to Mark 4:26-29 Jesus said, "The kingdom of God is as if a man should scatter seed on the ground, and should sleep by night and rise by day, and the seed should sprout and grow, he himself does not know how. For the earth yields crops by itself; first the blade, then the head, after that the full grain in the head. But when the grain ripens, immediately he puts it in the sickle, because the harvest is come".

In my early Sunday School years when I was told by my teacher that Jesus is perfect, I knew He must have loved gardening.

My own garden!

7

My brother, Clyde, felt God calling him into the ministry of the Gospel "from the time he was knee-high to a duck" as Daddy would say. We weren't allowed to open Daddy's trunk without his knowledge, but Clyde would slip around and get Grandma Daniel's old, worn and tattered Bible and hide between his bed and the wall to read it. Brother's heart was gladdened when he came home with a brand-spanking New Testament. The Gideons International Society had given one free to every fifth grader at school that day. He laughed when he told Daddy he wouldn't have to borrow his anymore.

Clyde was the one who persuaded Mama to let us kids walk four miles to Boughton Baptist Church on Sundays. Even though we walked to school during the weeks through the winter, we were bouncing down the same dirt roads because the church was close to school. The rocks seemed to be scrambling more than usual as our pace exceeded our usual gait.

We arrived in time for Sunday School. My first teacher was Mrs. Mildred Ingersoll Johnson. I was mesmerized when she stood in front of the five of us first- and second-graders and told us the story of baby Moses being hidden in bulrushes. She kind of left me dangling. I didn't believe he would ever be found. The next Sunday she told us he was discovered safely and grew up to be a true leader. Mrs. Johnson was a very good teacher. I was beginning to read, so I asked Clyde to find that Moses story in the Bible for me. When he did, I could hardly put that book down. I read it over and over.

Mrs. Johnson raised a big family of six children with her husband, Willie and lived to be a hundred and two years old. She was blind for the last part of her life, but had obeyed Godly instructions, "Study to show thyself approved unto God, a workman that needeth not to be ashamed; rightly dividing the word of truth" (II Timothy 2:15).

I had never been privileged to sit in such an elaborate building as Boughton Baptist Church. I saw lots of ornate carvings on the individual pews and on the altar furniture. When I got home, I told Mama and Daddy about the "curly" furniture I saw.

When Milton was honorably discharged from the Army, he came back and moved Bonnie and Dwayne into a small wooden "shotgun" house. It was called that because the three very small rooms sat one behind the other in a straight row. The house sat on land that belonged to Mrs. Georgia Haynes. She agreed to let them live there if he would work in her orchards. They were scattered all over her farm and were prolific every summer. She and her manager, Mr. Henry Hignight shipped peaches all over the United States, as well as plums, pears, apples and many vegetables. Folks came from near and far to purchase the Haynes peaches. The business got bigger and bigger.

The orchards were about a mile from our sharecropper's house. We were still privileged to cross Cold Run Creek to get there. Our cotton crop was growing well when the peaches started getting ripe. Mrs. Georgia asked if Daddy and the boys could come over and help her until his crops of cotton and corn reached harvest time. Our landlord was still Mr. DeLaughter. We had farmed for him longer than for anyone else, and he and my family got along really well. Even though he was "boss", he called my dad, "Mr. Daniel".

The first time his wife, Mrs. Maude, drove her big luxury car up in our yard and honked, Mary and I just about exploded with excitement.

She asked our mama, "May the girls go to my house and help keep the boogers out while Mr. DeLaughter is gone to a farm convention in Memphis?" Thank goodness, Mama agreed to it!

My heart was thumping with anticipation as we climbed into her light blue sedan. She asked, "Where are your overnight bags?"

I explained to her that Mama said we would just wear the same clothes the next day. As we left our dirt road and tall timber, we rode about five miles on 67. I never forgot how light I felt after my first ride in an automobile circa 1943. I thought I would just float through the air, but I didn't.

Her home held the finest collection of "stuff" I had ever seen. She seemed to have way too much furniture and decorations for only two folks living there. I didn't ask any questions, though. She led us through a room that had a bed in it, among many other ornate fixings. Then we went into a smaller room with what looked like a shiny, white horse-watering trough and a matching ceramic chair, half-filled with water.

Mrs. Maude walked around that spotless mule trough and flipped a lever. Mary and I jumped as water started pouring from a silver spout. We could see steam starting to rise from the water.

So many questions rolled through my mind. How did she do that? I barely heard her whispering voice telling us to remove our clothes and hop in. She handed each of us a pretty, pastel pink wash rag and a delicate matching towel, the likes of which we had never laid eyes on before.

Mrs. Maude excused herself and left the room. As we rolled our bodies down the inside wall of the tub full of water, all I could do was sigh. Mary yelped, "Whoa!" Anybody who knew my sister knew about her shyness. That was a big exclamation coming from her!

We washed all over first then played and pretended to be fishes. When our hands and feet had wrinkled like a sundried raisin, we reluctantly got out of the still-warm water, dried, and dressed. Our hostess came back in and showed us how to drain the "big machine" and return the bathroom to normal. I thanked her more than once and Mary just smiled.

I told her that was the first time we had ever seen a bathtub or water running inside a house or water in a white chair. She explained that the chair served as an outhouse. Well, now she was speaking our language! My bladder was about to pop, so I immediately plopped down on that chair and "let'er fly".

"I'm gonna call this the wonder room!" I exclaimed as Mrs. Maude laughed out loud.

She then led us into a bright, cheerful room where the afternoon sun was shining through two windows and highlighting the beautiful sunflower curtains. Mary was clasping onto my dress sash, and walking slightly behind me, as usual, and probably hoping she wouldn't have to say anything or pull her clothes off again.

It was a kitchen! My jaw dropped in awe of all the gadgets I saw. I saw a white box built lower than the safes, and I suspected since it had a shiny spout that it could explode with water at any moment. There was a little white table with four chairs near one of the windows. A smooth table cloth with smaller sunflowers graced the table.

Mrs. Maude motioned for us to sit. "I made you some sandwiches. Do you like bologna and cheese?"

I wished that just one time, Mary would speak up so that I wouldn't have to answer. All she could do was fidget!

"We love cheese," I said, "but I don't know what that other is."

We bowed our heads while our hostess asked God to bless us and our food. It made my heart feel good to know how easy she talked to

Him. When we tasted I quickly told her how great it was. "I like it very much and thank you for doing this for us."

She glanced at Mary, who was taking huge bites and had hers half-eaten. "What about you? Do you like it?"

I saw my sister's face get redder and redder as she kicked my leg under the table. I knew she wanted me to think and speak for her, so I said, "She likes it too," as I had always done.

I had never seen bread like what we were eating, so I asked her what kind it was. She told me it was light bread. I was wondering how many new things I could soak up in one day. Oh—so good!

Without thinking too much about it when we stuffed our bellies to the point of nearly popping, we quickly cleaned up the table and stacked the dishes in the white sunken box Mrs. Maude called a sink—huh!

She told us, "Just sit down. I want to show you girls something I think you will like," as she slipped out of the room.

We sat on a soft, long seat that was almost the size of a bed. It was rose-colored and velvety with large flowers as big as I was. Our eyes were "bugging out" as we kept adjusting ourselves to sit with our feet on the floor. I half stood and pretended to be floating with excitement just as Mrs. Maude scurried back into what we later learned was called the living room. At home, we called it the front room.

She was loaded with two stacks of folded cloth. As she unloaded a stack in the lap of each of us, she explained that these were feed sacks and flour sacks that she had collected when purchasing feed for cows, goats, chickens, geese and a couple of horses.

I held all white sacks with colored labels printed on them, announcing what had been their contents. The first one I picked up revealed bright, orange and yellow plumes of wheat and the words, "Shawnee's Best Flour—25 pounds, made since 1906 in Shawnee, Oklahoma."

I told Mrs. Maude, "This much flour would last about two weeks at our house", as I displayed the large cloth sack.

I also explained that we had some white sacks like this. "When we wash them, the printed letters go away. Our sister-in-law, Bonnie helps us sew our underwear from them. They turn out pretty and white. We don't have elastic for the waist of our unmentionables, though. We heard that it couldn't be manufactured because of the war using most of the rubber. Bonnie learned how to sew a cloth waistband on and work a buttonhole and apply the button."

Mrs. Maude pointed at the colorful stack on Mary's lap and stated that she was hoping Bonnie could help us construct some nice dresses and skirts using them. Mary smiled big, and I jumped up and hugged

29

Mrs. Maude, which made her laugh. I told her "thank you" so many times without remembering I had already said it. We just sat there, admiring our new wardrobes and smiling. I had many visions of how I would dress up in those pretty prints.

Our hostess was ready to show us our bed. We followed her so closely, I accidentally stepped on her heel. I think it must have hurt, and I told her how sorry I was. She said she knew I was tired and needed to rest. After she finished ruffling through all the extra pillows and the tiers of lace on the covers, we slipped off our clothes and slid under them as quickly as we could. Our bodies were the cleanest ever! Can't say that about our flour-sack petticoats, but we slept in them. For once, we were both speechless. I opened my mouth, but no sound came out. My eyelids were heavy, and they closed on a day I was hoping would never end.

When I awoke, I could see daylight through the open crack in the curtains. Goodness, we were always up, dressed and finishing our breakfast by the time daybreak arrived. Mama usually made her good biscuits that pleased the whole Daniel family. They were scratched out of the big, wooden biscuit bowl, which contained remnants of several mixings of that good ol' Shawnee's Best flour. She piled it in the bowl and bored a fist-sized hole in the middle, into which she placed a pat of hog lard and a swiggle-and-a-half of buttermilk, then very gently mixed it with her hand. It only took a minute or two before she pinched off pieces of dough about as big as a sausage patty, and skillfully rolled them out with both hands till they were round. She then plopped them in a big, square pan that was always greased and ready.

On a wood-burning cook stove, there is no oven temperature control or timer, but our trained noses could detect how close those biscuits were to being done. Wow! Mouth-watering! We always managed to be in our places around that homemade 'eatin' table when meals were ready, three times a day. There was no snacking at our house. The only time food was saved for later was when a job kept one of the men from making it home on time.

I missed my family! They must be fixing to head out to the fields right about now, and Mama would have to lie back down for a while. She had to rest often.

I eased out of bed and tiptoed toward the window light. Peeping out, I could see that the cars on 67 still burned their lights. They were zooming east and west, meeting each other on the two-lane black-top road to everywhere. I wondered how far they could travel on that road, and who would they be meeting at the end?

Just as Mrs. Maude knocked on our door and called, "Breakfast..." I spotted an old red truck coming up the driveway. On the door I could see the words, "Miller's Dairy" written in white with a black and white cow painted underneath them. He drove on around near the kitchen door. I jerked my dress on and entered the kitchen just in time to see a man handing Mrs. Maude two glass bottles of milk, and her giving him some change.

"Humph," I thought. "She gets her milk from an old red truck. We get ours from a Jersey cow."

She poured some of the milk over the three bowls of Kellogg's Corn Flakes. Mary and I had already lapped ours all up, when I noticed Mrs. Maude was sugaring hers. Another first for my short lifetime. After breakfast, we listened to her radio for thirty minutes. It was some silly character who called himself, 'Howdy Doody', and it was his time. We sisters had many questions to ask each other later about radios. I enjoyed this time at the boss's house so much, but I was glad when the lady of the house said she must take us home, because her husband was returning from Memphis, and she wanted to cook for him today. On our way out, she grabbed a stack of *Progressive Farmer* magazines and a few *Kansas City Star* newspapers for our family to look over. There would be plenty of room for them in that big ol' car. This made me happy, because I loved to read anything I could find. My sister—not so much. We loaded the feed sacks in the car, also. I could hardly wait to show Mama what we got. Oh—another most delightful car ride home!

As she slowed the car from what felt like flying to gliding, and turned into our yard, I saw the front door of our house opening slowly, and Mama stepping out onto the porch. I had spent my first night away from home in my whole life! I jumped from that beautiful car as quickly as I could and ran to my mama! She bent to hug me and I jumped up at the same time. My head bumped her front tooth and it cut her lip and made it bleed. My head bled too, so I guess we became blood kin or something.

Mrs. Maude thanked Mama for sharing her daughters, and I hugged her and told her how happy we were to get to visit her. She smiled and asked if we might come again. Mary looked at her and nodded her head up and down.

I laughed and cried as I told Mama about everything—the big, beautiful car and house, and all the unbelievable contents inside it. Daddy and my brothers came home from the cotton fields. They had been pulling out some bad weeds, called cockleburs, that were entangling the cotton plants which now held almost full-grown bolls of cotton. The only way to get rid of the cockleburs was to pull them up by their roots and burn them. They grow spiny burs with hooked prickles, which cling to clothing.

I ran and met them before they put the wagon and team of mules up. Ruby and Dan, the mules, were always fun to watch when they were unharnessed. They would lie down on their backs and roll from side to side with all four feet kicking strongly up in the air. They spread their big mouths wide open and showed their huge teeth. It looked as though they were laughing heartily. It was a mule workout.

At supper I told the boys, "Betcha can't guess what all we did at Mrs. Maude's."

Bob replied, "You were only gone one night. Why don't y'all go back?"

I think he was jealous. He said that we owed him, because he was the chief dish washer while we were gone. I brought in cook stove wood for him that night. I didn't mind that chore because the wood was cut into smaller sticks than regular fire wood for the fireplace.

The fire compartment was only about 6" x 6" x 15" in one end of the cook stove. Our 15" long sticks were about 2" x 2". Daddy knew exactly how to split the wood with a chopping axe so it would fit. He always started a fire there and got his coffee percolator ready to go as the stove got hot. He usually cut off some meat for breakfast the night before. There was an awesome supply of bacon, ham, or sausage in the smokehouse most of the time.

Daddy was considered an expert on salting, sugar-curing and smoking meats by several folks in the community. We often assisted neighbors with hog-killing, and they returned the favor to us.

Mama's expertise was making them homemade biscuits, which we always had with fresh pork tenderloin on hog-killing day.

8

When Daddy came in on Friday night for supper, we all gathered round our favorite spot, the eatin' table. As usual, Bob complained the sisters were hogging the bench. One look from Daddy convinced us to scoot down and give Bob half the bench.

If there was one thing I was good at, it was detecting a twinkle in my daddy's eye. "What's up?" I asked him.

He guzzled down a good, long swig of milk, then looked at us girls and told us Mr. DeLaughter was leaving early in the morning for Kansas City. He had been elected to serve on an important farm committee for the president or someone that really mattered.

"You may get a honk from the Mrs. tomorrow," he said.

Mary and I were so thrilled that we just might get to go and protect Mrs. Maude from anything or anyone who possibly might want to harm that poor, rich woman.

We were too excited to eat or sleep, but we tried to do both. We arose from bed the next morning before the biscuits were in the oven. Mama told us to get some warm water from the tea kettle on the stove and wash our bodies and put on clean clothes. (She called this a "spit bath"). In warm weather, we mostly had tub baths. We would let the sun heat our water in a wash tub outside and hide it in a good place. Then we'd take turns cleaning ourselves! This normally happened on a Saturday, so that we were clean for church on Sunday.

We each donned a flour sack apron to eat breakfast, clean up the kitchen, make the beds, and sweep the floors. The men had already vacated the premises and took up the barn and pasture chores. There were fences to be fixed, stalls to be cleaned and mule harnesses to be mended. They all worked fast with their hands, so the work was quickly taken care of.

Sometimes my middle brother, Clyde, was accused of shirking a little when it came to physical tasks. Daddy told us if we wanted to know how many airplanes scraped the sky that day, just ask Clyde. He said Clyde could tell you how many and what kind went over. He read the Bible and any other materials he could come by, pertaining to Christianity, and was a very good student in school. Clyde also took a liking to birds and could identify most southern U.S. species by their appearance or their songs. He and Roy were both scared to death of snakes. That wasn't my greatest fear. I was totally frightened out of my wits one day when the boys found a nest of about a dozen newborn field mice and rudely packed them down in the posterior opening of my shirt. I ran through the sedge grass pasture until I collapsed face-down, crying. They all got extra chores for a month for that evil deed. I am still afraid of mice.

"Honk, honk!" Our beautiful, blue, horseless carriage arrived. Mrs. Maude stepped out momentarily to ask Mama if we could spend the night with her again.

Mama said, "I hope they don't cause you any extra trouble".

Mrs. Maude assured her that we kept her from being afraid and that she enjoyed our company immensely. This time we each toted a brown paper sack, which was made ready the night before. After we floated on air up 67 and arrived at her home, she showed us where to set our sacks down. It was the same room we slept in before.

"This is my guest bedroom," she said.

Our eyes rolled at each other when she wasn't looking. She picked up a white cardboard box from a nearby chair and handed it toward us. I reached quickly to see what was inside. I pulled out a lovely soft garment the color of my blue-green eyes.

When I stretched it out on the bed I said, "A dress! Is it for me"?

"No," she said. "That one is sized for Mary." Her eyes were the same as mine. I yanked another soft clump from the box that was the prettiest blue, velvety dress I had ever seen in any catalog. The box showed the word, "Spiegel".

The only catalogs we ever had were *Sears and Roebuck* and *Montgomery Ward*. They were hand-me-downs from some folks whose house was on our school road. We called them our wish books. We named some of the models who starred in our catalogs, cut them out with scissors, and pretended all sorts of activities for them. On a rainy or snowy day when we didn't have to go to the fields, we often had a paper-doll wedding while our brothers laughed and made fun of us. I'm surprised my eyes didn't pop out of their sockets when I saw my first ready-made dress. It looked like a princess dress I had seen in a storybook I had borrowed from Mrs. Clark, my teacher. It had long sleeves that were puffy at the top and snug with lace at the wrist.

Mrs. Maude must've known my thoughts. She asked if I would like to try it on. Whoopee! Off went my clean dress and on went my store-bought one! She tied the fluffy sash for me, and I whirled about gracefully, with the full skirt standing far out around me. When I glanced at Mary, she was shaking her head to the negative sign. I knew that was code for "I'll try mine on when I get home."

We both hugged the generous lady and told her how much we "'preciated" what she had done for us. I was thinking that when Daddy is owing somebody for a good deed, he always says, "much obliged", but I didn't exactly know what that meant.

She fixed us sandwiches again with real light bread and called them tuna. We gave each other a questioning look. I could tell, Mary didn't know any more than I did about that word. We stuffed down two whole sandwiches, while we wondered what the strange smell was. When Mrs. Maude asked how we liked the tuna fish, we then knew what had died. It surely tasted good!

After we drank some of her store-bought milk and cleaned up the kitchen for her, she bragged on us for doing such a good job. She disappeared for only a moment and returned to the kitchen to tell us she had another surprise.

This time she held two small packages, which she laid on the table and went back for an apron. I examined one of them and tried to pronounce the words on it. "Ch, Cha, Charm, C-U-R-L".

"Charm Curl," said Mrs. Maude. "We are going to curl your pretty hair."

She had us to go wash our hair with Lady Godiva Shampoo, and gave us a big, fluffy towel to wrap around our heads. We ordinarily washed our hair at the well in a dishpan with soap.

I hopped in her chair when she asked who would be first. She surely knew by now that Mary was bashful. She soaked my hair in a strong-smelling lotion and divided it into small twigs. Then each one was rolled from the ends up to my head on some kind of a cardboard roller and fastened with bobby pins. When she finished rolling all the twigs, she allowed me to look in a mirror. We all laughed and laughed—I felt like an ugly boy with my hair greased up tight!

Next up was the shy one. Her hairdo took a shorter time because the stylist said she knew better what she was doing. All of this primping consumed about three hours. She gave each of us a pretty glass jar of Pond's Cold Cream, and suggested we rub some on our face and neck every night before we go to bed. We used it sparingly, so it would last a long time.

She told us to let the rollers stay in our hair until morning. We told her we brought our new gowns that Bonnie and I had made. When I took mine from the sack, she exclaimed, "Oh, my goodness! It's so beautiful and so pretty and white."

I told her they were made from the feed sacks she gave us. Mary went in the bathroom and put hers on. I guess she was in a hurry to sink into that luxurious, ruffled bed. Mrs. Maude told us goodnight and thanked us for being there. I said, "We are much obliged, Ma'am".

I admired my new gown and the nice way it fit, as I pulled it gently on and snuggled into bed. The hair curlers on my head were a bit uncomfortable at first, but I don't believe they caused me to miss any sleep.

We awoke the next morning to a loud ringing somewhere in the house. I jumped out of bed and walked toward the kitchen door, and I could hear Mrs. Maude talking and laughing. I figured it must have been the telephone we heard. She later told us that Mr. DeLaughter called from Kansas City to "check on his three girls".

When Mary arose and we were about to make up the bed, we both started laughing. There were two sunken ruts in the bed. It appeared we had slept all night without even turning over. I wish I could sleep like that nowadays.

We dressed and quickly went into the kitchen just as the phone conversation ended. She was laughing and told us some of the things her husband had told her, and we all laughed.

"Oh, my sleeping beauties!" she said, as she began to unwind curlers from Mary's head. I was admiring her pretty hair, and I was definitely not disappointed when Mrs. Maude led me to a mirror to see my own. A new me!

Our permanent curls didn't last forever. I don't know if our hostess knew, but her acts of kindness, our first perm and many other favors, caused both of us girls to be more concerned about looking nice and taking better care of our hair and skin. I was born when Mama was 35 and she had suffered from her undiagnosed illness most of my life. Mary and I just did what we knew how to do for the most part, with some help from Bonnie.

We learned many things in our short visits to the mansion on 67. God blessed us when he made us sharecropper's daughters.

9

All of us kids learned early on in life that we weren't to ask repeatedly for or beg Daddy for things we wanted. He had his way of making sure we had plenty of fun times when farm work wasn't looming.

One of those super-fun days happened after Daddy took a poll at breakfast, to find out how many of us wanted to go fishing at Middle Creek. Everybody got excited, but Roy. He volunteered to stay with Mama because she said she didn't feel like going.

After Daddy announced we would get hungry before this trip was over, we started looking for grub to take. Mama gave us some tips about what to carry, and we were packed and loading on the wagon in no time. We even carried a meal for the mules. We must be ever grateful to Dan and Ruby for bearing all our burdens!

Our bedrolls consisted of one large quilt for each participant. Even though the nights were quite warm, we would have to roll up in cover so as not to be eaten up by mosquitoes. The men folk took care of the fishing gear, a big jug of water, and other odds-and-ends. I was sure we would forget something. Oh well.

The mules were rested, so it didn't take long to get down the road a couple of miles toward the river. We stopped at a boggy place across the ditch and sampled the dirt for worms. We hit the pay load and dug the biggest worms we had ever seen. Some of them were ten to twelve inches long and as big around as a pencil. When we had filled a tall coffee can, we took off to our campsite on Middle Creek bank.

Daddy was tickled when I caught the first fish. He said he gave me a special hook because I was the baby. It was a multicolored perch big enough to keep and eat. I was cautioned many times to be quiet or the fish would all run away. Sometimes I forgot about that and allowed my thoughts to be spoken out loud. Then my brothers made more noise than I did, telling me about it! I caught a lot of fish, anyway.

While Bob and Clyde cleaned the fish, the rest of us gathered twigs and chunks of rotted wood and built a big bonfire. After it burned down to coals, we got out our cast iron skillets, pots, and percolator for coffee. We peeled potatoes and chopped up onions in them, then fried them in the black skillet until they were golden brown. I hope I never lose the memory of that aroma.

The boys fried fish, fish, and more fish. The large, brown paper sack of biscuits were already baked. We all ate and swatted mosquitoes until we couldn't hold another bite.

Mary and I cleaned up the mess, stowed it all back in the wagon, and covered it well. Meanwhile, the others had started to put the trot lines together for night fishing for catfish or whatever kind the Lord blessed us with. Daddy managed to get his post-supper dip of snuff, so all was well with the world!

We followed the men, who were winding along the creek, depositing the trot lines loaded with large, baited hooks. We had no boats in which to cross the wide creek. Several times during the night we would get up and check for fish and re-bait the hooks.

There was only one old, rusty lantern that burned coal oil, and it was filled and ready for dark to come. Mary and I snuggled up in our quilts in the little space that was left in the wagon, while the rest hovered around the campfire, rolled up in their quilts. We all kept our shoes and clothes fastened tightly to discourage snakes, ants, and such.

Daddy fashioned a fish stringer from a strong cord and a forked twig or two. We started loading it on our first check with the three big, jughead catfish we hooked on our lines. Then, it was back to bed until our fearless leader moved again. We followed them every step of the way, because we were cowards and didn't care to stay at the camp alone in the middle of the night with no lantern.

We crawled back into our respective napping spots. I was truly grateful that the mules had earlier been unhitched from our wagon bed, so they could wallow and then lay their enormous bodies down to rest. Our heads were lying on the end of the wagon where their rear ends would have been if they were hitched. If our blessings continued, we would have a slew of cats to take home tomorrow.

The next sound I heard was the crackling of a limb on the ground as Daddy stepped on it. The rest of our clan wasn't hard to awaken in the wilderness. We were following the leader again—this time it was Bob. I held tight to the back of his shirt tail, because I knew he wasn't afraid of anything. I was second in line as we all dodged brush and limbs and trapesed along the creek bank. We would go to the farthest hooks first, so we didn't have to carry our fish there and back.

I softly asked Bob, "Don't the Bible say there ain't no friend that sticketh closer than a brother?"

He laughed.

Clyde spoke up and told me I said it backwards. He said in Proverbs it says, "there is a friend that sticketh closer than a brother," meaning Jesus Christ. Clyde knew a lot about the Bible, and it seemed like it was on his mind often.

Some of our lines were jumping up and down as we moved along. We knew we would find a big fish there when we came back by.

Suddenly, I yanked down on the tail of the shirt I was latched onto. Bob stopped quickly, because the tug almost brought him to his knees. I raised my shaking hand and pointed toward two shiny eyes that I spied in the dark. When Bob saw them, he turned around fast and told the others he didn't think we needed to check that first hook up there, because it wasn't shaking, and we could get it next time.

We stood still as the others walked past us, getting ready to pick up the line which was still quite a way ahead of us. They didn't make it to the line before Mary let out a blood-curdling scream that stopped them in their tracks.

She whispered, "Look! I've never heard of anything having eyes that big!"

We all stood very still and quiet as we saw the eyes move slightly in our direction. Clyde placed his hand on his scabbard around his leg that contained a knife he used to clean fish for supper.

Daddy was the first to move. He slipped closer to our hook as he remarked he had seen such as this before, and that it would float away because it was scared of us too. He leaned over the water and retrieved a huge mudcat. Then he unfastened the line and wound it around his arm. The humongous eyes began to rise higher in the air and float away from us until they were no longer visible due to the forest.

Daddy said, "I'll tell you what I think it is later, but right now, let's just take up our fish and our hooks and go cook us some bacon, sausage and eggs."

I was so glad the two brothers had accompanied us on this short camping trip. They shuffled the left-over coals in the fire and managed to get Dan and Ruby hitched back to the wagon just as we opened the biscuit sack and served up a breakfast fit for a king. Our olfactory senses woke up our taste buds for sure! Thanks to the Lord, He brought daybreak just in time to make this togetherness circle just perfect.

Daddy said the coffee was simply the best he had tasted as he took a sip and breathed a good sigh. He then emptied the pot into four more cups and passed them around the buffet on the ground to all of us. He quietly loved us and the feeling was mutual!

The boys lifted the three stringers of fish from their resting place in the creek and tied each one on the outside of the wagon to drip the short distance to home. We had about twenty catfish and an eel or two. It was meat for two or three days. We had no way to keep it cold, so we would have to cook it all at once to prevent spoilage, then eat, eat, eat!

It seemed like a long ride back up the hills to the house. We weren't as peppy on returning home as we were when we got ready to go to the creek. We were anxious to hear Daddy's true story about his encounter with eyes.

When all the camp amenities were washed and put away, it was lunch for a bunch. Mama surprised us with a Johnny cake she had made the last time the oven was heated. She had covered it with a cloth and kept it hidden two days, deeming it a miracle that it wasn't found and eaten.

We opened jars of peaches, pears, plums and blackberries from our canning pantry. Sugar was still rationed and scarce, so we only sweetened them slightly.

Milton, Bonnie, and their kids, Dwayne and Jeannie, came and ate dinner with us, so we had help afterward cleaning and frying the fish. When all was done for the day, we gathered under a walnut tree in the yard. The four kids that fished had our eyes fixed on the head of the house, waiting for an explanation. Most of us found a bucket or a big rock to sit on. We only had four straight-back chairs, with seats made of heavy strings woven together.

Grandma held the baby granddaughter, Jeannie, in her arms, and the grandson, Dwayne, sat beside her. Even after bearing eight babies of her own, she still liked to be near the grands every chance she got.

Grandpa sat on the ground and leaned back against a fence post, while our milk cow nudged his back peacefully. When I moved closer to him, he told me to sit on my fist and lean back on my thumb.

Daddy cleared his throat like our preacher always did, and he started by telling all of us that we had a little excitement at the creek this morning, right before day...

"It was dark enough that all we could see was about fifteen feet in front of us. When we run the trot lines the last time, there were two round lights about the size of a plate. It scared me for a minute. The kids all thought it was eyes. Well, I knowed it had to be a huge monster to have eyes that big. My heart was banging pretty hard till I saw them 'eyes' moving separately. That's when these young'uns were 'bout ready to take flight instead of fight."

He then told about when he and his brother, Henry, went out on a date with our mother and her sister, Lizzie years ago. After they walked the girls home, and headed back to their house in the dark, they encountered a light that floated alongside them in the woods as they walked in the dirt road. He said every way they turned, the light did the same. They hid behind two trees on the other side of the road, and after a bit, the obstacle floated up above the trees and disappeared.

A few days afterward, he and Henry were in Emmet at the feed store and overheard a fellow talking about seeing a moving light on that road along the same place they had seen it. The stranger told them that he knew a radio man who said that kind of light can be seen in the fall of the year, right around Halloween, so they nicknamed them jack-o-lanterns, just like the pumpkins.

He told them that the radio guy said it occurs in boggy, swamp-like areas, and that some kind of gases rise up out of the bog and form a balloon-like formation that sucks in the gases, causing it to be shining and floating.

Milton reached over closer to the tree we were under and handed me a pumpkin from our pile. Ha!

When we finally got to go back to school, I told Mrs. Clark about our scare, and she said, "Let me read something to you right here."

She motioned for Mary to come hear it, too. She read that according to an Irish legend, jack-o-lanterns were named for a man called Jack, who couldn't enter heaven, because he was a miser. He couldn't enter hell either, because he had played jokes on the devil. As a result, Jack would have to walk the earth with his lantern until Judgment Day.

"I wish I had a book like that," I said. She told me that the big book was called a *World Book*, and that I might look at it anytime I liked.

I told my teacher that Jack didn't have to walk the earth all the time. He can float high and fast. I knew he wasn't just a legend! We all saw him!

10

There was a noise in the kitchen and I sat straight up in bed. I shook Mary awake, realizing daybreak had come. Wow! A whiff of percolating coffee drifted through closed doors to my nostrils. Daddy and Mama are up already! I flung the door open to see it was only Daddy in the kitchen. He didn't look up, just kept on at the task before him. He was attempting to make biscuits, just like Mama, for the first time. He said she didn't feel like getting up this morning. He asked me to get a skillet and fill it with the ham he had cut off and brought in from the smokehouse the night before.

I had always been tickled to please my father, and this time was no different. I placed the pieces of beautiful pink ham precisely in the battered, old, black skillet, until it was full. I set the heavy creation on top of the wood stove to wait for the fire in it to start heating the ham through and through. I had been told that pork must always be cooked thoroughly to prevent illness. It is never to be eaten when cooked rare.

I ran outside to the hen house, grabbed an empty lard bucket, and gathered up a sufficient number of eggs for all of us. Mama taught me how to crack an egg when I was helping make cornbread a little while back. Only two eggs were miscracked. The others, I managed to crack and scramble with Daddy eyeing me carefully and warning me to not touch the hot stove.

I was told to go wake the boys, so we could all eat and get ready for church. This was the chance I'd been waiting for! I snitched an artificial bird feather from Clyde's Sunday hat hanging on the wall in their room. I started with him, tickling his nose from every direction with that feather. Each time, I would duck down to the floor so he couldn't spot me. He finally woke enough to find me.

I went on to tickle Roy and Bob. It was so much fun aggravating my brothers, I forgot to tell them why I came in there. When I announced that breakfast was ready, they were up fast as lightning and headed for the eatin' table. Not a one of them seemed to suspect that I had anything to do with cooking breakfast until Daddy told Mary she could wash the dishes because Nora helped cook!

I pitched in and helped wipe up the kitchen, so we could hurriedly get into our store-bought dresses, and go on down to church. We always made sure our bodies were thoroughly clean, and our hair was shining, late on Saturday, because we knew that Clyde would see to it that we went to church on Sunday morning.

Our steps may have been a mite swifter this day, because breakfast wasn't on time. When we got within hearing distance of the building, we heard the church singing, *When the Roll is Called Up Yonder, I'll Be There*. We ran, and I was the first one to reach the doorsteps. Clyde had cautioned us to respect the house of God, because He is our Heavenly Father and He would be there with us!

We walked in very softly and took the first empty pew for our seats. The congregation sang again, and I steadily looked for God, but I didn't see him. I asked Mrs. Mildred Johnson, my Sunday School teacher, where God was.

"He is in Heaven, but He's right here with us, too, because He is everywhere."

She also said that I won't learn everything right now, but if I keep on coming to church, I will learn something each time. I loved going to Boughton Church, and indeed, I did learn some scripture, which I can still recite. Mr. Joe Beavert led the singing, and Mrs. Lizzie McDaniel played the piano. It truly did seem like *Heaven Came Down and Glory Filled My Soul*.

I don't remember the preacher's name. He preached loud and long, and I had to sit still, or my siblings would tell my parents and I wouldn't get to go again. I was relieved when he would call on Mr. Trosie Formby or Dr. McDaniel to dismiss us.

One of the deacons, Mr. Cue Johnson, asked us where we lived. When one of my brothers told him, he volunteered to take us home if we didn't mind riding in the back of his Ford pickup. Wow! We were all delighted, and crawled right in. There were only three vehicles parked in the church yard. Dr. Mac had to have a car to make house calls to attend to the sick. Mr. Formby had his farm and grocery store pickup.

Mr. Cue's wife, Alta, and his two sons, Thomas Cue and Prentiss, were in the cab of the truck with him. What a quick trip home! We thanked him really good.

He got out and tipped his hat to my daddy, then shook his hand. He said, "Mr. Daniel, I could take your children to Boughton and bring them home every Sunday if it would please you and your wife."

Daddy told him he would appreciate it because they worried about us walking there and back. Just one more handshake and it was done! What wonderful news! We all loved the breezy ride in the back of the truck, although Sister said it tangled her hair. We laughed at her.

Sunday dinner was peas, potatoes, and a pan of cornbread. It was eaten quickly while I was giving our folks every detail about the truck ride. They had never had that privilege to ride in a truck before. It was hard to clean up the kitchen when our bellies were so tight, but we knew it was our job and it couldn't wait.

11

When all was clean and put back in place, our dear father announced that we should get our swimming clothes on. We grabbed cut-off overalls, khakis, and shirts, and we were on the road in no time, headed to Little Missouri River. Clyde stayed back with our mother this time.

While walking on the rough, rocky road through the tall timbers, Daddy explained that we would soon have to hit the fields for fall harvest. He said he thought the corn crop would be gathered first, because if it rained too much, it would mildew and might poison our livestock.

I hoped that we could get the corn and cotton out of the weather before it ruined. I didn't know how to pray exactly, but I did ask God to not let my daddy get sick, and to let us get everything done the right way so he would be pleased. I was unhappy when Daddy's face looked worried.

To this day, as I write in my latter years, I can truthfully say that it grieves me to the gut when I fear that I have not pleased my awesome Heavenly Father. My greatest worry is that I might be guilty of the sin of omission. I regularly ask His forgiveness for this and beg that he might help me not to worry.

I was delighted to find that Milton and his little family were already there at the river. He asked me to sit in the shallow edge of the water and watch his children while he and Bonnie swam. I accepted the responsibility and enjoyed just cooling off on a very hot day. The kids obeyed me, as usual, and entertained me considerably, just helping me make roads and rock dams in the ankle-deep water.

For the first time ever, I was glad when Daddy gave his loud command, "Outta the water!"

We knew better than to argue with him—we were headed for the bridge and straight home. Little Mo didn't produce the excitement that I anticipated that day. I still had my mind on helping our family with the much-needed harvest that we were told would start tomorrow.

First order of business after breakfast for us girls next morning was clean up the kitchen, make beds and sweep floors. We also found some canned beans, squash and mixed pickles in our fruit shelves that held big half gallon jars of beautiful produce that we had canned at various times during gardening season. These sealed jars could quickly be opened and heated while cornbread baked for supper.

The men folk proceeded to the barn crib and retrieved the cotton-picking sacks that were stored there in a rat-proof box when the harvest was finished last fall. Daddy mended the holes that had been caused by simple wear and tear. He handed out a good, strong sack to each of us. They all laughed when he gave me the last one—the smallest. He knew I probably wouldn't fill it anyway.

If our field was close to the house, we all went to work. When he asked me to go see about Mama, I would take fresh water back to the field. When we worked far from the house, we carried a large milk can filled with water on the wagon. The water got warm on hot days (and most of them were), but as Daddy said, it was still wet.

When the gang was harvesting far away from the house, one of us kids stayed with Mama when she wasn't feeling well. Usually it was me, because I wasn't worth as much in the field as the bigger ones were. Mary got a hundred pounds in her sack sometimes, so I thought maybe I could in four more years. Daddy and the older boys could manage to grab over two hundred pounds in a good crop of cotton. Each full sack was weighed. The weight was recorded for each person and totaled at the end of the day.

We emptied our cotton sacks into our open wagon and stomped it down until the wagon was so packed, that it couldn't contain any more. It was ready for the mules to be re-hooked and pull it to the gin in downtown Boughton.

Daddy was our boss, so he allowed us to take turns riding on top of a wagon with sideboards loaded with cotton. It was a ride that almost equaled Mrs. Maude's fancy car ride. Except for the clopping of mules' hooves, it was like what I imagined riding on a cloud would be like.

We traveled the four miles at a slow pace, so the cotton wouldn't blow. As soon as the gin was in sight, we knew we would have to wait in line behind a few other loaded wagons. When it was our turn, Daddy parked the loaded wagon in the designated spot. A long metal tube stretched from the gin out to our wagon and sucked all the cotton into the gin. There, they removed all the seeds and trash from the cotton and pressed it into a 480-pound bale about the size of a modern-day refrigerator.

Our landlord had made a contract with the ginning company about where to ship it and who to sell it to. The cotton belonged to Mr. DeLaughter. We would, hopefully, be paid when our crop was all ginned and sold.

Daddy met a few farmers that he was already acquainted with, and a few who became friends after meeting them at the gin. Every time he went, he met some new folks. Our family hadn't thus far, been overly-friendly enough to go visiting our neighbors often. We liked them and were friendly upon meeting, but we were taught to mind our own business. Because he had to quit school at a very early age and get a job in the log woods to support his widowed mother and three younger siblings, he taught all of us the importance of keeping up with our jobs around the farm, and not allowing our work to push us. That way, we seldom got behind.

Once when we brought back the empty wagon from the gin, Daddy let the mules run down a steep hill on the road. Their mouths would spread wide open as if they were smiling. Back in the field he hollered, "Whoa!" loudly. When the pickers looked up, he grinned and yelled, "Fill-er-up!"

Just about sundown, he motioned for us to board the wooden vehicle and go in. Bob drove the team this time, and allowed them to step a little faster, since the wagon was light. It seemed like they almost giggled when they were turned loose to wallow. Poor old Dan and Ruby had been hitched all day. Bob fed them well for their reward.

We all washed up and entered the back door to the wonderful aroma of hot, fried potatoes and ham, and some cornbread with home-canned, wild plums for dessert. The plums were tart without sugar.

The next time our wagon was packed with the freshly packed fluff, Mary rode atop the white cloud that would soon be ginned, and its seeds that were removed reserved for planting next spring. The seeds from most of our bales were sent to a mill in Texas where cottonseed oil was produced from it, then the remainder of it was used for cow feed.

12

When we had three bales processed that year, Mr. Landlord said we had surpassed our record for the previous year for the number of bales we had picked. He also commented that our yield-per-acre was much improved.

He and Daddy talked in the front yard for some time. After they shook hands again, he left. Daddy came in and announced that we were shifting gears again. Mr. DeLaughter thought heavy rains were headed our way, and perhaps we needed to let the last field of cotton bolls open up more, while we harvested the corn. Daddy was a topnotch weather predictor, as far as his children knew, and he didn't anticipate rain at this time. But Mr. DeLaughter said get the corn in the barn, and so we would!

We were up and in the fields of dried corn every morning shortly after daylight, until every corn stalk had been robbed of its ears. All of our corn cribs in the barn were filled with premium ears when Mr. DeLaughter came in his pickup truck. After several trips to his barn, the boys had his cribs full.

The next job was to cut all the corn stalks down completely and stack them in the barn loft, to feed the animals during the winter. They loved to eat the fodder.

We hadn't felt the rain yet!

On Sunday morning, this time, we ate and finished our chores hurriedly. Mr. Cue Johnson had told us he would come and pick up us kids for church. We had moved up a notch in our world. No new scratches on our good shoes. They didn't touch the rocks! Mrs. Johnson commented that our dresses were very becoming. I didn't know what that word meant, but I told her, "Thank you. Mrs. DeLaughter gave them to us."

She smiled and slightly rolled her eyes at her husband.

I really liked my Sunday School class. For once, I was the only Daniel kid who fit this age group. I delighted in the Bible story cards Mrs. Mildred gave us to take home. I had one of Jesus hanging on a cross that I stuck on the only mirror in our house. I didn't understand why he was crucified, until many years later. I did know that He was God's only son, and that He had the power to stop the killing. He chose not to stop the crucifiers, so that His Father's will might be perfected.

We memorized John 3:16 and recited it to the whole congregation. I never forgot, "For God so loved the world, that He gave his only begotton Son, that whosoever believeth in Him should not perish, but have everlasting life."

When we finished reciting in unison, a corner group of male voices said, "Amen".

I supposed that was the Amen Corner I had heard about. When we went home, Mama usually asked us what the preacher said, I think just to see if we paid attention at church. Or maybe she just wanted to "go along for the ride." I listened to the preacher carefully this time. He asked us to turn to the gospel according to St. John, fourth chapter and thirty-fourth verse.

I don't know if the preacher realized that some of us didn't own a Bible. I quietly stepped over Mary and scooted in by Clyde, so I could look on his Gideon Bible with him. All I could remember to tell Mama was where he read from, and that he was talking about cotton farming and sharecroppers. He said for us to, "lift up our eyes, and look on the fields; for they are white already to harvest."

I went on to tell her what else he read that the sower, who is my daddy, and the reaper, who is Mr. DeLaughter, will be happy together.

That being said, I skipped off toward the kitchen. Daddy reached out and slowed me down. It was often that my quick feet (or mouth) got me reprimanded, but I knew I could blame it on being the baby of the family.

In the kitchen, we found out Daddy had killed two fryer chickens while we were gone, and Mama had cooked them and made gravy, potatoes, green beans. and biscuits. Another Sunday feast. We usually settled for fresh milk and bread for supper.

❧❦

Monday morning always rolled around too quickly. We had to rush through breakfast and our morning chores and hit the wagon. Daddy brought in a huge cowbell and told our mother that we would be in the back field today. He rang the bell once. The deafening sound would certainly get somebody's attention! He instructed her to ring it if she needed us.

She knew it had to be all hands pickin' till this last patch of cotton was done. It was the story of her married life. She very rarely complained about anything. She didn't speak idly, only what needed to be said. We had the greatest mother in the world! I asked God to be near her that day, but I didn't know if he heard me.

Dan and Ruby jostled over the creek and through the tall timber like they knew we were rarin' to get the job done. Finally, we rode through some tall weeds and there it was in plain sight. Our young driver, Bob, said, "Whoa," and the wagon was still.

We all just sat there for a minute, with our eyes fixed on the white field in front of us. It was truly God's amazing beauty! John Wesley Daniel said, "Praise the Lord"! He said he had never seen a new snowfall that white or that solid. Our family efforts were rewarded ten times over. It was a blessing to see such a bountiful crop after all these years. White already to harvest!

Daddy yelled, "Let's go grab 'em bolls, Young'uns!" and that we did!

None of us had a timepiece, so we watched the sun and took a break mid-morning, at dinner time, and mid-afternoon. Cloudy days dragged by slowly. We just ate when we figured it was noon. Our belly told us it was eatin' time.

We tried to snatch the full bolls as fast as we could, because Daddy said this was a special cotton patch, and that's why we were blessed with such a bountiful crop. He told us maybe the rain will hold off till we're through. He added that it didn't look like rain to him.

He was right. The day we scrapped over the barren cotton stalks and got the last few bolls that opened late, it hadn't as much as sprinkled rain on that field. We stopped by our house to see about Mama, and she was OK, but said she didn't feel like going with us in the wagon.

Our leader suggested we all climb aboard and ride to the gin. He grinned as he spat out the last of his snuff and climbed in the driver's seat taking the reins. The rest of us snuggled down deep in the cotton with only our noses sticking out.

Mules are generally described as dumb, but Ruby and Dan danced along as if they knew this was their last trip to the gin this year. They took us right on into Boughton and across the Missouri-Pacific railroad tracks fast. They finally slowed as they neared the gin.

Daddy didn't act like he was surprised that Mr. and Mrs. DeLaughter were there awaiting our arrival. They were smiling and making small talk until our cotton was vacuumed from the wagon through the long metal tube and carried all the way through the ginning process. They called Mr. DeLaughter inside. When he came back out, all the gin staff and a crowd of spectators began to clap their hands and yell.

They came close to us and our wagon as Mr. DeLaughter delivered the statement that we had produced the most cotton per acre of any farmer in Boughton township, whether owner or sharecropper. The gin manager told Mr. DeLaughter and Daddy that we had the softest and cleanest cotton, also, meaning it would bring a top price. I was so happy for my daddy!

Several men came and shook hands with both men. When all was said and done, and Daddy held a paper check in his hand from our owner, (including a bonus) we climbed back in our carriage. The mules responded to the click of their master's tongue and started moving with less urgency now.

We didn't know what to think when Daddy directed them to the front of the Boughton Mercantile. He told us to stay there as he entered the store. When he returned, he was carrying something big we had never seen. It was red and about two feet long and approximately eight inches around. Our imagination went wild, and none of us guessed correctly. Daddy didn't reveal his surprise until we got home, so Mama could enjoy it with us.

Indeed, it was something that had never been in our house. It was a whole stick of bologna with a round, wooden box of hoop cheese. He didn't need to make a speech about his appreciation for us. We all immediately started slicing and eating it with the fresh baked bread on the table.

We didn't make any thank-you speeches either, but our parents knew we liked it. The boys had never eaten bologna, and none of us had ever enjoyed cheese before.

Daddy admitted that Mr. DeLaughter had told him we were in the running for top cotton farmer in our area. That's why he insisted we all make this last gin trip. Huh? Last?

෴

Our family had been taught that early to bed and early to rise makes a man healthy, wealthy and wise. Before we went to bed that night, Daddy told us we could sleep a little later. The next morning, we took the wagon down by the river and turned left to a large field. He told us that in the past, there had been a big field of pumpkins planted there.

"Sometimes," he said, "a few seeds that had lain dormant for a few years will awaken and sprout."

He was right. Many long vines meandered through the sandy, river-bottom soil, climbing over brush piles, and yielding a wagonload of bright, orange pumpkins. We left the green ones to be picked by the next family that wandered through the bottoms.

The pumpkins were piled under the walnut tree at the house. I made a sign from a piece of cardboard: "Pumpkins 25 cents". Benevolent-minded Clyde thought we should give them away to anyone who wanted them, because the Master (God) grew them without any work from us. I told Clyde to just go on and put the mules up!

About the time I finished arranging the beautiful pumpkin pile, I was startled to see a black, flatbed truck turn into our front yard. It had a man driver and a man passenger in it, and nothing on the back. The door next to me opened, and my daddy stepped out! I didn't even know he had gone anywhere. The truck turned around and went back in the direction from whence it came. When we entered the house, Daddy asked us to sit around the eatin' table. He motioned for Mama to sit, also.

He stunned us with his first statement, "Get the stuff packed. We are moving tomorrow"!

He told us that Mr. Henry Hignight had stopped him on the road by the bridge at Cold Run Creek one of the times he was going to the gin. He had asked Daddy to be thinking about coming to work for him at the Georgia Haynes orchard. He said they would have work for him the year around and they would pay him according to the number of hours he worked each week.

Mama asked if he was letting the DeLaughters down by leaving them. He told her he had spoken to the landlord already, and he thought it was a good deal for our family, but he surely hated to lose his award-winning cotton growers! Mr. DeLaughter said he was always happy to see his sharecroppers move on to better themselves.

I, the worrier, thought sadly about leaving this place where Bob and I were well-acquainted with every stump and hollow. I hoped that Mrs. Maude would still need Mary and me occasionally, and she did!

Daddy told us we would get the moving done quickly because Mr. Hignight would send his big, flatbed truck and two men to help us. He said the orchard folks were providing a house for us as long as he worked for them. He had been to look at it, and it had good well water. Daddy was really happy that it was very close to church and school for us. He said he was so glad we wouldn't have to walk those four miles each way anymore.

Roy and Clyde drove the mules and wagon to our new home with our two cows and a calf following by being tied to the wagon with a rope. By the next evening, everything we owned was at our new place, except some of our corn crop. This new place wasn't a farm, and we didn't have enough storage space in the barn. Daddy started the boys off building some corn cribs onto the barn. They were able to finish them in a few days and bring the corn on home.

"Pumpkins 25 cents"

13

Daddy took us around the corner in the middle of the little city of Boughton to get us all signed in to school again, but nobody was there. We turned around and stopped at the Mercantile. The clerk in there seemed surprised that we hadn't heard.

"Heard what?" Daddy said.

The next words that fell on our ears shocked us all. The Nevada County School District had consolidated some of the smaller schools in the county, and Boughton was one of them! There would be no more school in that beloved little, red-brick building.

Not a word was spoken on the few hundred feet that Dan and Ruby trod to take us home. They would get more rest now. I ran in and blabbed to Mama that we didn't have a school anymore. When the others came in, Mama had plenty of questions. "Right when we get the kids moved closer to walk, things change so drastically!"

We found out at church the next Sunday that one of our deacons was on the Prescott School Board now, and he announced that a school bus would pick up all Boughton students the next day. It would deliver them to the front door of the school in Prescott and bring them home at 3:30 or 4:00 in the afternoon. And parents may ride with them the first day, if they choose.

Only four would be boarding the school bus from the Daniel house. Our sweet and timid brother, Roy, was forced to drop out of school earlier in life because of his speech impediment. He had attended Redland School before we left that community. His teacher sent a letter home with him for Mama. The note simply read that she was having to spend too much time with Roy because she couldn't understand anything he said. She recommended that he be kept at home, and Mama teach him. Mama was devastated, but she tried her best.

Roy was emotionally scarred, and he never could understand how he was different. It was difficult for us to realize that his speech was impaired, because we heard and understood every word he uttered. That teacher surely disturbed our family.

Roy was twenty years old at this time. When Mr. Hignight came to pick Daddy up on his first work day, Roy went with them. That's when he got his first job. He sat in the cab of that truck like a gentleman! Roy worked right alongside Daddy, who was just learning the trade, also. From then on, he held his head high, and worked like a man. He was Mama's son!

∽ᓚᘏᗢ⌒

The first day of school we were up for breakfast early, way before the two men left for the orchard. One fact that we were sure of—eating was a family event. That's when we revealed those small details about our lives that otherwise, wouldn't be told.

Mary and I wore new dresses that Bonnie made for us when she heard we would start school. She was fast becoming a good seamstress on our sewing machine, and I tried to watch every move she made. I wanted to sew good like her. She used some of the feed sacks Mrs. Maude gave us and trimmed them with pretty colors of rick-rack. We swirled around in them, knowing we must be looking good. The boys wore their Sunday khakis and chambray shirts. We told them they looked good, too.

Standing on our front porch, we heard a loud roar, coming around the corner. A gigantic yellow monster was fast approaching! It came to a screeching halt in front of us, and the driver stretched his neck out the window and asked if we're going to school. We marched around the front of the bus, looking for a door.

I was shaking all over with fear and excitement as I stumbled up the three steps. We knew the driver from church. He told us to take the first empty seats we came to. About middle way, Mary and I sat together. Clyde and Bob shared the next seat. I didn't want to look at the others just yet, so I looked at my well-worn, brown oxfords with miss-matched laces. I felt dizzy.

I whispered to Mary, "My head feels like it did when I tasted Milton's home brew…"

She slapped her hand over my mouth in a hurry. I didn't say another word. The bus traveled down several side roads, picking up children and some parents until all the seats were full. I had to scoot closer to Mary and let another girl sit by us. Then we went up 67 all the way into town.

I stared out our window at all the pretty store windows, as we drove through Prescott. Our first stop was the Prescott Elementary School. The driver got up and turned toward us and told us that everybody who would be in grades 1, 2, 3 and 4 would get off the bus and head to those red doors right there.

I stood up and tugged on my sister's dress, and she gave me a negative head shake. Clyde leaned up and told me to go ahead and get off, and somebody would show me where to go. All my siblings were going to another school! How could they???

I stepped off that monster much more reluctantly than I had climbed on. I felt as if I had left my whole world back at the house with Mama…Mama?

As I finally dashed through the doors, the first lady I saw was Mrs. Nellie Clark, my teacher from Boughton School.

"You're one of mine!" She hugged me and wiped my tears. Then she led me to my second-grade room, which she said was her room, also. I loved her even more now. There were several other consolidation-second-graders that I knew in "my" room. I smiled.

When we were somewhat settled in, Mrs. Clark told us all about our new school. The most interesting to me, was about the lunchroom at the end of our hall. She said three ladies cook lunch for us every day, and if we bring fifty cents on Mondays, we can eat there five days a week. I didn't know where I could get any money. Then she finished by saying she knew we were used to bringing our lunch to school, and that would be just fine if it suited our mothers. Our teacher paid for five extra lunches that first week.

She then escorted us down the hall and showed us the lunchroom. I was beginning to like this place. Back in the room, she gave each of us a small reader, and went around the room having us to read one page each. As I started to read my part, she paused and told the class, "I brought my best little reader from Boughton".

There were five of us "Boughtonites" in her room, and when the bell rang for recess, she went outside to show us where we could play and introduced us to the city kids. They were in their own little group and acted like they couldn't care less about us. Their eyes scanned us over good, from our hair down to our worn oxfords. It was obvious that they had won the style competition for the day. We five stuck together from then on.

I liked this room, because it was second graders only, and we got all the teacher's time. We stayed so busy, the day passed quickly. At the end of the day, Mrs. Clark made sure we got on the right bus, and I was so glad to see my family already onboard. We were going home. I had so much to tell!

I have tried numerous times in my lifetime to recapture the feelings I had when we stepped inside our home after that first day in the city. Mama was cooking supper with the oak-filled stove blazing. She had her hands in the sticky dough, filling the old, wooden biscuit bowl. As usual, she had sweat on her brow, and her face was beet red from the cook stove heat. She was prettier than any of those town kids' mothers, and I wanted to stay home with her forever! She was definitely a stay-at-home mom, as were most of the moms we knew.

Roy and Daddy came home from work, telling us how they learned to graft fruit trees. Of course, I was the one to ask, "What's that?"

Daddy explained, "You take a small branch from an excellent fruit bearing tree and attach it with tape to a limb of a tree that bears bad fruit but has good roots. Somehow it eventually bears the better quality of the donor tree. There are thousands of fruit trees in her orchards, but not all of them need to be grafted."

Roy expressed his gratefulness for a job.

14

Bob and Clyde hitched up the wagon and team and went to our old place to move the pumpkins. I went along. About half the pile had disappeared. I knew why, when I saw my sign for 25 cents each had been turned around to read "FREE". Clyde laughed. He was the culprit. I told him it was OK because folks needed pumpkin pie for Thanksgiving. Bob commented that most of the folks that traveled this road past the pumpkins were going right across the river bridge into Clark County to buy whiskey from a well-known bootlegger. Nevada County has been a dry county (no alcohol sold) as long as I can remember.

Some people who frequent that road were also going to fish at Rice's Lake, which is about halfway down to the river. Nobody swims at the lake, but fishing is great. Legend has it, that a woman fell in years ago. When they searched for her body, they decided there was no bottom to the lake. The signs clearly stated, "No Swimming".

On the way home, I told them I wanted to sell two pumpkins a week so I could eat in the lunchroom at school. The next morning, I was pleasantly surprised when a log truck stopped out front right after daylight. Daddy stepped out, then came back in and told me I had a customer. The kind man said his wife wanted a pumpkin or two. When I went to the pile, there was a beautifully decorated sign there that read, "Get your pumpkin here for 25 cents". I think Clyde did that. The fellow handed me a dollar and told me to keep the change. Mary would have lunch money, too.

When we got home from school that evening, Mama had collected three more quarters for me. I hadn't even thought about who would sell when I wasn't home. I surely didn't want Mama to have to go outside and do that.

Clyde helped me out again. We found an empty coffee can to set on the porch, then he printed another cardboard sign that read "Honor us with your quarter and take any pumpkin". Mama said she would take the money into the house after the customers left. It worked out well, and I really didn't mind if someone took a free one.

When Saturday rolled around, Daddy went to the store to buy paper and new pencils for us. I divided my jack-o-lantern money with him. We all liked school, except recess when we were expected to interact with kids who seemed to not want us there. I know they didn't think we were better than them!

The men broke up a large garden area and planted a turnip patch. Daddy said the soil had been resting a few years, so it would be excellent for the spring garden when the right season came.

I asked, "Why did the dirt get tired?"

No answer.

We all changed into our old home clothes as soon as the bus delivered us, and promptly hung our school clothes on nails that had been driven into the raw wood walls in our respective bedrooms. We had only about five clothes hangers that had been left in this house from the last tenants. Metal and plastic were still scarce due to the war. Even though we wore our clothes more than one day, when it was difficult to find clean ones, Mary and I knew wash day had come. We had been waiting for the wash pot to be raised onto big rocks to allow space for a fire underneath. It was close to the well where we drew the water up with a rope and bucket from about twenty feet in the ground. We then just dumped the well bucket into the pot. Daddy was right—we had good water this time! Our clothes were boiled in the pot, then splashed into a nearby tub and rubbed with our homemade lye soap on a rub board. Then they were rinsed in another tub and hung on our new clothesline in the back yard.

Later, we had another pot of clean water heating over the fire. We all took turns taking a washtub bath in the smokehouse. There was no meat smoking yet, so it seemed very convenient.

The boys' Sunday shirts looked so nice and white when we brought the dry clothes in. I always heard that clothes can't define what a person is inside. That was true for us, country kids, who endured a mighty culture shock in 1944 when we were forced to be integrated in school with town kids. I thank God, still, that Mrs. Nellie Clark was on this little second-graders's side.

I won't further lament on the culture shock problems, except to say that when we went to church again, the deacon who was on the school board took statements from most of us students who were there. He asked how we liked our new school, and he wrote our answers on a tablet. I told him that I loved the school, and I wished the kids who were already going there would like us Boughton folks, but they don't!

When he got around to Bob with the same question, my brother quietly told him he gets asked silly questions all the time like, "Did you ride your mule to school or walk?" or "Where'd you park your wagon?" or "Why are your britches so short?" or "How come y'all don't eat no lunch? Don't y'all eat nothing but turnip greens?"

All of that was written down. He said he was going to let it be known, and I suppose he did. We had much less intimidation after that. I learned to just concentrate on how much better desks, chairs, blackboards, and the whole building was. Also, I had a good teacher and some old friends there. I so appreciated the hot lunches I earned that year, and we all would rather ride a school bus than walk. I felt so blessed because I loved school! Several times a day, though, my thoughts drifted back to Mama and Daddy.

It was always good when we would come home and see Bonnie and my nephew and niece visiting. One time she had brought more new dresses for Mary and me. Her talent to look at a picture of a dress in a catalog, then cut fabric and sew it up to look just like the picture, without using a pattern was, in my mind, unsurpassed! Mama told Bonnie how grateful she was to have her for a daughter-in-law and thanked her many times for all she did for us girls. We tried the dresses on at once, and they fit us to a T!

Daddy and Roy said they let their bosses know that they were so pleased to have their jobs. Some days they worked with Milton, but most of the time he was driving a truck. Neither of them had ever been behind the wheel before.

When they got their first paycheck, they caught a Greyhound Bus over on the highway, and went to Prescott. It was a rare event and didn't happen often. Roy bought Mama a lovely, yet practical, new dress. He said he was hoping she would feel up to going to church. Not this Sunday. Daddy brought us a bigger skillet so we could fry up more potatoes. That's one thing we could always find in our barn—more taters to peel.

Daddy opened up a bank account, also. He never had enough money to worry about it being stolen before. He has been "banking" on the advice that Jesus gave in Matthew 6, "Lay not up for yourselves treasures upon earth, where moth and rust doth corrupt, and where thieves do not break through and steal: but lay up for yourselves treasures in heaven."

Our family was never destined to be wealthy. Neither Daddy nor Roy bragged about their wages from Georgia Haynes Orchards, but we had plenty to eat, clothes on our backs, and love for one another and our neighbors. What we lacked wasn't missed, because we never knew anything else. We all considered ourselves blessed!

15

One Easter morning we siblings were getting dressed for church, when Daddy called Clyde aside and asked him to get Dr. McDaniel to come to our house after church. Mama didn't feel like getting out of bed today.

Dr. Mac, as he was known all around our area, did most of his doctoring by making house calls. His tiny office was on a corner near the church and his home just across the train track. Trains through there were numerous because this was a main route east and west. The elderly doc was blessed with safe crossing of the track several times in a day and night. We heard some folks say he gave just about every patient the same triangle-shaped pill, no matter the ailment. He was a family medical doctor and loved by all.

I reminisced recently, with Jack and Georgia Johnson, who moved from Boughton to Chicago. Jack confided that Dr. Mac smoked Chesterfield Cigarettes (unfiltered then). He said he would see him light up one as he traveled in his little black coupe. He would quickly throw the smoking stick down if Mrs. Lizzie was outside. She didn't care for his smoking. Jack would scuttle across to get the cigarette just as the doc entered his house. He said he got at least six good smokes a day at a very young age.

Another story Jack told was that you could set your clock (if you had one) by the four men who arrived at the same time every Saturday morning at the store that Mr. Shope ran. They each pitched in a certain amount of hard-earned money, then one of them made the whiskey run across the river near Okolona for a gallon of moonshine.

I wish I could verify all the good and the not-so-good stories I've heard. There were some noted murders in and around there. But we were fortunate not to have a radio or any other form of communication. We were spared a lot of grief by not knowing about all the bad news. In some ways, I long to have that time back again.

∽ৡ৶

After church that day, our dinner was very quiet. Mama didn't come to the table. When Dr. Mac's little black car drove into our yard, Daddy invited him in just as I finished the last dish and hung my rag to dry. We, kids went to sit on the edge of the front porch. My dangling feet in the rocks underneath the leak of the house got on the others' nerves. I was told to "stop it!" That was a frequent response to things I did or said. I didn't want to be their age or their level of intelligence. Loudly, I reminded them that the preacher said we should keep our minds on Jesus on this Easter Day.

I got up and found some round rocks and went around to the back porch, and got the two crayons I had found there when we first moved in. I colored my rocks really dark and pretty and begged the boys to hide my Easter eggs for us girls to find. We didn't find the one in the woodpile till much later. Bob was a good hider.

Suddenly, the door opened, and the doc and Daddy stepped out. Their conversation seemed to be about the war, so I headed in to see the patient.

"You look mighty healthy." Dr. Mac patted the top of my head.

I wondered what he had in the black bag. He swung it like it was heavy.

When I stepped in to see my mama, she was crying. I asked her what I could do for her. She wanted a little water to take one of the pills he had left for her. I brought her a drink of water, quickly, and handed her a pill. Yes, it had three corners—a small, white pill.

Daddy just told us that Dr. Mac thought she had ailments associated with her present age. He told her most women feel similar to what she described, at around forty to fifty years old, and that these tablets might give her the boost she needed.

Since we lived so close to the church house, we started going for the night service, also. We knew the house would be quiet for Mama while we were gone. She said she hadn't slept in two nights.

16

School was out the first week in May. I had already planted my garden, which was a bit bigger than planned. I called it my garden, even though they all had done more work in it than me. They all went to work in the orchards, even Mary. I wasn't old enough. I decided to become a nurse for Mama. She didn't ask for much help. Most of the day, she was able to be up, so sometimes I had to just pretend to be a nurse. I always told them I would love to be a nurse or school teacher when I grew up.

Every morning before it became too hot, was weed-pullin' time. Sometimes the other five kids and Daddy helped me with the garden work when they got home. Daddy said it looked good—words of a master, truly spoken.

I was learning to cook, and the work crew bragged on how good it was (when they didn't know I cooked it). It was a good thing we all liked vegetables, because we were running out of pork in the smokehouse. We'd have to wait for very cold weather before we could kill hogs again.

The crew carried some kind of lunch with them every day if they were far away. If they were close to our house, they stopped in for leftovers from the previous supper. We seldom had leftovers, though. It was difficult to cook for a big family. At that time of year, we had an abundance of food. There was lots more slop for the hogs with the excess from the garden, and we also divided veggies with our elderly neighbors.

Mary had bought a card of bobby-pins for us to use in our hair with some of her money. She told me about her day's work. A wholesale truck brought new bushel and half-bushel baskets to the peach shed in preparation for packing and selling peaches and plums. Her job was to count them as they were unloaded and placed in the storage room, so the owner wouldn't have to pay for more than she got.

"I bet your job is exciting," I told her.

Her reply was, "Well, it is not!"

∽ଚ ଚ∾

When it was just the two of us, Mama and me, our favorite food for lunch was wilted lettuce. I picked very fresh leaf lettuce and simply poured on it a generous amount of bacon grease that stayed warm on the back of the stove from breakfast. Mama loved chopped onions and icicle radishes mixed in with it.

One year, there was a bumper-crop of extra big, nice cabbages, thus we decided to make sauerkraut to last several years. At work, Mary told Milton about our idea. That evening he and his family came over for supper. Afterward, we all went out to gather cabbages. We cut about forty of them. The children, gleefully, helped me carry them to the well, laughing and playing, as if it was a game. The family circle was really "cutting up". Mama, Bonnie, and Mary did the fine chopping of the cabbage, as I packed it into the churns.

Eventually, three large pottery churns were full. One was salted down well to wait the nine days for the contents to ferment fully. Mama had decided we could only handle one churn a day when it came to canning, so that's why we salted each churn a day apart. The first one salted would be the first one canned. There would be kraut for all of us and plenty of cabbage to cook the next few days.

After nine days of just sitting in the salt, the first churn seemed to be well-fermented. I replenished the stove wood to the breakfast fire and got the boys to lift the first churn up to the eatin' table. Then I squeezed the soured cabbage in my hands, a little at a time into the biggest dishpan we had. When all the kraut was in the pan, it was washed and poured into another pan to cook on top of the stove.

I wasn't sure I could manage the rest of this major undertaking alone, so I asked if Mary could stay home and help. Just about that time, Milton drove up and let Bonnie and our favorite children out.

"I can help you today and tomorrow," Bonnie said, "but I have an appointment, so I can't help with the third kraut churn."

We later learned that it was a doctor's appointment where she found out her third child was expected. All of us got excited again!

Bonnie kept watch on the heating pan on the stove, while the kids and I found canning jars in the smokehouse. We scrubbed them carefully and placed them into a clean tub. They would be sterilized with boiling water before being packed with our precious product, then capped with new lids and not-so-new-rings.

It was time to drag out the "monster". Pressure cookers had been provided by the government to prevent food poisoning among the canning public. Bonnie loaded it by Mama's instructions. I was so thankful that best friend, Bonnie, was there to do the hot stuff. I took the kids back outside to make sure they didn't dart under a hot jar and get burned. I had found a little red, metal car under the porch when we moved. We made a road, round and round in the sandy yard, under a huge oak tree. The kids played there all day.

The "Monster".

When all was cleaned up, we were looking at eleven half-gallon jars of beautiful, healthy sauerkraut, plus enough saved out for supper. For this meal, we added fresh beans and newly dug potatoes, boiled and creamed. We also fried some dry-salt meat and used the grease from that for seasoning.

Mama and Bonnie were sweltering from the kitchen heat. They moved to the porch with the little kids and fanned, while I finished up the meal and set the table. I brought in wooden crates for seats, so as to accommodate our bigger family. Then I carried Mama a wet rag for her red face.

The workers from the fruit fields liked the supper and ate it all. While we were eating, I told them that the beets were about as big as the smallest cotton pee. We decided that our beet pickles would just have to wait till we finished the other two churns of sauerkraut. Early to bed…

The second day and the second churn were a repeat of Day One—uneventful, except for twelve more family-sized jars of kraut, and eight quarts of white, patty pan squash. Daddy smiled when he saw it. I told him I was concerned about tomorrow when Bonnie couldn't come. He said he believed Mama and I could do it. They were picking the early peaches right now in the orchard and were rushed to get an order to its destination. Otherwise, he said, he could have taken off work to help. Off they went again, to the west forty, as he called it.

I did the preliminary procedures in the house and got the pan of washed cabbage on the hot stove to cook. All the windows and doors were open, but the usual east breeze couldn't be felt at all today.

Grabbing my rags from the small clothesline on the back porch, and the pans and tubs on the floor, I knelt in the morning shade of the old smokehouse to wash the jars. I vividly remember singing loudly, the stanzas I could recall from a church song "What can wash away my sins? Nothing but the blood of Jesus. What can make me whole again? Nothing but the blood of Jesus…" Then it turned into, "What a Friend we have in Jesus…What a privilege to carry, everything to God in prayer."

Finishing the washing and rinsing, I wagged the big dishpan of clean jars up the steps and across the porch to the back door. I had to set it down to open the screen door. Mama usually met me and opened the door.

I stepped in and suddenly tripped over something. I saw my only mama lying on the floor, eyes closed and her lips and fingers blue. I called her and got a wet rag and wiped her sweaty face. She finally opened her eyes, but her breathing didn't sound right.

"Go get your daddy," she spoke softly. I tried to get her up, but couldn't, so I put her pillow under her head, and flew out the door to find the orchard crew.

The mail carrier had already passed that day, and I was pretty sure there wouldn't be another car passing anytime soon. Through the fence I crawled, then ran over a cow pasture. It was eaten down clean, so the running was easy. Another fence loomed ahead. I squeezed through and was then running through neck-high sedge grass. I had to stop. My side was hurting badly, and it was hard to breathe. I stood there a minute to get my breath again, then I hollered as loud as I could, "HELP!"

Was that an echo or a reply? I heard it again.

Daddy yelled back, "Come on, Baby!"

I ran again, thinking, "What a privilege to carry everything to God in prayer. Can you hear me, God?"

When I reached the field they were in, I couldn't talk. I motioned to the direction of the house.

Daddy guessed… "Is it your mama? Is she sick?" I nodded, and Daddy motioned for Bob to come to the old orchard truck. He pitched me in before him, and we took off, bouncing down the gravel road.

When we got to Mama, she was unable to tell us anything. Daddy told us to go to Boughton and get the doctor. Pulling up at the little office, Bob shoved me out the truck to go in to get him. I told him that we needed him right now for our mama. Dr. Mac grabbed his black bag, and jumped in his little Ford, beating us there.

The three men picked Mama up and carried her to her bed. Her eyes were open now. Dr. Mac took a long, funny-looking tube from his pack, and plugged it into his ears.

"How will that help her?" I thought.

Daddy asked us to step out on the porch. I could tell that Bob didn't want to. Neither did I; however, we knew better than to disobey him. I went around to the back door and slipped in to see if the kraut was burning. It wasn't. Mama had managed to slide the pan to the cooler end of the stove. I would wait for Mary to get home to help me finish. I slid the heavy pan back to the stove's hot spot, so it would be ready to pack in the jars when everybody got home.

In a few minutes, Dr. Mac was leaving with a disturbed look on his face. He said Mama had a heart attack!

My heart sank, and I blurted out "Is she gonna die?"

He handed Daddy a bottle of pills and told him he would bring her a different kind as soon as he could get to the drug store in Prescott and get it.

Then, he replied to my question, looking straight at me. "Nobody knows when anybody will die. I think she has a good chance to live, with this many caretakers around here."

He went on to explain, "She needs to eat good vegetable meals, and take it easy. No heavy work. Keep her as cool as possible and give her plenty of water to drink. Keep her in bed for a while. Put a fan on her if you can, and I'll be back before too long."

I knew someone had invented a fan with blades that turn swiftly enough to mimic the wind. The hold back is that no one had electricity to run one.

Mama's Almanac was in the dresser drawer. It was the only calendar we had. I marked the heart attack on June 15.

The working ones had come home for supper. After relating Mama's situation, I churned the clabber milk, so we could drink the fresh buttermilk with cornbread, and have butter on our biscuits. I opened a jar of newly-made blackberry jelly from the berry patch Roy had found.

Mama had been given the famous triangle pill, and she was resting well with an occasional chest pain. I peeped in on her. She had dozed off, with Daddy holding her hand, of course.

We didn't go into the front room that evening. We just did our PM chores, and caught up with some gardening.

"Lord, are you hearing me? If you are, much obliged!" I whispered.

Dr. McDaniel made another house call later that week. He commented that we were doing a great job of nursing Mama back to health. She said she was feeling a little stronger than she had in a long spell. The doctor told Daddy that her blood pressure and pulse were pretty close to normal.

As he came out on the porch, Daddy followed him, reaching into his overalls bib pocket for a small roll of bills. He had just been paid by Mrs. Haynes the day before. He asked Dr. Mac how much he owed him.

"Dollar and a half each trip, and if you need me for anything just get ahold of me."

Daddy handed him the bills and a sack. "Much obliged. We picked you some vegetables, too."

Even when times seemed hard for some folks and money was scarce, it was vital for my daddy to keep up with the debts he made and pay them as soon as he could. He was constantly reminding all of us that "money don't grow on trees."

Take that from a man who has been enveloped in hard work since he was twelve. He told me that the orchard job was the easiest one he's ever come across. He was modeling to us, his offspring, one lesson after another in honesty and humility. These two traits brought contentment for his family. He told us the fewer desires one has, the more peace he exhibits, and that dreams are good if they are coupled with wisdom.

Daddy was really smart, but I don't know if it came across that way to most folks. He didn't mix and mingle with people other than kin and a few others. He, for sure, didn't advertise his feelings or try to force his opinion where it wasn't asked for.

A young cotton picker filling her long canvas bag.

17

We always had buckets or tubs of garden produce on the front porch. Sometimes we all shelled the beans or peas or shucked the ears of corn together, but if some were busy with other duties, one or two of us could carry on as needed.

Often, we were blessed with fresh peaches, or apples to peel. We either canned them or sliced them in thin wedges to dry. This time we were drying the fruit and no appliances were needed. When we had overflowed two dishpans, despite the amount we managed to consume as we peeled, Mary and I went inside and found two slightly ragged sheets and brought them to the side shed on the smokehouse.

Daddy showed us how to spread one sheet on the hot tin roof and dump the pans of sliced fruit on it. We placed the pieces, gently, half an inch apart. This was all covered with the other sheet to prevent birds from pecking them.

We brought the drying fruit in at night, for fear possums and coons would taste and like it. They sometimes dried in a week, according to how much sunshine there was. When they were absolutely dry, we stored them in a clean flour sack hung on a kitchen wall till Christmas. We had the best doggone fried pies after we soaked the dried pieces of fruit in water overnight.

When we asked for God's blessing on our food, the fruit was frequently mentioned. God had generously supplied everything we needed to eat through Daddy's generous employers.

❧❧

Mama was improving but was cautioned by the doctor against exertion. I was so glad when she was able to just take care of her own physical needs. She could walk out in the garden and tell me the most urgent jobs to do. That was very helpful.

She was also able now to write many letters to her mother and her remaining six siblings, who were scattered to Texas, California, and all over Arkansas. Her mother and my granny, Sarah Annas (Ross) Bradford, lost her home and all but meager possessions when her husband and my grandfather passed away at a young age.

Granny Bradford took turns living with all her children. She hadn't shared our home yet. It seems that some of my mother's siblings thought that our house wouldn't be sufficient accommodations for her, so we waited.

Mama was anxious to let them know she was recuperating slowly. She asked me to "back" her envelopes and assured me she could write the letters this time. No one was gladder to hear this than me. I had to print them all when I did them, but I was about ready to learn cursive! Mama's handwriting was slow, but very neat. I mailed one letter a day with a three-cent stamp.

Just as I mailed the first letter and started back across the road, I saw a shiny light blue car approaching. As it got closer, I recognized the smile of Mrs. Maude. I didn't know she knew where we lived, and I told her that. She hugged me as she was getting out of the car and handed me a spectacularly wrapped square box with a neat little pink ribbon on it.

"I keep up with you, Girl!" she said.

I asked her to come in. She hadn't done so before. Mama was sitting with her feet propped up on a cushioned apple crate to prevent swelling from her heart failure. Mrs. Maude motioned for her not to get up, and I brought in a straight chair from the table for her.

I brought them both a glass of cool water and picked up the pretty box again. She told me to open it and I didn't lose any time. I was glad the boys weren't home. It was the most exquisite garment I had ever seen, much less owned. A white batiste petticoat with the most delicate lace on the bodice and all around the bottom. I was speechless! I hugged her and it was for real. She kept her arm around me and said, "Happy birthday, Lenora!"

I cried, not because I only got one gift. (It was the first wrapped and tied one I had ever received.) I didn't even remember that it was August 9th. We had all been too busy to look at Mama's Cardui calendar in her trunk.

Don't get me wrong. I nearly always got gifts for my birthday and Christmas, just not ones that could be wrapped. My siblings usually offered nice gestures and acts of kindness for the occasions just as I did for them. For instance, they would reverse the order that the food was passed around our table. Tonight, I would get the serving dishes first. I could choose the crustiest bread and get the biggest tater first.

One birthday, Mary almost busted a gut allowing me to wash instead of dry the dishes, and we didn't fight one bit. Bob whittled a cross from a piece of cedar limb he cut in the far woods. Roy picked the last berries he could find so I could make us a pie sweetened with honey. Clyde read Romans 10 to me one more time, at my request. Milton bought some fabric and Bonnie did the sewing. They gave me a fancy dress that I wore for a long time, letting the hem down as I grew.

My best treat was if Daddy uncrossed his legs and pulled me up in his lap for a tight hug. I felt as if I didn't get my share of that pleasure. As I said before, my family wasn't a hugging family, so that made it so special! I vowed under my breath that if and when I have a family of my own, we would be "huggy".

Mrs. Maude visited with Mama for quite a while. It really did help her feelings to have our guest say she would come and take her out for a ride one day. Mama perked up and awaited the treat. She wasn't disappointed. They rode eight miles over to Emmet. She was delighted to go when she found out Mama's mother lived there with Aunt Georgia, her daughter. Granny and Mama both cried, so I heard. They hadn't seen each other for about two years.

Mary and I made sure that pretty blue car was loaded with plenty of garden produce for Mrs. Maude when they returned. Mama talked about her trip until we all felt like we went with her. Her health seemed to be improving. In her words, "I give thanks to God above."

18

I began to notice how life seems to happen in cycles. In our case it was a long, hard summer of work, then everything changed rapidly as we went for a final swim of the year. This time, Mama rode down to Little Mo in the wagon with us and sat in a "poolside" chair to watch and laugh as we performed our aquatic capers.

It was our most enjoyable outing ever! Two days later, we were back in school. Not much changed from last year. We were a grateful bunch because we didn't have that eight miles a day to walk to school and back.

Clyde said, "Better to be thankful for all things, or some of these privileges might be taken from us."

I didn't understand that—I don't know about the others. He added that we need to be thankful for the not-so-good things in life, also. He went on to tell us a story about a woman named Corrie Ten Boom, whose most famous book, *The Hiding Place*, recounted the events involving her family hiding Jews in their home so they could escape the Nazi holocaust. She and her whole family were arrested and placed in a concentration camp along with many others. When the guards came to the cell where Corrie and others were waiting to be taken to the chop block, they saw that it was working alive with fleas. They passed on quickly because they decided they were far outnumbered by the fleas.

Corrie shouted, "Thank God for the fleas!"

I thought, "Thank God for my big family and a good house… Thank God for a bus to take us to school… Thank God for giving me this life that nobody else is fortunate enough to have!"

I still loved school. The good in it outweighed the bad. We weren't heckled by the snooties anymore, but sometimes a few kids looked disapprovingly at our shoes and clothes. We just ignored them. I wondered why their parents didn't teach them how to be good to folks around them.

We started cursive writing in third grade, which I enjoyed a lot. We also began spelling bees. The whole class lined up while the teacher went down the line and pronounced a word from our speller to one student at a time. Then she asked them to pronounce it and spell it. If you spelled it correctly, you remained standing. If you missed it, you were to be seated. The last one standing after everyone else misspelled a word, was declared by the teacher to be the winner and received a certificate to take home. I had no problem spelling. I could spell a word looking at it once. The picture stayed in my mind making it easy to spell aloud. There were a bunch of certificates tacked on our bedroom wall.

The only thing I didn't get an A in was history. I didn't like sorrowful subjects like wars and stuff. The cycle of life seemed to pass somewhat slowly. We repeated a lot of life month after month and year after year. It was school from September to mid-May. One week out for Christmas and no other breaks—except when Mary and I had to miss a day to delete the pile of dirty laundry.

We only required a couple of days to celebrate Christmas in a mighty way. I loved going to church on or near Christmas Day. The teacher would delve deeply into the Bible story found in Luke chapter two. We sang many songs about Baby Jesus, the angels, the wise men, shepherds, and such.

Christmas Eve was the longest day of my year. Couldn't do nothing but wait! This was the time of year to bake plenty of sweets. Daddy would buy all the sugar we needed. We already had the cakes and pies made so far ahead of Christmas. They were pretty dry when we got the go-ahead to eat them. Tupperware wasn't around yet.

I managed to do the little details on Mama's list. Most of Christmas Eve was spent crawling round and round Daddy's metal trunk. He started buying hard candies of all kinds in October, and by December the trunk was totally packed with the candies, apples, and oranges. We couldn't open the trunk until Christmas Eve. All we could do was crawl around it and sniff. I still expect that special scent of his trunk at Christmas time.

All of us contributed homemade decorations for the tree, which was a pine or cedar we found in the woods. We grew our popcorn and strung about twelve feet of popped corn around the tree, eating more than we strung. The next day the boys started snitching it off the string, so Mary told them we had dragged it through the ashes. That stopped them.

Daddy brought a fresh, hairy coconut home from the store for this special occasion. I had never seen the inside of one or tasted it. It was hard to imagine that anything looking so ugly could taste good. I had heard a rhyme on Milton's radio: *Baker's Coconut—Coconut for Sale!* I started repeating that phrase over and over to Daddy, hinting for him to get a hammer and break it open. He finally got aggravated and told me if I didn't hush that, I wouldn't get a bite of it. I hushed!

Another homemade decoration for the tree was fairly new to us, and Mary and I did most of it. Bob went to the woods and gathered a water bucket full of sweet gum balls that fell off the tree in late fall. We had collected aluminum foil from empty cigarette packs we found along the roadsides as we walked. It seemed like the doctor and Jack Johnson weren't the only ones puffing smoke in Boughton. The shiny foil was pressed around those gum balls. They really made our Christmas tree light up, even without electricity.

We didn't need pretty electric lights or store-bought presents to celebrate a day set aside to honor Jesus on His birthday. We were always home as an extended family. No alcohol, football games, or movies were involved. If Santa Claus was ever talked about, it must've been before I came along. I guess they got tired of that game by the eighth child. When I started to school, the teacher passed around paper sheets of a mimeographed Santa for us to color. I made his pants and shirt brown and white. The whole class laughed at me. I had never seen him, not even a picture. How did everybody else know he wore red? Well, he never came to our house!

We surely did stuff our bellies with good food for two or three days, though. I sometimes ate enough oranges to make me regurgitate. God was good then and now!

19

In the dead of winter, there wasn't anything to be done in the orchards. The boys were on Christmas vacation. Mr. Hignight and all the Daniel men did a lot of hunting and trapping for small, wild animals.

In this era, wealthy and fortunate women were enjoying wearing fur coats, stoles (shoulder wraps), hats and muffs. They were made from trapped furs, like the men were catching. We never heard anything about PITA or any other protestors then. There were plenty of "ooohs and ahhhs" when a lady was seen wearing a real fur.

A whole, untorn hide from a mink was worth twenty dollars or more. That brought out much envy from the non-trappers or non-hunters. Coon, rabbit, and possum hides were in demand, as was the meat. Squirrels, wild ducks, and geese were considered delicacies, also.

The men enjoyed the sport of all the hunting, not to mention the winter income from it. They skinned the animals, always keeping one foot intact on the body, so that the purchaser could identify the animal, and preserved the hides stretched tightly on a wooden board, wrong side out. When the drying rack in the barn was full, they made a trip to Prescott to sell them. They nearly always came home wearing a wide grin, and bloody clothes for us to wash.

My brothers kept coon hounds for the purpose of chasing down coons for the hunters. Bob got two blue tick hounds and even when he went to school by day, he loved taking Ruff and Tuff coon hunting by night with the men gang. Hunters were required to buy a license to hunt fur-bearing animals.

On one trip they took to nearby woods, they were all sitting around a bonfire listening to the dogs in hot pursuit of a fleeing coon. Mr. Hignight told his buddies about an idea he had whirling around in his mind. He was thinking of a plan for getting all the young men and boys in the community involved in a profitable pastime that just might keep their mind off moonshine and getting into trouble.

He said he knew of a place in town where you could rent a deep freeze by the month. He asked what they thought about pooling the coons they kill and freezing them till they had enough to feed the whole country close around us. That's what they did, and Mr. Hignight built a pit for barbecuing, and made large buckets of tomato base barbecue sauce.

The men announced there would be a barbecue coon supper for all. They told the place and the time, and nearly the whole community showed up and ate coon! That was his way of getting the attention of the youth. It worked so well, he made sure it happened every winter for years.

A few times in the summer, Mr. Hignight barbecued enough goat meat to feed a community gathering. We furnished bread and others brought vegetables. After the togetherness meetings, started by the boss, we heard of many folks offering to help neighbors, friends or mere acquaintances, just to pay forward the good deeds of a generous man.

Daddy was invited to go fishing with Mr. Hignight one Saturday, late in the evening. They stayed so late that all of us were in bed asleep when he returned. The next day after Sunday dinner, he confided in us that Mr. Hignight had asked him if he would be willing to pull out from Haynes Orchard and work for Hignight Orchards, if he could borrow enough money to get a hearty business started. He also said if he would be willing to come on with him and help get the whole project planted and growing, he would build us a new house near his house and orchard. He knew that Daddy's goal in life was to have a roof over our heads. He wanted his own place, so that no landlord could ask him to move.

Mr. Hignight told Daddy if he got a chance to buy his dream house, he wouldn't hold him back, and that he would be happy for him. He said he didn't know of anybody who deserved his own place as much as Daddy did. He truly had worked all his life with that one aim in mind.

Near the end of his announcement, he reminded us we weren't to mention these plans to anybody. Mr. Hignight also told Daddy it looked like the end of World War II was in sight. There was still little news about the war except for word-of-mouth. We did hear of some of our close acquaintances being killed in battles at Iwo Jima and Okinawa, but no one knew until their bodies were returned to the United States for burial.

I read in World Book Encyclopedia later that the Allies planned to invade the Japanese home island, but July 26, 1945, the heads of state of the United States, Great Britain and China issued an ultimatum to Japan.

They called for unconditional surrender and a just peace. They planned to occupy Japan, restrict Japanese authority to the home islands, disarm the country and bring its war criminals to trial.

Japan ignored the ultimatum, and our country used the atomic bomb! The invasion of Japan was no longer necessary. A B-29 called "Enola Gay" dropped the first atomic bomb used in warfare on the city of Hiroshima. More than 92,000 persons were killed or missing. Three days later, another atomic bomb was dropped on Nagasaki, killing some 40,000 Japanese. The injuries were figured to be about the same as deaths.

On August 14 (in the US), the allies received a message from Japan, accepting an agreement offered earlier in Pottsdam. Army General Douglas MacArthur was appointed supreme commander for the Allied Powers. His signature was important to declare the war was ended.

President of the United States, Harry S. Truman, proclaimed September 2 as V-J (Victory Over Japan) Day. Three years, eight months, and twenty-two days after the war began, when Japan bombed Pearl Harbor, World War II ended in 1945.

The only memory I have of that awful war is the deep furrows on my daddy's brow when he worried about the outcome. I had some friends at school whose fathers didn't make it home from war alive. I hardly knew Dixie Ann, until I heard that her father's life was taken in the war. I loved her then for the rest of her life. Her tragedy really made me appreciate my father more.

20

After all was said and done, we knew we would be changing houses again soon. Mrs. Haynes told Daddy we could continue to occupy our present house until we had another place to live. She asked if he thought fifteen dollars a month for rent sounded fair, and he agreed.

Mr. Hignight's plans were progressing toward building his own orchard about a couple of miles south on 67 Highway, where his new home was already built. It was a lovely sight to see. There was no disagreement that I knew of between any of them. Neither of the men were young any more, and Mrs. Haynes said she understood that "a man's gotta do what a man's gotta do!"

She looked Daddy in the eye and said, "Your stall will still be open if you and your family need to work for me again—just let me know."

Milton and Bonnie decided on the same move when asked if he could help build simple houses. They found a rent house that was readily available directly across the highway from the Formby Grocery Store, just one-half mile south toward Prescott. The men moved the furniture. Mary and I straightened up everything while Bonnie and the two kids watched. Just about two or three days later, she delivered her third child, with the help of Mrs. Lily Ruth Formby. The doctor arrived later. Bonnie said the lady was so sweet, she was going to name her baby Ruth Ann.

The substitute midwife was elated. She said, "I have three sons, and now I have a daughter!"

She treated Ruth Ann like her own. That store held many treats. Ruth Ann later got the nick-name Polly.

The makeshift crew of builders did the best they could with the supplies they obtained. In a matter of weeks, we moved into our brand-new, never-before-lived-in house. It smelled so good. It was built from pine slabs from a nearby sawmill.

There were a few cracks in the single walls, where the slabs had shrunk a little on one or both ends. Of course, we brought our flock of chickens with us. We were greeted each morning by their clucking as we spied them under the house pecking for worms in the new ground. Yes, we had cracks in the floors, too, but it was unanimous—we all liked our new home.

Our brand-new, never-before-lived-in house on the Hignight land. (Left-to-right seated: Jeannie, Dwayne, Bonnie, Lenora, and Mary. Standing: Roy, Clyde, Mama, Bob, Ruth Ann, and Daddy)

The boys quickly assembled a fence for Dan from barb wire we bought from the old place. Ruby had gone to a new family at Boughton. We weren't using the wagon much, so Dan could pull light loads and plow a garden all by himself, and it would take less feed. Dan seemed happy chomping down on his new plot of grass.

We demanded a clothesline be stretched soon because washday would surely come here, too. The chickens finally got a new house with plenty of nests to lay eggs in. The boards fitted together better than our house, so that when we fastened the door at night, no varmints from the near woods could infiltrate our hen house. There was one big beautiful Rhode Island Red rooster, who was as sneaky as a snake! When I went to feed the chickens or gather the eggs, he always managed to creep up behind me and flog me on my back or legs. I could have killed him! As a matter of fact, I did! We ate him in a pot of dumplings. I had learned the art of butchery! Watch out world!

We had to put Mama's bed together and get it ready for her to lie down the day we moved. She had too much exertion and was suffering with those old chest pains again. She said they weren't as bad as before.

We, girls opened up good ol' jars of canned goods until we got all of our stuff unpacked and put away. Somehow, we had accumulated stuff in a substantial amount since we last moved our household. There was a little bit more money since the bread-winner had been working the year round. We still didn't ask for money, though.

As soon as we were moved in, we had to think about how to catch the school bus. We heard from our boss that it would come right up the highway, and if we were out near the road, he would stop for us.

We scrambled through the bushes and briars the next morning, and the bus stopped right by us. We were surprised when we noticed it was the same driver we had before, and lo, on boarding we beheld the glowing faces of the same bunch of rowdy kids we knew before. We were glad to see them. The driver told Clyde that the road up to our house wasn't wide enough to accommodate that big bus to turn in from the highway.

I heard my brother say, "That's quite alright—we've walked a lot further than this."

My sweet brother, Clyde, would never argue with or question an adult. He had been known to quote Proverbs 16:32 to his brothers and sisters often: "He that is slow to anger is better than the mighty…"

Another couple of verses that often crossed his lips when we were quarreling as kids was "Let all bitterness, and wrath, and anger, and clamor, and evil speaking, be put away from you, with all malice," and "Be ye kind one to another, tenderhearted, forgiving one another, even as God for Christ's sake, hath forgiven you."

Our trail to the highway was through the fenced pasture we had made for Dan and Bessie, our milk cow. Daddy sold one cow and calf before we last moved and saved the money in hopes to buy a motor vehicle. Bessie was in a dry season, which came around annually after she weaned her calf from last year and was no longer producing milk.

We wouldn't have any milk until she calved again. This might happen any day now—woowee!

The grazing pasture was in front of our house, and Mama told us if she walked out to the pasture fence on a pretty day, that Bessie would come a-running to get a pat on the head. I was glad Mama got outside and walked around a little. I thought about her often while at school, and worried about her being alone all day. Fortunately, Daddy's crew was working pretty close to our house.

Mr. Hignight decided to build a very small house for Milton and Bonnie. He said Milton made a good hand for general everyday jobs. He thought he would be an asset to his farm. Milton asked us how to spell "asset" and I told him. I remember his saying, "Well, I hope I can be more than the first three letters of it."

He was inclined to spout off adages like that just when a laugh was needed. He would have never said that in Mama's presence. When one of his daughters first started talking, we could point at her pants and ask her, "What's this?"

She would always reply something that sounded bad but wasn't. "Sonnie beeches!" (Sunday britches).

We found a shortcut to our same church by walking through the woods behind our house the way the boys had led Bessie and Dan when we moved. They didn't want to go around on the busy highway—the boys, that is. The animals didn't say. As we walked, we came into another graveled county road that eventually led us across Boughton Creek bridge!

We stopped at the bridge. Mary and I washed our feet and put our shoes back on. The gravel could ruin them quickly, and they wouldn't be replaced until fall. We entered the church yard from a different direction this time, but I was glad to see the same loving faces in the congregation. I knew it must be the same God there as before.

After the benediction, Clyde announced that he consulted with our parents, and they gave permission for us to invite the whole church and community to come to our new house for an Easter egg hunt next Sunday after lunch. He told them we would color some eggs, and we would like for each family to bring as many colored eggs as they'd like and hide them, too.

I could hardly wait! Many church people showed up and several brought eggs. We had more eggs than our big washtub would hold. The men folks complained that it was just too many eggs to hide.

Daddy told them we only had one mule and one cow in the pasture and that they were welcome to hide them out there. Mary and I instructed all the kids through teenagers to follow us to the barn, so the grown-ups could focus on hiding the eggs.

We lined the kids up into two groups and explained the game "Mother-may-I" to them. The ones who weren't interested in that were given a calf rope and told to exit the barn at the back and play jump rope until they got a signal to hunt the eggs.

"Ready to hunt!" We were having so much fun we didn't even hear them calling. They had to send someone to the barn to get us. I probably cracked and ate more boiled eggs than anyone at the big Easter egg hunt that day. I feel sure that I threw up more times than anyone else in the crowd. I guess that was the first time in my life I got all the boiled eggs I wanted. It was a long time before I even wanted to look at one after that.

We made many new friends. It seemed like everybody had fun, and Mama said it was so good to hear the laughter of good kids at our new place.

My mother on the front porch of our house at
Pleasant Hill

21

After Easter, it was all-hands-on-deck to get the garden planted. It's hard to start one in a patch of weeds and grass where there has never been a garden before. However, virgin soil is excellent for growing vegetables, once you're rid of the unwanted growth. Daddy and Dan worked the plow while we were at school. We all changed clothes and planted when we got home.

I cried one day when I got through helping plant beans. When I went toward the shed to put my hoe where it belonged, I found a small plowed spot in the back yard, and I knew it was my garden.

I sobbed out, "I love you too, Daddy!"

After supper, I spent some time before dark in my own garden, just me and the dirt.

❧❧

Out of the blue one Sunday morning, Mama said she was gonna walk over to that highway where all those cars and trucks rushed back and forth day and night, and wave down one. She said she had sat on our front porch and watched the big blue and silver contraptions appear over the hill and just glide right on down the highway, seemingly without an effort.

As tears flowed down her cheek, she went on to say she knew if those huge vehicles stayed on the same path, they would be going very near her mama's and sister's house in Emmet.

She said, "Sometimes I just want to see my mother, and hear her tell me that everything's gonna be alright like she used to do. I won't stay long."

Daddy's mind was full of questions. "Are you able to make a long trip like that?" (It was about eleven miles from our house). "Do they know you are coming? What if you have one of your heart spells?"

Mama told Roy the water bucket was empty and asked if he would draw some cool water from the well. He promptly got up and went to do it. Her every wish was his command. That's when she broke down crying and told us she aimed to take Roy with her. She said she could always use a good escort. Then she managed enough words to tell us that Roy had tried to go visit Granny Bradford by himself. She said he got all dressed up in his Sunday clothes and stood by the road until the bus topped the little hill, then he waved his handkerchief until the driver pulled the vehicle off beside the road. She said he stepped up when the door opened and held out a handful of change to the driver. He told the driver he wanted to go to Emmet to see his grandma. He asked Roy to repeat, and he did.

He did repeat several times, then the driver told him, "Get off the bus. I can't understand what you are saying."

Mama went on to tell us she was watching and saw Roy hide behind some bushes for a while. In a few minutes he slowly walked back to the house. He told her what happened, she said, and they cried together.

For once, I was silent. I wanted to ask Daddy to give her some money for the bus and tell her to go on to Emmet with his blessing. I could tell from his expression he was giving it serious consideration. I believed he was talking to God. I surely was hoping God would say yes. I didn't want to see my mama cry again, ever. I hated to think about my brother crying just because he was born with his mouth not cooperating, like everybody else's. It is just not fair! He had asked Mama to not tell us at the time it happened, but her decision was always best. That we knew!

As I started to walk off, Daddy reached his hand in his overall bib pocket and pulled out some money, handing it to Mama, and telling her to go get ready. She told Roy the same thing, and in no time, Daddy had walked the two of them to the highway to wait for the Trailways monster to top the hill. I'm sure he asked her at least three times if she had her heart pills in her purse.

This time when the bus rolled to a stop, Daddy climbed aboard, and let the driver know that these two wanted to ride to Emmet and the driver simply said it would cost forty cents. As Daddy was handing him the change, he asked the driver how they would stop the bus to let them off when they came back. He helped them on the bus and showed them a cord that ran above the windows, all the way back. The driver said that they would only have to pull down on the cord once and the driver would stop.

When Mama and Roy were seated, Daddy backed off the bus and it headed south. It seemed like Daddy was loaded with a mighty burden when he was walking back across the cow and mule pasture. With his shoulders slightly slumping forward and his arms hanging straight down, he managed to slowly put one foot in front of the other until he reached the front porch, where he sat on a wooden tool box that had been at every sharecropper's house we occupied.

The rest of us kids prepared ourselves outwardly for church. The inward part was doubtful. Clyde asked our daddy to go with us, but he declined.

"Not today," he said. "But pretty soon. I think I'll just rest today."

Nobody at church knew our house felt half-empty. This was a place of happiness. The songs of cheer and gladness rang out pronouncing a risen Savior. I wished I could get an understanding of what all those pretty verses meant. The music was smooth and beautiful, but what in the world did "redeemed" mean? After the sermon, we sang, *I Surrender All*. I could read the words in that old-looking, musty-smelling song book now, but for the life of me, I didn't know what most of them meant.

When church was over, Mr. Cue Johnson offered to take us home. Clyde suggested to him that since it was such a pretty day, we could ride with them to Mr. Cue's house, then walk through the woods the way we came. They agreed. When he was stopped at his house, Mrs. Cue stepped out and handed Mary and me an object that was wrapped in clear cellophane. Each was a beautiful floral umbrella. They were mid-size, so we could handle them well, she said. We both said a big thanks and I hugged her. She always wore the nicest dresses with gorgeous necklaces, and she smelled so good!

When we started our little jaunt through the woods, I lagged behind the others a bit, and whispered out loud, "God, did you tell Mrs. Cue that we were sad because our mama was gone? She sure cheered us up, God!"

I told him if it's raining when Mama comes back, I will meet her with my umbrella. Late the next day, they came back. It wasn't raining, but I showed her my umbrella anyway.

22

After school, we walked through the pasture, now growing lush, green clover and several other grasses. The grazing animals ate from early morning until after noon every day. I asked Daddy why they quit eating and laid down nearly every day. He told me when they laid down that early, it was a signal that we didn't need to go to the trouble of going fishing. He said when the cows lie down at noon time, the fish aren't biting that day.

Mama asked if we saw Bessie anywhere as we came through there. I told her no and took off to look for her. I didn't want to skin up my shoes, so I removed them and my socks, and set them on a tree stump.

As I walked, I called the cow, "Sook, Sook, Sook!"

That was the universal bovine language for, "Come on, Cow!" I mooed like a cow, and waved my arms to no response, cow or otherwise. I had started back to the house to set the table for supper, when I remembered my shoes. I circled back around and found them. When I sat down on the stump to re-shoe myself, a low moan could be heard. I followed the sound until it became more audible. Bessie was under a big oak tree that had fallen back in the winter but was still was covered in brown leaves. She sure found a good place to hide from wolves and buzzards, and anything that intended to harm the calf she knew would soon come.

I ran as fast as I could to tell Daddy that our calf was half out and couldn't come on. He followed me back down there. He told Bob, who came with us, that he couldn't figure she was in trouble. This wasn't her first time to calve. As we got closer to her "delivery room", Daddy assured us that she was alright. Bessie was standing up, licking her little Jersey bull, which wasn't moving yet.

Bob hovered over the newborn and rubbed its legs and arms, until it tried a few times, then successfully stood on four wobbly legs. God had blessed our family and Bessie again. We left her there with her son, Harry S. Truman, completely covered by an oak arbor.

As soon as we got home the next day, Mama told us about Bessie strolling up to the yard fence to show off Harry, who was wobbling beside her. Then, she had to tell us about her new joy. She had thought our prettiest dommernecker hen was missing, and I guess she was for about twenty-one days. She came up that same day with a dozen baby chickens. Mama said they were already able to scratch in some loose dirt in the yard. When I found her, she had them all up under her wings, hovering over them. Isn't that just like a mother hen?

When I hear of near-term abortions today, I remember that half-born calf, and wonder how any mother could possibly want to kill something that perfect.

23

Our garden was growing, in spite of us. The men had all been working hard on the house on the other side of our garden. Mr. Hignight was directing them to build it for Milton and his little brood. It would bring a lot of joy to all of us, especially Mama and Daddy. They so loved having Dwayne, Bonnie Jean, (her nickname was Jeannie), and Ruth Ann around.

When we moved them in, we invited them to share the vegetables we had growing between us. They were to share our well, also. Every time we walked down the garden rows to their house, we carried them another jug of water. I guessed you can't have too much water when you have three kids to keep clean, and Bonnie did that well.

School was out for summer again. I cried when I told my teacher, Mrs. Overstreet, goodbye.

She hugged me, and said, "You may see me again."

I loved school because of all the books I could borrow. I missed getting to read in the summer.

We canned for both families at the same time. All that work went so much faster with the extra help. We grew every vegetable we had seeds for growing, and we canned all that we couldn't eat fresh. Because of the heat, we always asked Mama, nicely, to leave the kitchen when we were canning or cooking a lot.

Mr. Hignight came by one day when we had cooked a lot and were about to eat. At our persuasion, he sat down and ate with us. The boys had lengthened our table and made a second bench long enough to seat four. That day, we had butterbeans with ham, cornbread, fried corn, cabbage, deviled eggs, potato salad, raw onions, and sweet tea.

Our guest ate more than the brothers, as he grunted and groaned and dipped just a little more in his plate. I told him we don't have cakes and pies till Christmas because Daddy didn't like to buy sugar, but my mama said we will probably have peaches to eat pretty soon.

He said, "That we will, and I'll be back for some dessert at Christmas."

After we finished eating, he said he'd dropped by to ask our parents what they thought about planting a big patch of okra in that orchard that wouldn't be bearing fruit this year. Also, he was thinking he could turn it over to Mary and me, so we could make a little money. He told us what little bit of okra he had last summer sold really quickly, so he would plant a lot more this year.

Well, he did, and we did! When the stalks grew and started bearing, it looked like the whole world had turned to okra. We started gathering the long, green pods when the boys and men began their odd jobs around the orchard and shed, shortly after daylight. There was no fruit to pick yet, but the trees needed lots of care year-round.

We never finished by lunch time. I learned that most folks called it "lunch", and they called it "dinner" at supper time. Most of the time, it was around two o'clock when we got home to eat. There was always plenty. Mama and Bonnie took turns cooking and tending to the children early in the day, so the house would cool off from the wood stove.

We were told the okra would, most likely, need gathering every other day, except when that day fell on a Sunday, we could get it on Saturday. He knew we went to church and he didn't mind about the okra on Sunday. Our hands were already bleeding where the okra split the skin. We wore old socks on our hands until the boss told his wife about it, and she bought us some gloves. Hand-me-down long sleeved shirts and bonnets kept the sun off. Bonnie made them for us.

Mary and I didn't want to look like field workers when we started back to school. We wished we could be really white like the town girls were. Then we found out that the town girls were stretching their bodies out in the hot sun, just trying to get brown. My dermatologist recently asked me if I laid out in the sun to tan in my younger days. I told him if I was in the sun then, I was holding a hoe, or pulling a cotton sack or picking peaches. In spite of my efforts, I have had sixteen cancerous or pre-cancerous skin lesions treated on my face and arms.

Not only was the "girl patch" flourishing with okra, but the young fruit trees that had begun to bear were, in Mr. Hignight's words, "astonishingly bountiful".

He was grinning from ear to ear when he drove up at *our* house, which truthfully, was *his*. We all were surprised to see him arrive for a visit so early. He just tipped his hat and walked up to the porch and propped one foot up on the doorstep.

"I got some good news for y'all this morning. I was invited to a meeting at the court house last night, and I am happy to inform you that all of us will soon be offered electricity. I've already accepted the offer for my house and the peach shed, and for these two houses over here on this side of the road. I'll be paying all the bills for the first six months, and after that, you can keep up the bill or have them to turn it off."

I looked at Daddy's flushed face. He had told us before that he didn't want anything such as that. He said it would create more problems than it was worth. We all were expecting a big let-down if he told him no, but we didn't dare voice our own opinions. I was thinking negatively to myself that the only time the kids' opinion registered around here was when we were asked, "Do y'all want the potatoes fried or boiled?"

About that time, Daddy turned around and asked us, "What do y'all think?"

I was sort of dramatic, I guess, when I screamed and clapped my hands loudly. Mama quietly stepped out on the porch to see what was going on.

Daddy told Mr. H, "Much obliged and I'll be ready to start in the west orchard in a few minutes."

He directed his crooked pointer finger at Mama and told her she was gonna have electric lights. I thought she would clap or move or do something to show excitement. She just smiled!

Roy had recently bought Mama a battery-operated radio, and she listened to a couple of stories on it in the weekday afternoons when we were all gone to work. Even if we were there, we couldn't hear her radio. Somehow, she thought the battery would last longer if she kept the volume turned down real low. I remember her stories were called *Stella Dallas* and *The Guiding Light*. Later on, they and many other daytime radio dramas became known as soap operas. Some of her stories survived for years and were eventually visualized on television.

I went to sleep, finally, that night after allowing my mind to jump from one electric idea to another. I could only imagine reading after dark. Clyde would certainly benefit from not having to put his Bible down at dark.

The electric line installers were directed to start at several different points in Nevada County. It just so happened that one of those points was at the Clark County line, about four miles north of us. While Arkansas Power and Light Company was building the lines, Mr. Hignight hired an electrician to install the needed wiring in the loft of our wood frame houses.

Our houses were ready to be connected by the time the lines were completed out our way. It didn't take long for that process to happen. The AP & L truck made it to our place late in the day. However, it wasn't dark when the switch was pulled at our meter. The light fixtures in each room consisted of a small circle of porcelain that had been fastened to the crude ceiling with two screws. A light bulb (25 watt) was screwed into the porcelain. The pull-chain with a twill cord attached to it dangled from the porcelain.

We were told by our generous daddy that those bulbs wouldn't show a light when it was still daylight, so do not turn them on until dark, ever! Roy, Bob, Mary, and I each had a cord in our hand just waiting for Daddy to pronounce "dark".

My arm got tired and I turned the cord loose just to rest a minute, and he yelled "dark". Of course, Mary would be the first one to turn on a light at our house!

I looked out our bedroom window, past the garden. The little Daniel house was all lit up, too. "Much obliged, Lord. I am joyful!"

24

The countryside was beautiful, and our good Lord was generous with rain and sunshine to make the bounty grow from the efforts of all the farmers.

I wondered who could see the growing crops flourish, and not even think about God and man's cooperation making it happen. When I watched my nephew and two nieces growing and learning new things, I knew that God was surely the inventor of every good thing, but I didn't know where he was or how he knew where we were. I thanked Him anyhow.

Daddy often expressed to us how thankful he was for all the life around him. Watching his garden grow was a must for him to mark the seasons of the year; but he absolutely didn't like to see grass and weeds growing in our yard. It took in a lot of space, but he thought it should be kept clean as the wood floors in the house.

After sundown, we all helped him pull what we could of the weeds and grass in the yard (After we had the garden looking clean). What wouldn't pull up, we scraped off with a hoe. We hadn't heard a thing about lawn mowers then. Most of the time, we worked or played outside until it was dark enough to pull the cord!

Mr. H said he had driven around the community just watching folks enjoying being an electricity family. He had an idea that he wanted to invite the whole surrounding community, plus all the folks at Boughton and Piney Grove, to come celebrate the Fourth of July with no fireworks, just electric lights. He told us to tell everybody we met that he will furnish the barbecue and the lemonade and the ice cream. We were to ask the women to bring bread or green salads.

Nearly everybody came with a smile on their face and a covered dish in their hands. The host had strung electric lights all around in his front yard, and all the ones installed in his peach shed were turned on, too. I had never seen such a bright world!

There were many children and teenagers. We divided ourselves and began to chase, tag, and cavort into age groups. Some of the older teens just stood or sat around a bonfire and talked. I don't know what they talked about. They always hushed quickly when we younger ones stopped near them. I believe every last man and woman was speaking about all the electric appliances available at the Prescott Hardware Company.

Daddy was almost as quiet as Mama tonight. I knew he was thinking about how much money them new-fangled appliances would cost, and how much trouble it would be to keep them running. Must have been the smartest man around!

When all had eaten to the brim, Mr. Hignight started rolling out four army-green, cloth barrels. He turned on a string of red, white and blue lights in one corner of the shed, and kids flocked from every direction. Some adults walked up, too. He said he had forty gallons of ice cream from Southern Ice Company. Then he named four flavors and told us to form a line behind whatever flavor we wanted.

He and his wife, Nona Bell, and his son, Jimmy Dale took their place behind an insulated can of ice cream. He asked Clyde, who was the same age as Jimmy Dale to serve the fourth can. They served cones to the kids and bowls to the others. My, my, was I dreaming? 'Twas my first taste of ice cream, and I imagine it was a first taste for many there that night.

I chose strawberry flavor, and I really was wondering what the vanilla tasted like, and the chocolate, and the black walnut. Mary got strawberry, also. She was right behind me in line.

&⟨⟩&

I found a half-gallon jar almost full of dried flower seeds we had been saving from last year. While the front yard was shaved clean, I decided to cover it with flowers. I slightly trenched it in rows, going every which way. I pulled a cool bucket of water up from the well and carried it inside.

Mama was napping, so I just got a good drink of water and tip-toed back out to the porch. I sat on the steps and cooled off a bit. My head was spinning with thoughts of a yard full of blossoms, so I got up and grabbed the jar of seeds and started flinging out hands full of seeds into the breeze. It had begun to thunder lightly in the west. That's where most summer showers come from. When I had sown seeds over the whole yard, the jar was empty.

93

I took the garden rake and ever-so-lightly covered the seeds with dirt. No one knew what I had done. I had to hurry to put the rake back where I got it. Daddy said when we used tools, we must not leave them where we got through with them. I wish everybody had been taught that. The thunder shower came, and I hoped for flowers.

Within four days, I started seeing some green foliage sprouting up in the front yard. I didn't want to reveal my blooming surprise yet, but I didn't want everybody walking on my tiny flowers yet, either.

Daddy and Bob had built a stile over our pasture fence in front of the house where most of the crossing was done. All we had to do was climb up three wooden steps and walk down three steps on the other side. I sat down on one of the wooden slabs to think about solving my problem.

I remembered how helpful the signs were with selling my pumpkins, so I jumped up and found a small pine board and a few crayons. I crafted a friendly sign for my family: FLOWERS, WATCH YOUR STEP! Problem solved.

Oh, well, I forgot that Ruff and Tuff couldn't read. They sauntered lazily by and settled in a cool, damp spot under the house. I looked sternly at them and thought "Just lie there waitin' till these flowers bloom!"

When the boys got home from the orchards, I was seated by a kitchen window, peeling taters for supper. I held my pose, knife in hand, waiting for them to read my sign. I was thoroughly impressed. Instead of walking over the stile, they all just followed the leader right on down beside that barb-wire fence till they passed my flowers, then they crawled through the barbs, all of them at the same time. Not one jagged tear in their shirts. Thank goodness! I didn't have time to mend any shirts torn because of my surprise flowers. I had to have the dish pan full of taters ready to boil as soon as my stove gets hot. It was my choice this time, whether to fry or boil, and I boiled. It was easier.

Mama helped me shell some whippoorwill peas. I washed them and she helped me lift the heavy pots to the stove. Afterwards, she laid on the bed to rest for a while. I dipped some cornmeal into the cooker pan and took it to the bed in the front room and told Mama I needed help. She told me to bring some salt, baking powder, and baking soda. She pinched up the amount of each one and placed it in the meal. She told me to melt a little lard in the oven skillet and pour a little bit of it into the meal, then wet the meal good with buttermilk.

"Stir it up good, pour it in the skillet and be careful sticking it in the oven. You won't need to put any more wood in the stove. It should have enough to cook the peas and taters," she said.

I never forgot my oral recipe from my mama for cornbread. I am grateful for a gas cook stove with an electrically-controlled oven now.

Mama was napping when we sat down to eat supper, and Daddy told me, "Don't wake her up. She can eat later."

I asked him if I could sit in her place this time, and he motioned for me to go ahead. I knew I would be second in line for the bowls of food because it was always offered in this direction first. We passed the bread first (it looked pretty good). Then came the whippoorwills, and next the taters that took me forever to peel. "Y'all are welcome," I thought.

I got the biggest potatoes in the pot and laid them proudly beside my peas in my plate. This must be my lucky day! I couldn't wait, so I stabbed the biggest tater with my fork and crammed it right on in my mouth. Selfish girl got choked! I couldn't chew or swallow or talk—or breathe. Mary said my face turned blue.

Clyde got up and ran to me and pushed my chest against the table as he beat my back. The big piece of potato flew across the table and I could breathe again! My brother was way ahead of Mr. Heimlech.

Everybody was looking at me. I thought for only a moment, then picked up my full plate and eased behind the head chair, and gladly claimed my end of the bench. I had no business trying to fill Mama's shoes or chair.

Back to the girl patch. Mr. Hignight told us we could pick the okra every day if we had time. I think one of our boys had let him know how much work we did around the house. He said the production of the okra surpassed his wildest expectation. He then told us it was selling as fast as he could get it on the counters at the shed. Some local folks bought it, along with a lot of tourists had found it. His roadside market that was growing by leaps and bounds.

Our next-door family was eating supper with us one night. Daddy mentioned that the girl patch needed more help.

Bonnie spoke up, "I would like to help out if I had someone to watch the kids."

Mary reminded Daddy that all our clothes were piled up waiting for a washin'.

Mama was the next to speak. She told us she loved them three children just like her own. I was tempted to break in with "more than her own", but I kept my mouth shut for once.

She looked at Bonnie and asked her, "Would you count on me to watch them? It's not for a full day."

We all looked perplexed, then she assured us she was physically up to it. Milton and his wife agreed it was worth a try.

I had created a playhouse that was fit for royalty behind our house under a shady sycamore tree. When I revealed it to everybody, I think it quickly passed evaluation. I had been the only one to enjoy it thus far. Mary didn't like to play house. She said she had done all the house work she wanted nearly all her life.

Daddy said he would take Mama a chair and plenty of water to the make-believe house. The next day, Mary stayed home to wash clothes and to make sure the first day of Granny-care went well, and it did.

When we planted okra that year, Mr. Hignight told us we could take home as much as we wanted. Bonnie took a peck of it to our house and fried it up for supper. Mary had picked butterbeans, and we had a bean-shelling together before we ate. I sliced fresh tomatoes and onions and sour pickles to round out our feast. Ours was country food, the only thing we knew.

The young-uns were so tired their eyelids were drooping by the time they finished eating and drinking their fresh cow's milk. Bessie was producing enough sweet milk, buttermilk, and butter for both families, that is, if we could persuade some people to churn the creamy milk when it soured. Roy and I were the only ones that half-way enjoyed sitting in a chair and pumping that homemade churn dasher up and down. If the temperature was just right, it only took about fifteen minutes of churning.

After that, I washed my hands as clean as I could, then dipped the fresh butter into a bowl, working it under and over with my hand, until I got all the milk out of it. Then I added a pinch of salt. Afterward, I dumped the bowl of butter into my Grandma Daniel's old wooden butter mold and kept pressing the wooden plunger down until the butter cooled off enough to remove a perfect pound of tasty, fresh butter. It didn't last long, though, at our double table. The milk that remained in the churn was poured up in gallon jugs. It was buttermilk—very good with cornbread and vegetables.

25

Every single person who laid eyes on my little hillside of flowers blooming in the front yard bragged on my artistry of spacing out the right colors to enhance the beauty. Many of them took pictures. We had no camera. I told them God did it all, even allowing a strong breeze to scatter the seeds he gave us last year. Then He sent a gentle rain, and later plenty of sunshine. I wished everybody would plant flowers.

When the summer season of peaches and other fruit and vegetables was waning, the men who weren't in school started learning there were many other jobs to be done while waiting. This year, they had become a landscaping team, with the supervision of Mr. H, who we found out later had been educated in that field. He trained them by completely re-landscaping his own yard—with Mrs. Nona Bell's direction. They were all enthusiastic in their new venture. They acquired many such jobs in town, and Prescott was looking good.

The okra just wouldn't give up. School was about to start, and the patch was still bearing an unbelievable amount of the emerald edible. Mrs. Annie Pruitt moved into the house across from Formby's store after the little Daniel family moved out. She had helped Mrs. Hignight out some at the house and shed. Mrs. Pruitt and her twin sons were hired to finish the okra crop. She was a widow, and a very hard-working Christian woman, well-loved by everyone who knew her. The Hignights knew she was a good hire, and Mary and I were glad to go back to school—well, I know I was.

I didn't get off the bus at the first school this time. I was told before school ended in the spring, that my grade would enter Park Middle School in the fall. I felt mature, staying on the bus watching the little kids get off at Elementary. It shocked me when Mary didn't get off the bus with me. I had forgotten she would be moving on, too. Boy, did that let the air out'a my balloon! Mary was more let-down than I. She was hoping to see me at recess. Now, she would have to make some new friends.

Park Middle School in Prescott.

I was no longer sad when I entered the rock building and found my room and teacher, Mrs. Hines. She told us she was adopting all of us. That scared me a little. I didn't quite know what that meant. I would ask my brother when we were headed home. All of them were at the same school. When I asked him about adoption, he just said, "forget it".

We all had earned enough money to buy our lunches and school supplies this time, and we all would go to town and try on our own new shoes this Saturday, compliments of Daddy. I loved the lunches and didn't understand why some kids complained about them every day.

I had a real art class every other morning with a real artist teacher. Right away I learned that I would never be an artist, but I surely liked to go the artist's room. I would get to go to lunch next.

I was glad to see that several of the girls I played with last year were in my room. We had a good time swinging at recess. I hadn't ever seen that many swings in one place. They were on a metal frame, and it was scary to me because some of the seats swung forward, while others swung back the other way. I got off. Somebody was gonna get hurt, but it wasn't gonna be me.

I got on a see-saw with Joyce Haynie, who became a really good friend, even though we lived far apart. She is still my friend, and now she is Joyce Tyree and lives closer to me.

This was a super-good school. After lunch every day, we went straight to the auditorium to meet our music teacher. She played the piano really well. I've only heard one pianist since then who could play better. She did a play on stage with our entire grade at Christmas time. I was chosen to be in a good role but had to drop out because they practiced after school every day, and I couldn't stay because if I missed my bus, I had no ride home. I never knew if I could have stood up there and said my part in front of all those people or not.

❧❧

Heavy frosts and repeated snows quickly put an end to our Southwest Arkansas growing season. The working men hadn't missed a day at the job, though. Mr. Hignight could always find something important for them to do. When snow and ice kept them from being outside, he and the crew was inside a small heated enclosure, building new bee hives. They would be ready to entice some of the spring flurries of bees to hang around and make enough honey to supply each of our families, and maybe have some to sell. He told them they would paint the hives bright yellow, which was more attractive to the bees, (so science said). Mr. Hignight was probably an entrepreneur before that word made it to Webster's.

Bonnie and her children loved the snow so much, and so did I. We created many games for the little ones and slid down our little hill many times on makeshift sleds we found around the house and barn. A shovel served the purpose if you mounted it just right. We kept sliding until the snow disappeared.

One evening in late winter, it began snowing sparsely and we all had to step out and enjoy watching what we thought would be the last flakes of the season. Bonnie had an idea. She had heard her sister, Christine Brown, speak of making snow ice cream. We had been wishing for some more of that miracle melt-in-your-mouth treat we had at the Fourth of July party.

99

She retreated into her little house and returned with her comfy, pink chenille robe she had received from her hubby. She spread it out on a clean spot of ground and said, "Maybe I can catch enough snow to make a little bit of that sweet stuff."

She said she had sugar and vanilla, and I volunteered to bring a fresh bucket of milk with cream on it. I went to bed that night hoping the snow wouldn't stop before we had enough on her housecoat to fulfil her daydream. Upon awakening the next morning, I immediately pulled back our feed sack curtain on the only window in our bedroom. Wow! Snow was all I saw in every direction!

I noticed Milton and Bonnie in their front yard. Getting dressed happened quickly. I grabbed Bob's huge rubber boots he left by the door and lit out into the snow. It came about half-way up on the boots.

Milton was laughing so hard! They couldn't even find her housecoat. It was well hidden in the deep snow. I ran back to get the milk and a dishpan. I woke everybody up to come on down.

Bonnie only combined a pan full of the soft, dry snow with sugar to taste, and a teaspoon of vanilla, then just enough milk and cream to barely wet the snow when it is all stirred. Wah-lah (Arkansan for Voila)!

There must be a first time for all things. This was the first and only time the Daniel family ate ice cream for breakfast. It took a while for Bonnie to warm up her chenille robe again.

The men went to work, and the school kids stayed home because the bus didn't come. I think Bessie, Dan and Harry S. Truman were happier when the last of that cold, white stuff was gone. Ruff and Tuff had been busy tracking rabbits every which way in the fluff.

Daddy and the boys, with Dan pulling the turning plow, had flipped the garden soil over early in the fall, skipping the turnip patch to allow it to absorb moisture from the rain and snow. They were also hoping when the dirt froze, it would get rid of some of the damaging insects. Soon, the icy sledding fun would change to gardening again, but that was entertaining, too.

26

I liked when Bonnie came to our house to sew after school. The kids were always fun, and they liked to eat supper with us. Jeanie liked boiled 'taters, and Polly like 'mater soup. Dwayne was a meat man. He often helped me butcher chickens for Sunday dinner. I was getting pretty good at dressing poultry, but Daddy said I couldn't do it as fast as Mary. I couldn't understand why he told us we couldn't get married until we could dress chickens and make biscuits. I was diligently trying.

This day, Bonnie made herself a pair of shorts. She wanted to be ready for spring. Daddy never said anything to her about wearing shorts, but Mary and I were forbidden to wear them because he said it made us just too naked. He believed women should keep their bodies covered and secret.

She had cut a shorts pattern from old wrapping paper, and I found it on the sewing machine when she left.

At school the next day, I thought a lot about which feed sack I wanted to use to make myself a secret pair of shorts with her pattern. Tomorrow would be Saturday, and I would have plenty of time to finish them. I hurriedly cut them out when I got home. Mama was resting and the house was quiet. Bonnie had left the machine threaded, and the bobbin was wound full.

Temptation overruled. I sewed the first seam. I would do it in the same order as I had seen her do. I matched the second seam and pedaled faster with my feet. The machine made a peculiar noise and stopped. I was hesitant to look at the needle. I was feeling sudden pain in my left pointer finger, the one that was feeding the seam through the presser foot.

When I did look, I felt a little woozy. I lifted the presser foot, removed the fabric and my finger, and stood up on two wobbly legs. The machine needle was still in my finger! The exit point on the bottom of my finger had broken, but the rest of the needle was still intact. I tried to pull it out and failed.

I showed my finger to Mama and begged her to not tell Daddy what I was making. She sorta panicked and told me to go let Bonnie see it. I ran as fast as I could. She was so good at problem solving, I knew she could fix it, and she did! She had some tweezers for her eyebrows, and they promptly removed the needle from the big end in the top of my finger.

I hurried back to the house to see if Mama was alright. She said I nearly scared her to death, and she didn't approve of me disobeying my daddy. I didn't reply to her statement, except silently in my mind I offered excuses. He only told us not to wear shorts, and I certainly didn't wear them. I have worn knee pants many times since then, but I never wore shorts, except to swim in. I felt like Daddy was watching.

◦⧼⧽◦

I told Mrs. Hines that I dreaded for school to be out all summer, because I didn't have books to read.

"Honey, you can go to the library and get all the books you want," she said.

When I told her we had no car, she started saving books up for me to take home this summer. That was one more worry off my mind. We only had three or four weeks of school left.

I decided I would plant my little garden when I got home. I secretly pulled my tablet from my desk and started mapping out what veggies would go where. I had already completed the math paper that some were still working on, and I had done my homework, too. I'll plant some beets here and some radishes…

The last bell of the day rang. We lined up for the buses in our proper places. I felt so tired. Soon I boarded the bus and sat next to my sis. I was holding my *Weekly Reader*, which was a national newspaper for kids my age, but Mary didn't want to read it. I had subscribed to it with some okra money. This was my first year to have it. I told her I brought it home to let Mama read about a real volcano. I also told her there's a pretty picture of a peony.

She laughed and asked, "What on earth is that?"

"Ain't that some name for a flower? It is pronounced "P-on-knee." I could hardly say it without laughing out loud.

When we got off the bus, I was always very careful crawling through the strands of barb wire. I was afraid the kids on the bus might see my underwear when I raised my leg to go through.

Our little president, Harry S., was lying in some honeysuckle vines, chewing like Bessie. I stopped and talked to them and rubbed their heads.

I heard Sister yelling from the porch, "Mama's gone!"

I yelled back, and asked her what she said, and then I understood, *Mama is not here!* I ran on up the hill so fast it took my breath away. All of them were upset.

Bonnie heard Mary yelling and started up the garden row, waving her arms. When she got to the house, she told us she came up to get water while her kids were asleep after dinner, and found Mama lying flat of her back on the plank floor of the back porch. She said Mama was unconscious, so she ran through the pasture, and called the men she could see in the shed. She said she went back to her sleeping kids, and in no time, the ambulance came.

"I saw Pa get in the ambulance, and the others went back to work," Bonnie explained.

I didn't even want to walk in that house. I sat on the plank doorsteps and cried until my shirt was wet with tears. Where is Mama? What's going on? Is my daddy crying too? So much unknown.

I stood up, securing my books and *Weekly Reader* under my arm as I opened the screen door. Realizing I couldn't share my newspaper with Mama, I stopped and cried again. Now I knew that the very saddest thing in the whole world must be a home without a mama. There wasn't even any warmth coming from the cook stove. The fire had gone out in so many ways.

27

The rattle of pots and pans reminded me that life must continue. Mary had decided we would have breakfast for supper. Clyde skillfully started the fire in the stove. He had a knack for many little jobs, and experience had prepared him for safely helping us girls out when he needed to.

Mary started on the homemade biscuits. She needed the practice! Bob did all the outside chores, this time, and brought me plenty of eggs for "breakfast", tonight and in the morning. I asked him to get a knife and go with me to get meat from the smokehouse. We cut off enough ham and grabbed a sack of smoked sausage. The whole family would be satisfied in at least one way. I set the table, as though everything was normal. That's what our family did, even if some of us were missing. There would be two empty plates tonight.

Roy came through the back door from work. We all stared at him, waiting to hear about what happened to Mama. I could see that the incident had taken its toll on my poor brother. He sat down in his chair and said, "What are we gonna do?" as clearly as anyone.

We waited for him to quit crying. Then he told us that Milton got Mrs. Hignight to call Dr. Mac. He said to call an ambulance and get her to the Cora Donnell Hospital in Prescott to see Dr. Al Buchanan. He told Mrs. H that he was afraid she needed more than he could offer her at home. Roy looked at the empty chairs, and his chin was quivering again as he asked about Daddy. We were wondering about him, also. Bob offered to hitch Dan to the wagon and go get him, but Clyde said Daddy would want to stay with her tonight.

The next morning, Clyde decided he would get permission to leave school and walk over a short distance to the hospital. He would have a complete report after school today.

I hurriedly found Mama's little book with her alphabetically listed kin and addresses. I found Aunt Georgia's and addressed an envelope to her and Granny Bradford. I wrote a short note, telling them about the emergency and where she was. I tried to do my best cursive. With it sealed and ready to go, I found three pennies in the dresser drawer. I grabbed my books and flew through the pasture with barely a "howdy-do" to Dan and the clan. I stuck the letter in the mailbox first, and then dropped the pennies in a jar lid we had placed there to hold our stamp money. I shut the lid, raised the flag, and took my place at our bus stop, just in time to see Big Yellow top the hill.

I didn't enjoy being at school that day. Everybody just went ahead doing all the usual stuff, like they didn't care if my heart was breaking. Seemed as if the whole world just would keep on with everything, without trying to find out if my Mama was alive or dead.

Mrs. Hines didn't get much attention from me that day. I was wondering what a hospital was like, since I had never seen one. I couldn't help but think about who was tending to her, and if she had her eyes open or closed. Who was helping her to the outhouse? Who was cooking for Daddy? Where did he sleep? Did he miss me? I bowed my head at my desk and told God I really would like it if He would bring all of us and me through this terrible time. *Please hear me…*

᪥᪥᪥

I heard the buses lining up out at the sidewalk. I thought that bell would never ring, but it finally did. I wanted to sit by Clyde, but that seat was already filled, so I took the only empty one I saw. I was feeling really disappointed when my dear sister reached over and pecked my shoulder and told me Clyde said Mama would be alright. Hallelujah! I bowed my head again. I had heard about reverence at church.

After we got home, Mary started getting ready to do laundry as soon as we could change clothes. Clyde lit a fire under the wash pot, and Bob fed the animals. I started drawing water from the well to fill the pot.

Bonnie and the young-uns came through the trail to enquire about our parents. The kids had plenty of questions about Pappaw and Granny, and Clyde answered them all. He said Mama didn't have to go outside at all. They had an automatic toilet like Mrs. Maude.

When we girls got all the rub-boarding done, and filled the clotheslines, we began to get whiffs of hot grease. Mary said it was fried

105

taters. That dear sister-in-law was cooking supper. She seemed to always be sensitive to our needs and try to meet them.

She asked to see my injured finger, and there wasn't anything to see. I told her I didn't finish the sewing, because I couldn't find another machine needle. Besides, I might not want to finish it.

Milton came up through the garden about the same time Roy got home. Supper wasn't quite ready, because the cook had supplied the sugar, and was making fried pies from some of our dried apples, and she put cinnamon in them. Ummm!

Roy got the milking done, and supper was ready. We all sat in our places and didn't mention the empty chairs. About that time, the front door opened, and in walked the head of the house! He said Mr. Baker Britt visited at the hospital and passed by where Daddy was. He told Daddy he was sorry about his wife and asked if he needed anything. He was a God-send, because Daddy knew Mr. Britt would pass right by the shed going home, so he asked him if he could ride to the house.

Daddy took off his felt hat and sat in his chair at the table. That made me feel some better, and I was anxiously waiting to hear about Mama's heart.

He said, "Doc says she has fluid around her heart. They're giving her shots to try and get rid of it. She'll have to stay there until she don't need the shots no more. Maybe two weeks."

No, no, no! I didn't speak aloud, but I surely talked bad in my silence. I still needed mothering. I could hardly remember what I ate for supper. As soon as the last pots and pans were dried, I got ready for bed, neglecting my homework.

The next few days were like I was just going through the motion of being Lenora. I answered roll call at school, and ate lunch, and rode home.

I asked if I could be excused from church on Sunday. My stomach really hurt. Nobody felt my forehead or offered any medicine. I laid across my bed most of the day. I didn't want to go back to school either, but the bellyache complaint didn't work.

Daddy said, "Ye can't quit school 'cause yore Mama's sick."

Well, I could try to keep up appearances. I tried my best to pay attention and get my work done, but I was the only one not finished with my math paper when we went to lunch. I cleaned my plate before any of the others did.

We were turned loose after lunch for recess under some trees, across a closed street where playground equipment was located. I didn't feel like playing, so I just sat on a big rock for a little bit, then walked to the front of the school house. It didn't seem to bother anyone that I wanted to be different. I started stepping faster, as if I were hop-scotching, until I got across the street where the buses would come later.

There was a hedge for a long way that hid me from the school street. I was picking up speed now, with one goal in mind. I walked on and on. My heart was beating fast, and it was hard to breathe. I saw a beautiful bed of irises under a tree with a bench nearby. Wait a minute! I already passed that once. I must have gone around this place before.

I saw a man walking with a cane, coming up behind me. I waited, and he asked me if I was lost. I told him I was trying to find Cora Donnell Hospital, because my mother was there. He said that was exactly where he was going, and he would be glad to have me walk with him.

When we started toward some steps, I stopped because I was scared to go in, but I was more scared of finding my way back to school. He held my hand as we marched to the front desk, and I told them who I was there to see. The woman pointed. I took off down the hall and found my mama.

She had a plastic thing over her face, but she could sure see me! I hugged her just as tight as she hugged me, before she asked me why I was missing school, and how did I get there. Then I noticed Clyde was sitting in the corner, looking worried. I told them all about how I got there, and that I wasn't missing anything at school. They were just playing.

He decided he wouldn't return to school, so he walked down the hall and bummed a ride home with someone who lived not far from us.

Mama couldn't talk much, so she didn't fuss at me, but boy I really caught some discipline from Daddy when he got home that evening. He told me what a dangerous caper I had pulled. I was as scared as I was during the ordeal.

I wanted things to get back to normal. I told Daddy I was afraid to go back to school, because I didn't tell the teacher I was leaving. He instructed Clyde to write an absence excuse for my teacher. He explained how sad I was that our mother was seriously ill, and had been in the hospital so long, and that I felt like I just needed to see her. He assured her that he was confident I would not do it again. Clyde signed it for Daddy, and I took it to her.

When the teacher read it, she called me to her desk.

Oh, no! I thought. All she did was put her arm around me and tell me she was so sorry about my mother. I was asked to never leave school by myself again, and if I will tell her when I need to know about my mom again, she would be willing to call the hospital and then relay the report to me. She told me to play like I'm her adopted daughter.

"I still have a mother, thank you," I said under my breath.

28

Some of my perennial flowers had returned after April showers. I pulled the weeds and grass out, so it would make Mama smile if she ever made it back home. When I looked down through the vegetable garden, I saw that it was somewhat like a flower garden. The rains had washed flower seeds downhill, and they were growing beautifully. I wondered if the pollen crossed between a potato and a marigold, if I would have a "pot-o-gold".

While weeding my little garden, I found three watermelon plants and three cantaloupe vines, just beginning to put on runners. Bessie's milk was decreasing, and soon she would be drying up to let her unborn calf have all the nutrients. Her gait was already becoming wobbly.

I was hoping to get a good price for Mr. Harry S. Would it be added to Daddy's automobile fund or house fund? Three mother hens hovered over about forty chicks, each hen trying to claim her own brood. I don't know how they identify their own, but I'm glad they do. Every chick needs a mother.

Laying down near my garden, I watched the fluffy, white clouds form imaginary objects. I began thinking how the seasons were planned, and how smoothly they marched in order from one year to the next. We must be having baked sweet taters for supper. I could smell 'em. I felt like I could devour two at least!

I had carried my new umbrella to the bus stop in the pouring rain, and so did Mary. My funny brother, Bob, said we looked like blooming idiots. Then after school, we both forgot to retrieve them from our secret hiding place in a bush at the bus stop. We usually brought them home after school. It would be difficult to tell Mrs. Cue if they got stolen.

I asked Daddy if I could run back to the bus stop to get our umbrellas. He nodded and I tried to see how fast I could run, but Ruff and Tuff ran faster. I knew Daddy sat on the step to make sure I was safe.

The dogs suddenly turned slightly off the path and started barking loudly. Daddy recognized their sound as a treeing bark. He hollered for Bob to bring the .22 rifle.

Daddy yelled, "Be careful… Don't run with that gun," as Bob leaped over the fence instead of climbing the stile.

Bob soon spied the object of all that barking. They had run a coon up a little persimmon sapling. He took aim and fired. The meat hit the ground, and the dogs had been trained to leave it alone. Bob always gave them what they liked best—the innards. He said his dogs could outrun and out-tree Mr. H's, and that was saying a lot.

I went on and picked the right moment to cross 67 Highway. Our pretty umbrellas were still in our hidey-hole.

Mary was happy. She scolded, "Next time, don't forget them."

As Bob got back up the hill showing off his prize, he stepped the stile this time and grumbled, "I think we are the ones penned in here. The mule and the cows have a lot more room than we do."

After the boys took care of skinning the raccoon and rewarded the dogs, they brought in perfectly clean meat. It was then mine and Mary's turn. It was necessary to go ahead and cook it since raw meat wouldn't keep overnight on a warm night.

❧

The next day was Sunday, and I was happy to tag along to church this time. Daddy asked us to pray for Mama. I told him, "I done been praying for her. Why don't you go with us, Daddy?"

He stared at his shoes for a minute, then said, "I bleeve I will." He said his overalls were clean, and he would get a rag and wipe his shoes off. We all had a smokehouse bath yesterday.

I just about forgot all about our troubles, as I skipped up the gravel shoulder of 67. Mary and I had a problem keeping up with all those long-legged men. I was happy with this much of my family, but I was trying really hard not to talk too much.

Instead of going through the woods, Daddy wanted to walk to the Formby's and ride on to church with them. Mrs. Lily smiled, and said they were delighted to take a truck full to church.

Mr. Trosie said, "I'm really glad to see Mr. Daniel is gonna worship with us this time."

When we piled out at church, Daddy shook Mr. Trosie's hand and thanked him "fer bein' so hepful bout gettin' these young 'uns to church. Is meant a heap to my wife and me, too, ta know all our boys are saved an baptized here. Thank ye for the teachin' and preachin'. Have a idy that one of um may wanna preach someday, too."

We went on inside as they started singing *Come Thou Fount*. I guess Daddy went on to tell him about Mama, because later after Sunday School, Mr. Trosie requested prayer for her. I know God was there that day. I felt Him.

When the truck pulled in at the store, Mrs. Lily and their boys got out to fix dinner, and Mr. Trosie carried us on to our house. He was such a good man. Our shoes were still clean. The stove had kept the coon meat warm, as well as the leftover baked sweet taters. I tried to substitute some muscadine jelly we had canned for barbecue sauce, like Mr. Hignight had served. Daddy liked it, and I didn't care what the others said. It was pretty good. We finished the whole jar of jelly with leftover biscuits and fresh churned butter.

The kitchen was to be cleaned up before we girls could leave it. I didn't argue, but I always got the job of drying! Daddy told us he wanted to walk over there and catch a bus to town while he was clean and go see his bride. I told him he'd better not tell her what we had for dinner. She'll hate she missed it.

I had brought a book home with me that Mrs. Hines offered for me to borrow. I laid across my bed to read it. I guess I fell asleep on the first page. The sounds of jars and spoons rattling in the kitchen awakened me. They were feasting on two or three varieties of canned fruit for supper. I pulled down another half-gallon jar of peaches and poured some in a plate. None of our pretty fruit was canned with sugar, but we weren't accustomed to eating sweets, so we thought it was good.

Daddy stepped off the bus, and Roy was watching for him with the only rusty lantern we had. It worked for us at the creek, and it shone brightly on Daddy's path home. I laughed and told him at least that lantern didn't conjure up a jack-o-lantern this time.

I waited until they were in the kitchen to ask about Mama. He sorta smiled and said she was feeling better.

He said, "She's a rarin' to come to the house, but she's a-smotherin' with that ol' fluid, still."

He pointed at me, and said Mama reminded him twice to not let me slip off from school and walk to the hospital again, and she meant it! I thought *okay, but you can't stop me from thinking about her!*

He said, "Betcha can't guess who 'uz ther when I got ther."

"No, who?" I pulled the light cord, so as to watch his face while he revealed Mama's secret guests. He said there wasn't just one, but four, and that our mother seemed very pleased. Who was it? The excitement was building. She hardly ever had company at home.

Then, he went on to tell us it was Granny Bradford, Aunt Georgia, Uncle Taft Osborn, and their son-in-law, James Spradlin, who had brought them there to see Mama. They said they had been there most of the day. Daddy thought it did her more good than a dose of medicine.

Daddy said, "I couldn't, fer the life of me, figger out how they knowed she was in the hospital. But whenever they gathered up to leave, Granny Bradford said to tell Lenora 'much obliged' fer writin' and lettin' us hear from Desser." (That was her nickname, short for Odessa.)

He looked at me, but he didn't say what Granny told him to tell me about the letter. Clyde walked into the front room and sat on the foot of Mama and Daddy's bed. He slightly bowed his head and closed his eyes. I sat next to him and closed my eyes, too. I knew God would hear Clyde's prayer because he had been saved and baptized. I guess I was hopeful that it would cover me, too, if I could scoot close enough. I loved my brother and he loved me. It was just not in our nature to say it out loud.

I was so happy to hear that Mama had company. She grew up in a big family, but they seldom, if ever, visited her. Her father died too soon, and naturally, the whole family was ill-effected.

One of Mama's sisters, Aunt Myrtie Prescott, who moved off to California so her husband, Ted, could work in a shipyard, or something, stayed out there and raised her two children, Cecil and Elizabeth.

On one of her rare trips back to Arkansas, she came to see us. She sat down next to me out under a cedar tree and told me more about my mother than I had ever heard directly from Mama.

She said they were pretty well off, financially, until their daddy, Harve Bradford, who was a gospel singing school instructor, died suddenly. His daughters hadn't worked in the fields up until then, and when they did have to pick up a hoe and join the ranks of a large number of women who had to work like a man in whatever needed to be done, it was really difficult to handle.

Aunt Myrtie was the third child, and Mama was his oldest child with Granny. He was a widower with one son, when they married. As the story goes, Mama suffered a low-grade fever for one whole planting and growing season. When she was finally pronounced able to go to work, she couldn't hold up in the field without passing out. Aunt Myrtie said her siblings helped Mama get back to the house many times, and she was sickly so often they just made her stay in, to do housework and cooking. Aunt Myrtie said she read a lot about rheumatic fever and how it affects the heart, after she moved out west. She told me she firmly believes that's what Mama had, and the other siblings agreed.

I was sorry to hear that Mama had suffered so long, but I really did love my time with Auntie. She and Uncle took us poor little Daniel kids for a ride in their brand-new maroon Ford car (circa 1947). He said everybody around them was making "real good money" out there in California.

She told me another true story that verified one of the first statements she made. She had said that everyone who knew Harve Bradford, my Grandpa, would tell you that his family was certainly his pride and joy.

According to her, his girls were mostly teenagers, and Mama, the oldest, was about seventeen, when he told them to get all gussied up to go to town with him. He told them he had money that was burning his pocket.

They went to a jewelry store, and he told them all to pick out any ring in the store that they wanted. She said the four younger sisters all selected one that was beautifully flashy, with colored birthstones. They all got a different color. Mama chose a solid gold, wide-band ring, like a wedding band, and wore it on her right hand. Auntie said theirs tarnished, and some lost the stones, but Mama's remained shiny, a lasting memory of her father.

Years ago, when her fluid problems began, Mama gained weight and the ring didn't fit her finger, so she hid it away in her trunk. She showed it to Mary and me once or twice, but she never told us the story behind it.

29

My days all seemed to run together. School was out, and I felt like I was in a square bubble that was bound to burst, sooner or later. I think I found out how orphans must feel—lost in space.

My siblings shouted out orders of things I should do before Mama gets back. Everybody was my boss now. Daddy acted like his mind was on something else, not me.

I believed I got more household chores than my share, because Daddy told me to do whatever Mary told me and left it at that.

I cleaned and straightened the dresser drawers, and the wooden shelves nailed on the kitchen walls, but I was told not to throw anything away unless I asked her. I had to clean the room where the three boys slept. It had barely enough space for two beds. We all slept on cotton mattresses that we made at a community project. The farm owners provided the cotton and the government furnished the other needed materials. Sharecroppers' wives did the tedious labor.

The boys weren't so reliable on making sure their clothes made it to the dirty clothes box when needed. I smelled all that were still hanging on their nails on the walls and took about half of them down to be rubbed clean next washday. They weren't too happy to find some of their good clothes were missing, but when they sniffed them right off the clothesline, they got happier.

Mary and I took two whole days getting the ironing done. That meant keeping the fire going in the kitchen all day to heat the iron. When the men came in from work, it didn't take them long to ask us why the house was so hot.

Mary said, "Well, if you would take a look, you would see that all your Sunday clothes are starched and ironed. Bet we worked harder than y'all these last two days!"

When Daddy caught a bus to town the next time, he made a stop at Prescott Hardware after he left Cora Donnell. He had purchased an electric iron with a cord on it. He handed it to Mary and told her that it was Mrs. Hignight's "idy". He told us not to keep it going all day—it might burn the house down. He also wouldn't allow us to plug it into the receptacle he bought to screw in above the light bulb, just yet. He didn't want to heat it up for nothing.

We may have rushed up laundry time a little bit, just so we could plug in that new invention in the front room. We ironed on a plank, rolled in an old blanket remnant, and laid across the high back of two chairs from the eating table. We had to take turns. It was so exciting!

That night, we couldn't wait to tell Daddy we didn't keep it plugged in all day. We were all finished by dinner time! He smiled and I stood there, waiting for a hug or just a touch—nothing. I wiped our shiny, new electric smoothing iron, and placed it on a high shelf. I surely didn't want any harm to come to it.

We sat down to eat in a kitchen that was warm, because it was summer, but not so hot from ironing those starched, white Sunday shirts. We had Daddy's clothes ironed for church, too.

Daddy dressed in those freshly laundered Sunday clothes, but he decided to go spend the day with his bride, instead of crowding into Mr. Trosie's truck for the ride to church.

All of us, kids, went and gladly took our nephew and nieces with us. Polly got tired of walking and required some assistance before we made it to the truck. Roy and I carried her piggy-back. All three of them loved the ride in the back of the pickup. We didn't have to ask them to go to church any more. They were rarin' to go every Sunday morning, and soon their parents were attending services, also.

Milton was the first one in our family to purchase a car. We were all thrilled, like it was ours. He soon taught Bonnie how to manage to keep that Model A Ford between the ditches and roll on down the road. She caught on to things like that as easily as she did with the sewing machine.

At church it was announced that Mr. Joe Beavert, who was our song director, would soon be teaching a Southern Baptist Convention singing school, right there in our little church. Those schools were mostly taught in larger town churches. I was extremely grateful to Boughton Baptist for covering the costs. Otherwise, my family would probably not go, but we all signed up. I was uneasy doing it without asking Daddy, but Mr. Joe said folks from other churches were already signing up, and he could only accommodate a certain number of singers.

I was so excited to tell Daddy our good news, but he had some news that topped mine. He started singing, "She'll Be Coming 'Round the Mountain When She Comes…"

"When WHO comes?" I shouted.

Daddy said the doctor told him they will observe Mama without oxygen tonight, and if he confirms she is ready, she'll be discharged tomorrow. He went on to say he talked to Mr. H after his bus ride back, and his boss insisted that one of my brothers use his car to bring her home. Daddy said he was glad to save the twenty-dollar fee for the ambulance ride.

As soon as he got through breaking the good news to us, that awful furrow returned to his brow. He walked over and unlocked his trunk and took out his checkbook. I knew what had shadowed his thoughts a moment earlier. I don't know if medical insurance existed then. I know it had never been offered to us.

Daddy said he had no idea how much the hospital bill would be. He was hoping they would accept a check and a promise. He never said another word about it. I didn't think he would be excited to hear our news right now, so I just held it in.

Ham and biscuits and honey made a good dinner. I was glad we had breakfast leftovers. Mary cleaned the kitchen thoroughly and straightened up with everything in its place. I worked on hanging up the boys' clothes that could be worn again, and then I piled up all the dirty laundry including Mama's bed sheets and the dirty gowns Daddy brought home. We knew she wouldn't want us to wash clothes on Sunday, so we would get up and start early Monday.

Mama and Daddy were strict about teaching us what the Bible says in Exodus 20 about working on Sunday: "Remember the Sabbath day, to keep it holy. Six days shalt thou labor, and do all the work: But the seventh day is the Sabbath of the Lord thy God: in it, thou shalt not do any work, thou, nor thy son, nor thy daughter, thy manservant, nor thy maidservant, nor thy cattle, nor thy stranger that is within thy gates: For in six days the Lord made heaven and earth, the sea, and all that in them is, and rested the seventh day: wherefore, the Lord blessed the Sabbath day, and hallowed it."

It isn't strange that the very next verse under the scripture just mentioned is: "Honor thy father and thy mother that thy days may be long upon the land, which the Lord thy God giveth thee."

First it was given from the inspiration of God, then it came from our honored father and mother, and their offspring believed it! We were convinced that catching or killing to provide food was work, and so we didn't hunt or fish on Sunday. I can't think of many times the "ox was in the ditch".

Milton and Daddy went to get Mama, and the other three men went to work very early on Monday. Bonnie got her children all situated in the playhouse I created for them. She could keep an eye on them by looking out the kitchen window. She cooked a feast for Mama's homecoming, including a beautiful plate of deviled eggs, which was one of her favorite farm dishes.

Mary and I strung the clotheslines full, and a soft breeze dried them in no time, so we were able to replace Mama's sheets before she got home. We scrubbed the porches and the front room floor, by pouring the soapy water from the wash pot onto the planks and sweeping briskly with a broom. They turned a shade lighter when dry.

We got the little ones cleaned up for dinner, and then waited and waited. What could be taking them so long to bring her home? They didn't have to wait on a bus.

Bonnie gave up waiting and fed the baby. She crumbled cornbread and covered it with fresh cooked beans from the garden and mashed and stirred it well. Polly was kicking her feet and smiling. All of the kids were good eaters.

Just as the baby was getting full, we heard a car. I was the first one out the door and saw Mama in the back seat. I was trying not to cry, but I burst into tears just when I got her door open. My mama was home again, and the whole world was right. I hugged her till I was pulled back by Daddy, trying to get her out of the car and in the house. She needed assistance, but she did stand up and walk. *Much obliged, Lord!*

They helped her across the clean planks right onto her chair at the table. Milton took the car back to Mr. Hignight. The other three brothers chased across the pasture and got in on the feast also. Clyde said a prayer aloud, and I thanked God silently for our bountiful blessings, as did the others, I'm sure.

30

Daddy had warned us that Mama could have only a bare minimum of salt, so Bonnie had cooked the dinner accordingly. It wasn't difficult to cook what she wanted. She liked vegetables, and that's what we had right now. Mama assured us she could shell beans and peas, and she would like to be busy, but we knew rest was important for the next few days.

After she took a nap, I brought her writing tablet and pencils, and asked if she could write the letters this time, and she did. I mailed one each day for a week. I knew it made her feel better, and it gave her hope that they would write back to her. She had very little contact with her family, except by mail, and a letter from any one of them made her day brighter.

I begged her to keep her tablet on the dresser by her bed, and start a diary for past time, but I don't think she ever did. I told her about the singing school, and she said it thrilled her heart. Mama laughed and said she hoped it was shape notes. It runs in the family. She said she learned to sing the scale and a lot more, just following her dad to the singing schools he taught. She never sang for us, though.

At the supper table, she talked about it again, and told Daddy she hoped all of us kids could go. That was good to know. I told her we had all signed up! We learned at church the next Sunday, the singing school would start in one week, and about a hundred people were registered.

❧❧

It was our busiest time of year. If we were to eat well through the winter, the garden stuff had to be canned now. The men continually fought a losing battle with the peach fuzz, and occasionally in a tight to fill an order, sought help from Mary and me to pick.

On any given day, I probably ate my weight in over-ripe peaches. Mr. H gave us bushels of over-ripes to take home. It looked kind of bad when the pickers weren't getting them to the packers in time to send them on their way. If they were to be shipped long distances, they were shipped half-ripe or green.

The men helped peel what we canned and dried, and sometimes Mama peeled too. Our shelves for canned goods were already filled and running over, but the fruits and veggies kept coming from a God-given growing season.

It was a relief to dip in a tub of sun warmed water, then traipse through the woods and onto the gravel to get to the "church in the wildwood". We met a lot of new folks, and most of them were country, like us. It was a happy group of people at the singing school, who had at least one good thing in common. We all loved church songs, and seemingly, loved singing them.

Mr. Joe Beavert was serious about not wasting our time or his. Most everyone there was so grateful to him for the opportunity, we listened to every word he said, and every do-re-mi he sounded.

The summer peach harvest.

I told Mama the next morning, that I was thinking if we still lived in that house near the church, she could hear us singing from her bed. She had many questions to ask about it all. I told her we really made a joyful noise unto the Lord.

The two hours passed so quickly every night, because we so enjoyed it. When it was over and we hurried to get our walk home done, was when our bodies began to wear down. Regardless, our hearts were light with the tunes we had sung.

We tried to slip in the house quietly, so we wouldn't wake our parents. In just a few hours, our wake-up alarm would be Daddy's "Get up, another day, another dollar."

⊰⊱

The summer work must go on. There was so much to do. I never heard anybody say, "I'm bored!" We didn't even know what that meant. During the second week of our musical endeavor, the teacher said he had noticed some potential for a quartet or an ensemble from the Daniel family. He pointed at Bob and said he had a bass voice good and low, and he just needs a little more power behind it. He pulled Mary out from behind me and told her that he was hearing a perfect alto voice, if she would turn it loose, and let everybody hear it.

Mr. Joe placed us where he wanted and had us give him a scale. He told us a number to sing, and I asked if Roy could come up and help us. He told him to come on up. I don't remember the song—I was so nervous.

When we finished, there was loud applause, and he announced to everyone, "The Daniel Family". After it was over, he gave us some tips for improvement. I was to sing soprano, Mary alto, Clyde tenor, Bob bass, and Roy was soprano, too, to make us sound stronger.

We practiced when all of us were home. Mama and Daddy laughed. They loved Bob's deep bass. I told them Mr. Joe asked us to sing a special for the Sunday morning service. We practiced a new song from the book he used for teaching. We had learned it in the past two weeks, and it contained specific parts for each of us.

In our best church clothes, we formed our group in proper order, and stood at the foot of Mama's bed. It was a command performance. When she got through crying, Bob told her we would try not to disappoint her again, so she wouldn't have to cry any more.

119

They both told us to "go on and 'sang' for them folks. Y'all are ready." That we did!

Some visitors from Gurdon asked if we could come to their church and sing.

The answer came from Clyde. "That's a little too far to walk. We don't have a ride."

I don't remember who the pastor was at that time, but I do know he and his wife paid us a visit that afternoon, along with the Formby and Johnson families. The pastor told our parents that we really would need some encouragement to keep up our singing, because he thought we were destined to serve the Lord in that manner.

After all the company was gone, Mama was tired and happy. I asked Daddy how he was going to encourage us to sing. Maybe get us a piano? He told me to go get his razor strap and he would start the encouragement right now, if I wanted him to. He and Bob were so much alike with their quick wit, but I didn't think that was funny. I had experienced the razor strap (whipping) before for my sassy mouth, and I didn't consider it a form of encouragement. My siblings laughed at me, and Mama told them to hush. Then she cast a not-so-happy glance at Daddy.

31

Milton acquired a better job somewhere, which meant they had to move our grand-babies away. Depression set in for Mama, but she was able to overcome it with much added attention from those of us who were still around.

Their little house was rented to Charles and Anna Bell (Holder) Andrews. I think they were newlyweds, a very lovely pair. She was timid when she came up through the garden with her glass jugs to get water. I offered to carry one of them for her, and she handed it to me. I was glad when she let me in the house. It was totally a different arrangement from before. I liked it. Her bed was piled high with beautiful princess dolls, wearing gorgeous crocheted gowns. That must have been my initial introduction to crochet, my very favorite hobby since 1981. She showed me a crochet project she was working on, and how she followed the written instructions. I wanted very much to learn that, but first, I needed to finish the small embroidery tablecloth I was working on. I didn't have much spare time.

We made it into another school year, and another snowy winter. Bob was faithful to meet the needs of all our four-legged family members. Harry S. Truman went to live with a friend of ours. Bessie had a female calf that year that we named Beulah, after a comedy character on the radio in the evenings. Daddy habitually turned it on early to hear Beulah. He always used the excuse that he was just trying to hear the news, which came on later.

The whole family loved the *Grand Ole' Opry*, on WSM station every Saturday night. It starred country and western performers and comedians like Minnie Pearl, Roy Acuff, Bill Monroe, Loretta Lynn, Patsy Cline, Hank Williams and many others. The show played until midnight, but Daddy usually shut-er-down at nine.

❦

Mary and I were experts at dressing chickens now. The hens raised more chicks than we could count, and we still had plenty of corn in the barn to feed them. One of the brothers chopped the heads off for us, if they were around, but we could do it if we had to. Daddy told us to scald the dead chickens to make their feathers loosen, then pluck each feather off and singe the remaining fuzz over a fire. He liked to eat the skin.

We only killed three at a time, so as not to let any meat waste for lack of refrigeration. The more meat we fried, the more they ate. One Saturday, we dressed six fryers for the Hignights, and took them to the Mrs. They had bought a new refrigerator. Mama said it was, "cause they had done so much for us." I wondered if they liked it as well as their goat and coon meat.

Mr. and Mrs. DeLaughter dropped by for a visit and brought Mama a small electric oscillating fan with two speeds. We didn't have any receptacles put in our house, so we unplugged the electric radio, and hitched up the fan close to her bed. They had heard she had trouble breathing, and this was a most helpful device.

I sat down in the floor next to Mrs. Maude's chair. I had thought of her often, and I loved and missed her. I knew she loved me, too. She told us she would be wanting to borrow us girls again soon. Mama told her anytime.

We had dressed two more chickens right before they got there. When they stood up to leave, Mama asked me to go in the kitchen and "get them chickens to give 'em."

Well, there's the chickens, right there… I thought. I didn't want to just hand them two naked chickens, still dripping. I searched for a container and found a bucket that was too little to hold them. Foil, Saran Wrap and waxed paper hadn't come our way yet. I'd not even heard of it. I spotted a classified news page Mrs. Hignight had given Daddy to give him an idea about how much land was worth. He had already read it, as best he could.

I wrapped the chickens in it, then packed them in the empty fan box. They acted like they were pleased. Mrs. Maude paid me with a hug that I was longing for.

I made it through another year of school. I loved my teacher that year, too. Mrs. Lucille Elgin had heard about the incident the year before, when I eloped from school to go find my mother.

She called me up to her desk and asked in a low voice about how my mother's health was. I told her there's no cure for her heart problem, but she was much better than she was. I told her she could walk and do small jobs around the house, but she wasn't strong at all.

Mrs. Elgin told me she was sorry. She said any time I need or want to talk to her she would be more than glad to listen and do whatever she could to help me. She read from Psalms or Proverbs every morning, and then prayed for all of us to have a good day. I could tell she was one of God's people, and His folks are good!

Mr. Hignight and his crew got a lot done through the winter behind the scenes, so to speak. They were ready for the harvest. Mr. Hignight told Daddy he hadn't forgotten their deal he made when we made the move up here to join his orchard team. He remembered that Daddy had told him he was looking for a house with a few acres to buy, because he wanted his family to have a roof over their head, where nobody could ask him to move, ever again.

He repeated, "When you find a place, just let me know. I will help y'all any way I can. I appreciate the good help that you and your family have given me."

Daddy replied, "I'm still lookin', but they're all purty high. I won't up and leave ye dry, tho. We'll try to git ye thew another season pickin' and give ye notice fore we quit an move."

He went on and told his boss he sure hated for us kids to have to leave our church. He hoped he could get a little place close by.

❧❧

We got acquainted with the Henry and Essie Page family. They lived close to where we came out of the woods and hit the gravel road, when we walked to church. They started walking with us some, and we all had a lot of fun together. They had several children near our ages. If we got our jobs caught up, we would go play at each other's houses. We played checkers and dominoes, and outside games, such as baseball with make-shift balls and bats.

Clyde was just about to make it from third to home in school. He would be in the eleventh grade when school started. Mama told anybody who came by, that Clyde would graduate in two years. He would be the first grandchild on paternal and maternal sides to graduate. Daddy warned her a lot of things could happen in two years to cause him to not go through with it.

Clyde had heard that his Junior class would have to pay down on their official class rings. He picked peaches and saved his money all summer. He wouldn't have to ask Daddy for any money. Clyde wanted to go to college. Nearly all the students in his class liked him, but he acknowledged that he hadn't one close friend and confidant.

While working that summer, he started smoking cigarettes, I think because all his peers at the high school were doing it. I reminded him how many times he had told us girls not to try to do things that others were doing, just to be like them and fit in. He said he planned to quit when he graduated. Nobody had ever warned that Junior class that quitting was easier said than done.

He really let his baby sister down. Clyde kept his smoking a secret from Mama and Daddy for a long time. Then he forgot and left an empty package on his bed one morning. He made a liar out of me. I told them I didn't know anything about it. He tried to quit then, but his money hadn't run out yet. Up until then, I saw him as perfect, but I learned Jesus Christ was the only one who went down in the Book as perfect.

Clyde was headed for his last year in school, and I was getting close to half way. He was seven years older than me. I wanted him to live in our house forever. I couldn't stay mad at him; he was so good to me.

Summer brought high temperatures and humidity, which made the peach fuzz more annoying when it went down in the collar. Even with a bandana around the neck, it was still miserable. Mary and I helped, alternately, in the orchard. Mama got most of our attention in the house. We had to be careful with how her food was prepared. She still wanted to come eat at the table with the rest of us. I removed the salt shaker from the table and hid it. She didn't need to watch us shaking salt. It was good for all of us.

The doctor had mentioned to her that she could breathe better if she could lose a few pounds. So, we cut her biscuits and cornbread in half, and gave her sweet milk, instead of buttermilk. Mama's portions were reduced so gradually, she hardly noticed. She mostly wore loose clothing, and we weren't able to detect weight loss, but she said she could. Daddy always remarked to her that he liked her just the way she was. I did too, but I hoped she could be healthier.

Our church family somehow became aware that Daddy was looking for a place to buy, preferably with a house on it. One man heard about a place down around Laneburg, and asked Daddy if he would like to ride down there and look. Daddy and Mama agreed that if he liked it, he would then take her to see it. Mary tried to fill Daddy's shoes, climbing the ladder to the high peaches that day, and the boys said she did good.

Daddy liked the place, but not the price. When he described it all to Mama, she just said, "I shore dread to move."

He didn't mention it any more.

32

Near the end of summer, Mrs. Hignight called Clyde in the shed, when he started toward home at quitting time. She said she just wanted to give him some encouragement to go ahead to school and get that diploma. Their son, Jimmy Dale, had graduated the past spring and had been working already, maybe at a power plant nearby or something like that.

Mrs. Hignight told Clyde, "We are so proud of you for sticking with your education, we want to give you an early graduation present to help you get through this last year. Don't tell anyone but your family."

She handed him an envelope. He opened it, and then gave her a light hug and a handshake.

He told her he had been saving his money for three summers and was earnestly praying and hoping to go to college. When he told all of us about the gift, I gasped.

Daddy was quiet for a minute, then said, "I'm sorry, Son. I wish I coulda been somebody important. I've been a mite too content with bein' a sharecropper and I like that way of life, but I've let my family down, I reckon. I'm seein' at most folks are able to do more with money than me. They must feel like they hafta help me."

Mama told him, "Mrs. Hignight wanted to do that for Clyde. She told me how she appreciated how hard he worked, and she was aware that he didn't run around like other fellas his age. She did that for Clyde, not for you or me."

Daddy's lament rang in my ears, as I cried behind the house in my almost spent garden. Tears fell as I thumped the remaining watermelons, pretending to check them for ripeness.

I had a hard time believing those words came from my father's mouth, and I know I never heard my mother speak up like that. She was extremely fond of her Bible-reading son, though. She depended on him for many things. He helped her out in guiding the rest of us through the do's and don'ts of everyday living.

I knelt beside my least melon, and audibly asked God to relieve the heartache my daddy must feel. I told Him I had read in the Bible where He said something about the least here on earth would be the greatest in heaven.

I begged, "Please don't allow my daddy to feel like he's failed. I want you in my heart, Lord. Help me to not ever hurt my daddy's feelings."

Mary cooked tomato soup with cornbread for supper, one of Daddy's favorites. I set the table and brought in fresh water and poured a glass where each bowl was set. Since it was a light supper, I sliced watermelon and cantaloupe from my own garden, but it was impossible to pull a smile out of any of them tonight.

"Pass the soup," was about the only words uttered at our table for that meal. Of all places, this is where our liveliest conversations usually happened.

Two girls cried in our bed after such a quiet, sad supper. My pillow was wet with tears of sadness. I continued to plead on Daddy's behalf that God would intervene and take some burdens off his back and get him out of this rut. I knew he had been through rough times, trying to go back and forth to the hospital, worrying about Mama's heart, and he was determined to fulfil his promise to all of us to buy us a home someday, which seemed to him to be just out of reach.

God didn't exactly speak to me, but I thought, *I feel relief this time.*

The radio announced the outside temperature was around a hundred degrees when the news was going off around six pm. Even with only one window in our room and no breeze to be felt at all, sleep was peaceful.

I awoke rested the next morning, and just about had the stove fire going when Daddy got up. I had named that old wood burner, Hellen. Why? Figure it out. She was hot!

Without any words being exchanged between the two of us, I think he knew that I would put forth every effort to help him any way possible. I could only wonder if he, too, had the feeling that God was working for us.

After everyone had eaten and gone to work, I bounded around like a chicken with its head cut off, cleaning and straightening the house and Mama's bed until I was satisfied with the way it looked. Then I found an old, worn-out gown, and disassembled it completely. I measured and cut new feed sack pieces from the old worn ones, just the way I had been shown by Bonnie. This was my first attempt to sew, since the left pointer finger had healed.

This may have been where I learned, "you rip what you sew". I did have to rip out some, but I was so proud to present the finished product to Mama. She smiled and bragged on me for making a gown so quickly. I don't know if she understood that I had so many folks to make happy, and so little time to do it in. That's the way I felt most of the time.

೮ಿ೧ಾ

We picked fresh turnip greens from our fall patch. The tiny, new leaves didn't fill the bucket quickly, but we stuck with it diligently until it was packed. The washing and looking for any foreign objects, such as grass, took even longer. No turnips grew beneath them yet, but maybe soon. Mama would enjoy the greens more than anyone. The men would be more fond of the last of the fresh whippoorwill peas we cooked along with a few patty-pan squash.

I pulled the pans off the direct heat to the cool side of Hellen. The kitchen was so hot. I fanned my skirt tail, took off to the front porch, then sat at my usual spot on the wooden tool box to cool, until the men quit at the shed across the highway. I saw Bessie and Dan running toward the far fence, as if they suspected it was quitting time at the shed. I was glad we lived close to their work. The boys came sprinting toward the house, but I noticed Daddy appeared to be thinking about whether to take the next step or not.

Clyde slowed considerably, until he was in step with Daddy. I noticed their heads nod as if they were conversing, as their steps got slower. My brother later told me he had planned to give Daddy the check he got from Mrs. Hignight, but Daddy refused it, saying if he really needed it, he would let him know. At the same time, Daddy showed him an article Mrs. Hignight had torn from *Nevada County Picayune* classified ads. A Mr. Tate was offering for sale a thirty-five-acre place with three fixer-upper houses in the Pleasant Hill community, approximately five miles northwest of Prescott on State Highway 19, toward Delight.

Daddy had asked Mr. Hignight about being off work one day to go look at it. He volunteered to take Daddy and Mama to see it. When they were in the truck ready to go the next morning, Mr. H asked the boys if they wanted to ride over there and take a look. They all boarded behind the cab, feeling so important to be asked.

Laundry day came too often, but we, girls knew the only way to get it out of the way was to just tackle it head-on. That was true with a lot of our jobs. Looking back through those years is sad. We worked really hard in our most formative years. Moving wasn't anything we anticipated joyfully. We went ahead with washing the clothes and replacing sheets on the beds. We didn't know the boys went house-hunting, too. *Oh well...* I thought. *The house was probably too high for us to buy...*

We were keeping supper warm and folding clothes to put away. I had started doing up the night work. I brought in water, fed the chickens and dogs, and checked on the pasture family. I penned up another half dozen frying chickens to fatten with all the corn they could eat, so they would taste good. Lastly, I brought in enough cooking wood for the next day.

The others wouldn't have anything else to do when they got back. *Where are they?* I remembered something I read in Mrs. Maude's magazine about what Corrie Tin Boom wrote, "Worry doesn't empty tomorrow of its sorrow, it empties today of its strength."

We sat on the porch to wait. They would have to drive up to our house because Mama couldn't walk from the shed. I brought out six jacks and a small red rubber ball, one of the few games Mary would play with me. She took the first turn and threw the jacks on the floor, then bounced the ball and raked up all the jacks in her hand and caught the ball before it hit the floor the second time. She kept doing that until she missed the ball, then it was my turn.

We saw car lights turn off 67 and come toward the house. It was the orchard truck.

33

I had been worried all day about Mama. She hadn't stayed up for a whole day since her hospital stay. Had they eaten?

The truck pulled on past us to the back yard gate, then we saw three brothers unload from the flatbed back of the truck. That's why they hadn't shown up from the orchards for supper. They had been to Pleasant Hill, no doubt!

Roy brought Mama in the back door where the steps were lower. It took all her effort to make it to the first chair in sight. My first question to these two was something like, "Was it worth the trip?" Silence...

I spread the supper out on the table and poured morning milk for all. The supper was cold and the milk was warm. I peeked out the window and saw that Daddy was still standing by Mr. Hignight, who seemed to be doing all the talking. They were flanked on either side by Clyde and Bob.

I fixed Mama's plate and encouraged her to eat a little if she could, before going to bed. She wasn't very hungry. I thought that was strange if she hadn't eaten since breakfast.

She was in bed when the others came inside. Her limits for this day had been exceeded. For what? I had made up my mind I wouldn't ask any more questions. Mary was quite puffed up that we didn't get to go see the place. She sealed her lips, too.

As we ate, Bob made useless conversation about the night chores. He should have known we girls had always covered for them. When need be, we did their work and ours, too. I told him we did all the jobs, except milking. We hadn't been trained to milk. We just turned the cow and calf together, and let the calf have all the milk.

Daddy went straight to bed, saying he would be getting up earlier in the morning. The radio was in the front room, so it would remain off for tonight. Our favorite program was Inner Sanctum, a scary drama. Oh well, not tonight. We hadn't anything else we could do quietly, so we reluctantly, pulled the covers over our heads to close out this long day, that still held so many questions.

I didn't want to move yet. I liked this house and its surroundings and our neighbors. I would much rather have Milton and Bonnie and their kids in the little house, but they had made a good move.

I loved going to worship at Boughton Baptist Church. We had many friends there, and it really stung my heart to even think of leaving them behind. I knew I spoke for all the Daniel kids, in saying it would be difficult to break in another bunch of school bus riders. It would take a long time for them to look past our outer appearances and see that we are all good inside. That, we knew from experience.

I wondered about the Hignights. Would they be hurt if we left this place? They were so good to us. As tired as I was, when I went to bed, I hardly slept at all. I was so afraid to think of change.

Daybreak lifted some of the darkness that seemed to hang over our house the night before. With me, unpleasant thoughts always seemed worse at night. If God is for us staying or moving, he must have special plans for us, and I will support them!

I was the first one out of bed again and was gathering together everything needed to begin the ritual of fixing breakfast for a big bunch when Daddy touched my shoulder and said, "I'll take it frum here."

I went ahead crackin' eggs, while he did the rest.

He said "I wisht y'all could have been with us yistiddy, but thangs jes happn'd too quick."

He told me he thought about it all night and was deciding to buy us a home. "And you are the first one ta know, Baby Girl."

Oh, how I hoped it would be a home that suited girls, too.

The whole clan fell in their seats around the table, and I dared to not say one word. The savory smell of bacon and coffee was a good waker-upper. Daddy gulped down his food pretty fast, then scooted back in his chair, and simply told us he was fixing to catch a Greyhound to town and buy his wife and kids a home.

He was meeting a man, who represented the owner, to sign the papers, but first he planned to talk the price down a little. He asked Clyde to go along for backup. Daddy could read some but was afraid he couldn't understand everything.

I called it smart when Clyde used some of his summer money to buy a Kodak. He wanted some tangible memories of his senior year. Fortunately, he preserved some memories of the Hignight place, too.

Roy and Bob went on to their jobs across the highway, and when Mr. Hignight asked what Mr. Daniel had settled on, they told him Daddy had taken his advice and left on a bus to meet a man at the courthouse to sign the papers.

Mr. Hignight said, "He'll do alright. He's got good common sense."

He went on to say he would take the crew over there and do a little patching up before moving day.

The buyers were back on the ten-thirty bus with a deed in hand, and a smile on their faces. They changed clothes and went on across the road.

We tended to collect all boxes in the barn throughout the years, and as a sharecropper family, had used them often. Today we had wagged some of them to the back porch, and filled a few already with unnecessary items we kept, but knew we wouldn't be using before the departing. I guessed it would be a long trip this time. I had no idea where Pleasant Hill was, but I could remember a girl at school, named Shelby Jean Harris, saying she lived there. It might be hard to find her if it's a really big place.

Daddy told us not to pack things we would be using yet, because he wasn't gonna get in a hurry. He wanted to get it in a better shape, first. He hadn't mentioned a well or water yet. Bob told us the two smaller houses had folks living in them and paying rent. He said they were told they could stay on, if they wanted to. He also marveled at an oak tree that was very near the road, which was encircled with an iron ring that had no opening. It was about three feet in diameter, and he was wondering how they got it on over the tree top. Bob told us about the barn, smokehouse, and outhouse, and laughed, "Ain't that all a feller needs?"

The long-awaited signal came one Saturday night, several weeks later, when Daddy and the boys returned from patching up the new place. He walked in and said, "Let's move on West!"

We all shifted into moving mode, but without the excitement we had exhibited before. We all expressed our regrets at leaving a place that we so loved.

When Daddy wasn't in the house, I told them to "act right and don't hurt his feelings."

They perked up and got up a good sweat. In a short time, we had the back of the flatbed truck stacked high with boxes, beds, and such. The mule was hitched, and the wagon was loaded with corn, tools and chickens. A rope tied to the back of the wagon led the cows through the back roads. Bob said that wasn't an easy feat, but we managed to avoid major roads.

Sis and I boarded the second and last truck load. We moved everything, even the light bulbs. I carried flower seeds in sufficient quantity. Every window and door was closed. My head turned around toward the house, as we drove off for the last time. I blew a kiss to my morning glories that continued to climb up strings on the side of the front porch. Their shocking blue blooms had closed for the day, but would show up again tomorrow, even if I couldn't.

We did all the moving on Monday, after we had told our beloved church bye, and gave them one last song from The Daniel Family, *In the Sweet By and By.*

Mama was already in our new home, and I certainly wanted to be where she was. Mary and I rolled pretty fast into a new world. My eyes were wide open, and my mind tried to imagine what unknown adventures awaited. At least I knew we would all still be under one roof. That thought made me hopeful.

Mr. Hignight talked with hand motions when he was excited, and I could see through the back glass on the truck that he was saying a lot. Ruff and Tuff had come over on the wagon atop the corn. That used to be where I rode. They rushed toward the dirt road, barking as we turned into the yard. I spied the iron ring around the tree that would now signal "this is home".

I saw another tree at the end of the long front porch that looked climbable, but to show my maturity, I saved climbing it for later.

There were two front doors and a single window on each side. I walked through the door on the right, and heard no bells ringing or anything exciting that announced that we were finally home in our own bought-and-paid-for house.

I surveyed the expressions on each face and knew that each of us had come to the same conclusion: Daddy had done his very best. He was willing to keep working till he realized his lifetime dream. I, for one, was eager to help that dream grow even bigger.

That afternoon, we started tearing down an old wooden shed that was about to fall in. Daddy said we had to build a shed and fence for the cows. They were still tied with a rope, so they wouldn't run off. He instructed Roy and Clyde to go in the house and get the bed steads set up, then come back out and dig some post holes. The girls were to get the beds ready for sleep, straighten up the kitchen, and fix everyone something to eat.

We were all good at team work, and before night fell, the cows were safe and the beds had the covers turned back already. We made the biggest bowl of canned fruit of every kind. There was lots of leftover bread that was brought with us. All our meat was in the house, though, since the smokehouse had yet to be made ready. The pork supply was low enough to buy some pigs. Daddy had waited until after the move, so they wouldn't add to the moving hazards.

One of the boys drew water from the well, tasted it, and proclaimed it drinkable. Maybe we would have some milk to drink by tomorrow. The calf wasn't able to reach the milk when they were in separate pens. We kids had known from a very young age, how to be flexible and learn how to get by in whatever circumstances we found ourselves in. We felt destined for successful living, as long as we had each other.

It was a fast walk through the calendar pages, and we were coming up on another school term. I got chill bumps every time I thought about a new group of riders on a school bus. I knew it would be a bunch who already knew each other and considered us outsiders. We would be guilty until we proved ourselves innocent.

While he was house-hunting, Daddy had noticed a Ford pickup truck wearing a for-sale sign in a yard, about a couple of miles from our house. He walked there to ask the price and was surprised to find that he had enough money in the bank to buy it. He ended up buying it, but still had to walk home since he couldn't drive. The boys all walked over, and Bob drove it home. He and Clyde had driven the orchard truck some but had no licenses.

Bob had become a jack-leg mechanic by his own will. He liked to be able to see the guts of how something was made. He hadn't tackled the starter, but he had discovered he could shift the truck out of gear and get all of us to push it while he attempted to start it by bypassing the starter. It worked. We all jumped in the back, while he tried it out down the road a piece. The cool breeze felt good on our faces.

34

Clyde had explored both directions on our road and found two churches—a Church of Christ in Pleasant Hill, and a Methodist Church in the Fairview community.

Mama said she grew up in a Church of Christ congregation, but didn't join that church. So, Clyde decided we would go there Sunday. They had a substitute preacher filling in, as their regular minister had resigned and moved away.

We told Mama plenty of people asked who we were, but nobody asked us to come again. Our new truck wouldn't start, so we walked, yet again, the next Sunday to Fairview. The church building was the only structure there, except for a few homes. No stores or businesses. The preacher spoke very softy and delivered an inspirational message. We met more friendly folks, but nobody we knew.

Pleasant Hill had a very small store, run by Carl Billingsley, his wife, Ruby, two daughters, June and Frances, and a son, named Herschel. We never bought a lot of anything, but we were so glad the store was near when Daddy decided to let us buy something. They had all flavors of powdered drink mixes in small packages, that we called penny-drinks, because we could get a package for a penny and mix it with a half cup of sugar and a half gallon of water. We all could have a glass of a fine tasting drink, if Daddy allowed use of the sugar. We ransacked the dresser drawers for pennies. It wasn't a terribly busy store, and sometimes when we found a penny, they didn't like getting out of the easy chair to sell just one penny's worth. I understand now, and I'm sorry we did that.

❧❧

The first time we filled the wash pot with water, the well went dry… There was just no more water in there. We went ahead with our rubbing, rinsing, and hanging to dry, while the boys stretched up the worn clotheslines one more time. Daddy was studying about what to do. He couldn't seem to get all his jobs done. There were always one or more new ones waiting on him.

The decision was to just dig a new well. One neighbor told him the water level around those parts would be down 'bout twenty feet. That's a lot of digging, when it's three feet in diameter! Digging started the next day. Each of the men dug fifteen minutes, then passed the pick and shovel to the next person. When enough dirt was loosened, somebody at the top would drop a bucket on a rope, and the person in the hole would fill it up and holler, "Pull it up!"

When their fifteen minutes of digging was up, they would step in the bucket on a rope, and get pulled up. The rope was on a pulley so it was a bit easier to handle.

Mary and I started taking turns with the men going down to dig. When all our combined efforts reached the twenty feet mark, there still was no water to be seen. The dirt was no more than damp.

It was almost dark when we went inside the house to eat. It was a silent supper. Bob said he was going to take Ruff and Tuff across the road to run a little, and I begged to tag along. I didn't like him going in the woods alone with a gun. He knew I would worry till he returned, so he told me to come on if they don't care, nodding toward our parents.

I was a happy girl when I was following in my bigger brother's footsteps. That way, he would see the snakes first. If I had made any money this summer, I would have bought Bob a better lantern. 'Old Rusty' was so dim, I didn't believe we could spot a snake with it.

Following the hounds, we came across a beaten path that forked off. We'd never been through there before, and we should've traveled it in daylight first, but I didn't care. I knew Bob would go the right way.

He stood there, looking at the fork, saying, "Eeny-meenie-miny-mo-which-way-do I-go?"

I told him that some famous person was known for his saying, "When you come to a fork in the road, take it." He took the *left* fork, and we laughed and said, "I hope we took the *right* fork."

A few more steps and we heard water trickling. There was a spring bubbling out of the ground. Bob called the dogs in and headed back up the hill toward home. He said we would come back tomorrow when we could see better. He had an idea, and he couldn't wait to share it.

Bob asked Daddy, "Wouldn't it be easier to take our laundry to the spring, than to bring the water up the steep hill in buckets? Till we struck water in the new well?

By the end of the next week, Bob had the wash pot set up at the spring, filled with water and a fire going on a cleaned area of dirt. We offered to let him serve at the rub board, but he declined. When we finished, Clyde and Bob carried a tubful of heavy wet clothes up the hill. I guess that was the most back-breaking job of our "spring" cleaning. It was a beautiful place around the spring. Many summer hours were wasted there.

❧❧

Foot by foot, we all made sacrifices to try to get the new well deep enough to find the water. Meanwhile, the men worked on applying brick-looking siding to the house and repairing or adding shelves and doors where there were none.

Bonnie came and helped us paper the inside walls with Carpenter wallpaper. It was very thick, to help keep the cold air out. We pasted it on all the walls. The pink floral patterns made it so refreshing in there. There were spaces between the wood planks that made the walls. Now, when an outside door was opened, it caused the paper to "sigh" and breathe out and in. I laughed as I opened the door repeatedly, just to watch the wallpaper breathe.

We eventually struck water in the well at about fifty-two feet. It wasn't an overwhelming flood, but Daddy said he hoped we hit the main vein. That was some scary digging. Mama couldn't bear to watch us going that deep. Mr. Hignight took Daddy to Texarkana, where he bought huge, hollow concrete tiles, enough to line the well and keep the dirt from caving in.

It practically took a village to get the tile situated one atop another, all the way up. A frame was built for the rope pulley, and we had "running water". Ha-Ha—Daddy said he would tell us when to "run" and get it.

In hot weather, when we wouldn't need to draw water during the night, Roy would pour the fresh milk in a lard bucket with a lid, then place it in the water bucket that was on the rope and let it down into the well. The cool water would keep it from turning sour.

కా౭ు

The two rent houses on our new land were both occupied. The little one closest to ours had Boyd and Helen Jones. A little further down the road was Boyd's parents, Sam and Beatrice Jones. They were all lovely, country folks. The women worked diligently in their yards. They both had beautiful, showy landscapes. I loved looking at their flowers and hearing them tell me about them. Their houses were fixed pretty inside, too, with lots of pictures and doilies.

Daddy was beginning to draw up his potential truck patches and gardens on a yellow pine board, that lay on the front porch. He wasn't schooled as much as he would have liked, but he could spell fairly well, using his self-taught method of sounding out words (Now called "phonics"). He mostly asked me to read and pay his bills. I wrote all his checks.

Cotton picking time, a family affair for many sharecroppers.

35

Mary and I practiced rolling each other's hair. Mama claimed we were improving. We rolled it on our rollers made out of tin strips wrapped in paper, then crimped the ends together. I liked to wash Mama's long hair and comb it dry in the sun. She always wanted me to make a braid on each side, then cross them over on top and pin it.

One day, we had many twisters in our hair, waiting for it to dry, when a long, shiny gray car pulled in our yard. The well-dressed, attractive, middle-aged lady who walked up to our porch, smiled and introduced herself as Era Gustafson. She told us she had heard there were several children living there, and she just wanted to come meet us.

Mama came to the door, and welcomed her in. I brought in a straight chair from the eatin' table for the nice lady. I was embarrassed that the bed was unmade in there. Mama had been in it all morning.

It was so good for Mama to have a conversation with another woman, although her side of it was somewhat quiet and low.

The visitor asked if we were going to church somewhere. She had been told we moved here from Boughton, where the kids had all been attending church regularly. Mama told her we had walked to a couple of churches nearby, but we were looking for a Baptist church. Mrs. Gustafson smiled big and reached for me and hugged me. She laughed and said, "Look no further!"

She said her husband, Gus, loved children, and would be over in the morning about 9:30 to pick all five of us kids up for Sunday School and church at Bethel Baptist Church. She said she didn't know how many miles it was, but we found out later, the church was about eight miles from our house, toward Blevins.

Our visitor spread the hugs to each one in the room, including Mama. She told her not to worry about the children, because Gus is a good driver. I don't think Mama told her that the kids who weren't there at the time, were grown kids.

We dressed in our best and were delighted with our curls. Mr. Gus was prompt. He got out of that long, sleek Nash, and stepped up on the porch to shake hands with our parents, who had come out to investigate who was leaving with their offspring.

Greetings were cordial, and we all climbed in, from the biggest to the littlest. The rocks from the gravel road flew fast and furiously, as we floated along pertly toward the northwest, a road we hadn't traveled before. I could hardly make out what the houses were like, because we were passing them so fast. I suddenly became nauseous. Mary looked at me, and then pushed my head down between my knees. She told me, later, I was green around the gills. I told her that what she did made me feel better and asked her how she knew to do that. She quickly let me know that she pushed my head down, so that if I threw up, it wouldn't get on her.

The church house was a beautiful, tile building with a white steeple on top, housing a huge bell. It was in a striking setting with woods behind it, and a well-kept cemetery to one side. The landscape was well manicured, presenting the look that God's people cared for this place of worship.

We exited the car cautiously, as we saw a few people coming from their cars to greet us. Mr. Gus seemed as excited as the rest. Mr. and Mrs. Ward and her sister, Mrs. Rhea Pye, ushered us inside, and took us right on down near the front of the sanctuary. I certainly felt welcome, and I was pretty sure my siblings did as well. I had been told that, "Cleanliness is next to godliness", and this place sure exemplified that statement.

I saw scripture plaques on the wall behind the pulpit. One of them said, "For by grace are ye saved through faith; and that not of yourselves: it is the gift of God: not of works, lest any man should boast."

I memorized that verse that day, and the Lord has helped me recall it as needed for these many years, for which I am grateful.

My family was split many directions for Sunday School. I wasn't with any of them, yet I felt comfortable with Mrs. Pye as my teacher. The room held many posters and colorful Bible pictures that piqued my interest at nine years old. She didn't read a story—she recited it. David and Goliath came alive.

We also did a Bible drill. The teacher called out a chapter and verse, and the students raced to be the first to find and read it. I didn't have a Bible, so the teacher allowed me to use hers. I had read Clyde's Bible often, and was able to find a few verses, but not in time to read them. I spoke to myself and said, "Self, you are gonna have to practice for this drill stuff and quit fooling around," and that I did.

I later found Clyde's Gideon New Testament. He had bought himself a full Bible with Old and New Testaments. He would call out verses for me to find, so I could learn where the books were located. I would be a lot more prepared next Sunday.

❧❧

The hard work kept coming around, and we kept doing what we could, with what we had. We had run out of space in the fruit shelves they built when they closed in the back porch. The boys had become fast diggers before they finished the well. They decided to dig a cellar under the corner of the house (under where Mary and I slept) to store our canned goods and root crops. They dug hard, and soon had the cellar deep enough to stand up in. This spot of ground hadn't been touched in a very long time. They even dug out doorsteps leading down to the cellar and made a galvanized tin door that leaned directly over them. Gradually, the jars of canned goods and the potatoes were moved in. One of the boys placed a canvas army cot down in the cellar to enjoy napping in the coolest spot on the farm.

❧❧

Our first deluge came in the late fall. Mary and I got the first shock when we were awakened by water dripping between us in our bed. I had wet the bed so many times in my younger days, naturally, Mary's first thought was to push me out of the bed with both feet. I knew better and proved it. She jumped up and got a dishpan from the kitchen to place between us. It was almost running over by morning, but we didn't wake Daddy.

When I heard him rattle the coffee pot, I went in to help with breakfast, and I told him about the roof leak over our bed. He said he would fix it as soon as the lightning let up. He said he thought it rained all night.

After breakfast, Bob brought the ladder around to our corner, while the others brought tin and nails for patching the roof. Bob placed the ladder against the house, then turned around and pushed out a loud, "Shhhhhhh! I hear water running!"

141

The whole bunch began to look around. Clyde leaned over the cellar door and declared the running water sound was in there. When the door was opened, the cot and a few other objects floated to them. The nice, cool cellar was more like a lake.

Daddy climbed the ladder to patch the leak, and told the boys they created that water hole, so they could clean up the mess. They took the floating objects out and stretched them on the ground. Then, they waded in barefoot with buckets, and started bailing the water out to the ground.

After a few days, the earth had dried, somewhat, and the spelunkers returned to determine the drainage problem. They filled in with dirt where they thought it was needed around the door, and packed dirt everywhere it would fit. It looked good, and the roof wasn't leaking, either. But it wasn't raining!

&⟩∂∻

The closer the time came for school, the more nervous we became about riding the bus. It came anyway, and stopped in the road, at the oak tree with the iron wedding ring. The driver mumbled something about the tree still being there, but I didn't wait to hear what else he had to say. My eyes were searching from one side to the other for an empty seat. The bus was fully occupied, except for one seat where a high school boy was sitting alone with his legs stretched across the entire seat. He looked at me as I walked past, and then later lowered his feet to allow Clyde to sit next to him. I stood in the aisle all the way to town, swaying back and forth from the motion of the vehicle. I braced myself with one hand and held on to my school supplies with the other.

I got off at Park School and found out my teacher was Mrs. Ross. She smiled at me as I entered her room. I wondered if she knew I ran away from school last year. I met a girl my age on the playground after lunch, named Shelby Jean Harris. She said she lived at Pleasant Hill and was on my bus. She also told me that her brother, Barney and her sister, Carolyn rode that bus, too.

This would be Clyde's last year of high school. His aim was college, but he was fully aware that it required more money than he had saved.

Bob confided in me that he might be in his last year, also. He was tired of being abused by one certain young man in his class, who was well known by the teachers as the class bully, yet no one put a stop to it. I knew my brother could end the bullying with one fist, but he chose not to make Mama and Daddy ashamed. I didn't talk about it.

The boy would gather a crowd, then shout out to Bob, "Whoa, mule, whoa", or "Did you have coon or possum for breakfast?"

Bob was never prideful about the way he dressed. Mary and I always suggested his school apparel. His grades didn't reflect his capabilities, because the bully adversely affected his concentration. His hands began to shake, involuntarily, and he was stuttering slightly when he had to speak in front of anyone other than family.

The final jab from Bully came when he asked my brother if country families all slept in one bed. Many students heard him but didn't laugh this time. Bob told me he walked out of that classroom, without looking back. He then walked to town and caught a ride with a student who had dropped out of school the year before and was now driving a gravel truck. He happened to be taking a load past Pleasant Hill. When Bob showed up at home and told Mama he had quit school, she cried, and so did he. He told her he wanted to finish ninth grade, but he just couldn't stay there any longer. Then he explained the bullying. She reached beside her bed and got her writing tablet and began a letter to the school.

When I got home from school and heard what had gone on with him, I cried too. He had taken to the woods toward the spring with the dogs, Mama said. She showed me the letter she wrote, and asked me to back it, and put it in the mailbox in the morning, so I did. We never heard from the school about poor Bob.

His nervous symptoms soon disappeared. He helped with the immediate jobs around the house. Daddy couldn't quite get caught up. Roy had gotten a job cutting pulp wood. He and the man who hired him used a crosscut saw and were making a little money.

Daddy talked privately with Bob about the school incident. We didn't know what he said, but they both were smiling afterward. That night at the supper table, both parents let Clyde know they would support his finishing school as much as they could. He had determination and his grades were good. He had also quit smoking and was gaining weight.

The ice man passed by our house, but we had no icebox yet. Roy said it sure would make the milk keep longer. A twenty-five-pound block was only fifteen cents. Bob asked Mr. Billingsley to stop the next time he's by this way, and he would be ready for ice.

Bob grabbed a pick and shovel and dug a square hole in the ground in the shade of a cedar tree in the back yard, then lined it with a piece of a ragged quilt. When the ice man came again, he bought a nice chunk of sparkling, clear ice. He lowered it a foot deep into the freshly dug hole and finished covering it with the quilt piece. He finished by placing a square pine board over the hole. We had an icebox.

Bob picked up some pieces that had fallen as our main block was chipped on the truck. He washed them and served Mama her first glass of ice-cold water. She told him it helped her to breathe better. We always looked for things to help her feel good.

I believed we had made a good move, after all. Good things kept happening for us at this place. Every Wednesday a peddler truck stopped in our yard. Mr. Mont Montgomery came from near Blevins. He stocked his truck there at M. L. Nelson's Grocery Store. The truck carried many small grocery items, as well as a variety of dry goods.

My favorite department was the fabric. I had discovered I could make a pretty full, gathered skirt with just a yard of calico print fabric. Sometimes I was allowed to barter with the peddler if we had extra eggs, butter, etc. One day, I traded him a freshly-picked bouquet of flowers for a yard of red plaid gingham.

There were wire chicken coops hanging on the back of his big box truck, for fowl he traded. He would drive up and drop down doors all over the truck to show what he had each time. It smelled so good! Mr. Montgomery also stocked hundred-pound sacks of animal feed in colorful cloth sacks. I loved to get those for sewing projects.

Someone I know very well said he always got 'guess-whats' from the peddler truck. It was two small pieces of candy, wrapped up with a different little surprise toy each time (We weren't allowed to buy candy). What a pleasant treat to have a mobile town come to us!

❧❦

I liked uneventful days. We all had our jobs to do, and for the most part, pushed our work so that it didn't overpower us. When I went to bed at night, I nearly always had a clear conscience that I had honestly tried to do everything that was my fair share, whether inside or outside. If we ever ran out of something to do, Daddy would point to the big pile of rocks that had been removed from the garden and yard and tell us to work on his mountain. It was easier to hoe in the garden after it was cleared of rocks, but every time it rained, more were uncovered. I nicknamed our garden, Rock City.

One evening, late, I was clearing weeds and grass along the garden fence next to the house, when I saw the weeds move close to my hand. A short, fat, gray animal of unknown species, was crawling low on the ground. He looked like he was carrying a turtle-like shell on his back. He had a pointed face with a long nose. I screamed, and my brothers came immediately, and chased it until it was in the road.

Bob wanted to turn Ruff and Tuff loose on that ugly creature, but Clyde wouldn't agree. Clyde said he had read about them, and he wouldn't hurt anything if we would leave him be and let him live his life. He called him an armadillo, and said some folks call them "grave diggers". We were fairly close to a graveyard. It was our first time to see such an animal, but they reproduced prolifically, and became thickly populated too quickly.

According to his garden map on the pine board, Daddy would be planting his truck patches soon, over on the opposite side of our land from the house. There were no veggies on his map that we didn't like to eat. The plan was to provide enough fresh eating, canned, dried, or saved crops for our family for a year. Some of the provisions we used every day in the kitchen were planted in Rock City. If somebody wanted to buy some of our vegetables, we could accommodate them, also, if the Lord blessed us with a good season.

So far, we hadn't scraped our yard. Daddy saw our neighbor using a weed slinger successfully, so he bought a used one for a dollar. It was fun, at first. Our neighbor, Mr. Jones, said it would cut our foot off, if we weren't careful. We took turns with it and kept the weeds down for several years. One of the boys eventually bought a non-motorized push mower.

❧

Daddy went to town with Clyde to find him a nice dress suit for commencement. He also got a new white shirt, tie, and shoes. When they got home, he asked if he could wear his new clothes to church, just to see if they fit alright. Mama said she guessed so—that was her usual reply.

Mr. Gus came early Sunday, and found us all in our best, but brother, Clyde, outshined us all. He looked so sharp. When Mr. Gus parked at Bethel, he asked Clyde to stay and talk a minute at the car. He told Clyde how good he looked in a suit and asked him if he would be willing to wear hand-me-down clothes. He said he had lots of clothes and suits that were too small for him now, and if he wanted them, he would bring them to him. Clyde said he would be glad to get them, because he was trying to make it to college soon.

Our classes went well, as usual. Mrs. Rhea told us a Jesus story in her lovely, story-telling voice. Mrs. Era led the singing. It was so easy for me to be still and listen attentively in that place. I felt like God was sitting right there on our row of chairs.

The preacher told us all about spiritual gifts, and he said we all have them. He read from I Timothy: "God hath saved us, and called us with a holy calling, not according to our works, but according to His own purpose and grace, which was given us in Christ Jesus, before the world began."

Then he read from the Bible about gifts: "Now there are diversities of gifts but the same Spirit; and there are differences of administrations, but the same Lord; and there are diversities of operations, but it is the same God which worketh all in all." (I Corinthians 12:4-6).

Clyde had his eyes closed, and his hand on his forehead. I guessed I would have to tell Mama he wasn't listening! Then, I saw a few tears fall from his face. I didn't know anything was bothering him. He used to talk with me when I was borrowing his Bible, but that hadn't happened lately. I figured he was probably just worrying about Mama.

The piano music started, and the invitation number for *I Surrender All* was announced. Clyde was no longer crying but his head was bowed, and his eyes closed. On the start of the second stanza, he turned loose of the chair in front of him and stepped his way carefully, to the aisle then on to the altar. He fell to his knees in prayer.

Several saints knelt with him, as we sang through all stanzas of the song, twice. When he stood up, he was smiling like his burden had been lifted. He shook hands with the preacher and said God had called him to preach! Shouts of "Praise the Lord!" came from all over the congregation.

Mrs. Era turned and addressed the gathering, "God has called Clyde to preach His message, and he has surrendered to do the will of God. We don't know where he will be called to go, but we can hold him up to God right here in this altar, any time. Clyde, would you come and stand here in the altar, and allow everybody to come shake your hand? I know all these folks want to wish you the best."

The pianist, Teresa Bonds, started playing *Where He Leads Me, I Will Follow*, as the entire congregation shook Clyde's hand. I was trying, unsuccessfully, to hold back tears, until I threw my arms around my brother's neck for the tightest hug I had ever given him. Then I quit crying and started squalling. I had to blow my nose on the underside of my ruffled skirt. Those Christian people clearly showed the love of God that day, not only to the new preacher, but to his siblings.

The pastor announced that a day would be set for Brother Clyde to preach his first sermon there in the near future. That startled me. He would stand up there behind the pulpit and preach! How can I help him? I will pray for him. That's the only way I can help. Lord, will you hear?

I felt a genuine tug at my heart. Maybe Jesus was knocking. I began to feel that tugging need each time I went to church, and sometimes in between. I asked Clyde if I could be saved, but before he could answer, Daddy told me I was too young to know about that yet. He was baptized and joined the church in his twenties.

Mama cried when Clyde told her he had surrendered to preach. She said she wasn't at all surprised, and that she had been expecting it. Then she raised up in bed enough to hug him. Daddy looked on solemnly, then asked him when he would preach.

I was tickled he had a nice, new suit. When Mr. Gus showed up again, he had many suits and casual clothes, and some study books that his wife, Era, had ordered especially for Clyde. The clothes were just a fit. I told him now he can dress like a preacher.

The church left it up to Clyde to decide when he would preach his first sermon, depending on whether his mother could come. Mama thought he might want to get graduation over with first, but he said he wanted to preach as soon as possible, because he had so much to say. He was anxious to get started.

36

When one of the Jones families moved out of the little rent house, Milton and his family moved in. We were overjoyed to have them and their three precious children close by again. Mama acted like she was feeling better right away. Interacting with the grandchildren kept her up and awake more in daytime, and it helped her to get more sleep at night. She was needing less pain medication.

Pappaw and Granny both loved to hear that patter of little feet on their front porch. Polly was a baby, but she remembers back some seventy years ago, knocking on our door and hollering, "Pappaw, 'et me in!"

Jeannie and Dwayne can remember getting to eat several meals a day with us. Their mother was a very good cook, and they ate at home, but they often slipped through the netting-wire fence, to see if we had "mater soup and boiled taters". They grew rapidly and were well-behaved with us.

Bob had worked diligently on that old Ford truck. He said he thought it would take a new starter, and they didn't come cheap. We could push start it for woodcutting, hauling dirt, and other farm jobs. He was hoping all along, to get to drive it to church to attract a girl, and he didn't give up easily. He was loving that old truck, and claimed it, because he bought a starter with his own money. Every spare minute he was cleaning and shining it.

All his work paid off when a new family decided to join Bethel. They had about eight children, with six of them still living at home. Bob took an instant liking to Floy, their third child. She had naturally blonde hair and green eyes, and as Bob commented, "a nice build". She was used to helping watch her younger siblings, and according to her mother, was also good at cooking and cleaning.

Bob sure did like picking her up in his truck. A cab full of her siblings usually went with them, too, and often Mary rode with them because Floy was her friend.

Bob and Floy were a couple mostly at church. He worked hard in the log woods, and didn't go many places, except church. He fell in love with her, and she stated she loved him, too. That's when the dating moved up a notch, and my brother seemed happier than ever. His sense of humor was so contagious that all the young folks in our crowd liked to hang around him.

When Floy visited our family, she just fit right in, and became one of us. Naturally, our family would love anybody who loved our Bobby. She said she hoped to be a nurse and was really good at making Mama comfortable. Mama told Bob she liked his girl and thought she would make him a good wife.

✥

A short letter arrived in our mailbox from Aunt Georgia, saying Granny Bradford was getting restless at her house, and wanted to come to our house to stay awhile. She said she wouldn't be coming until her next check came, in a little less than a month.

Daddy said he had been thinking about trading Hellen, our wood cook stove, in on a kerosene range, so the house wouldn't be heated from the burning wood all summer. He said he was hoping Bonnie would go with him to help select the right one. Mama said she thought it was a good time to do it. She thought it would make her mother happy.

Mama had written her siblings about the graduation and the first sermon that was forthcoming. I suppose Granny wanted in on it. Boy, did my mama think of a bunch of jobs to be done before Granny arrived! Mary and I got the worst end of it. As soon as we got off the bus and changed out of our good school clothes, we worked on all the jobs Mama could think up, as she lay in the perfect spot on her bed to see all the chores we had slacked off on. Progress was being made, though slowly.

Our new kerosene stove arrived via the old Ford truck and her faithful driver. Bob was the only licensed driver, so far, besides Milton, of course. I was trying to think of a name for her. She wouldn't be as hot as Hellen. Once she was in place, they filled the glass tank of the burner end, opposite the oven end with kerosene—that's what sophisticated folks called it. We just called it what it was—coal oil. It was the same substance Daddy dosed out to us in a teaspoon when we had a croupy

149

cough. I was the one who had to take it more than the rest. I had a bad cough every time I was outside in the wind.

As soon as Daddy turned the fuel line on and struck a match, I thought of a good name for it—Stinky! I didn't want him to think I didn't appreciate the new stove, so I renamed her Oily. It didn't smell as good as oak wood burning, and I could detect a slight taste of croup medicine in my boiled taters, but I didn't mention it. The fuel cost about ten cents per gallon, and that much lasted almost a month. We didn't have to bring in stove wood every night, although we still had to run to the well and back if we were to have "running water".

♣♠

Mrs. Era visited with Mama again and told us she would be coming for us while Mr. Gus was gone on a business trip up north somewhere. They discussed a time for the new preacher to deliver his first sermon. It was decided that they would announce the coming Sunday that he would preach on the following Sunday. He was rarin' to get started.

Word of mouth and US mail got the news out well enough. There weren't so many there for Sunday School, but when we came back into the sanctuary, the house was filled. I looked at the entrance, and people were continually filing in.

My biggest surprise came when I saw Milton, Bonnie, Daddy, and the young'uns all ushering Mama in. They brought her near the front. I moved to sit with them and got the last empty chair. The only song I could think of was *Hail, Hail, the Gang's all Here*.

One of Clyde's sermons stuck with me all my life, and I'm thinking it was his first one, but not quite sure. The title was, "Be Sure Your Sins Will Find You Out". He did it all so professionally. His voice didn't quiver, and his words rolled out like he was an experienced speaker. He had taken speech for two years in high school, but this seemed like the voice of God, the Great One, who inspired all the people who wrote the Bible, speaking through Clyde Daniel, the son of a sharecropper. I didn't let it be known that his experience began when he had his younger brothers and sisters take a stump and listen to him pretend to preach before he even owned a Bible. God can definitely use a "stump church" to prepare a country boy to spread His Word.

When he was finished, I realized he gave me and some others a lot of food for thought. He sat down, and the pastor extended an invitation for all who needed salvation, rededication, or to move church

150

membership, to come to the altar. Many came to pray when he stated, "The fields are white unto harvest, and God needs you".

Mrs. Era took us home again. There was no space in Milton's A-Model. While we were riding, she told Clyde that she and Gus had been seriously discussing finding a used church bus, since others over around us had expressed interest in our church but didn't have a way to get there. She asked Clyde if he would be willing to drive it if they found one. He told her he would see if he could obtain a driver's license. He did so in a short time.

It only took about three weeks for the Gustafsons to locate a used church bus and get it ready to roll. We rode to church in the pretty Nash, then rode home with Clyde in his initial drive of a bus. He had ridden with a school bus driver and received some vital tips for handling a jumbo vehicle like that.

Clyde drove it around our neighborhood throughout the week, seeking out all who were needing a ride to church. The Cottingham family had been going to church in a truck with a shelter on the back. It belonged to the company he worked for. Some of them wanted to ride the bus.

Edward Cooper, who was about to be a teenager, lived alone with his ailing, widowed mother. He was overjoyed to get a ride to church. For lack of a teacher, Edward was teaching himself the scales on an old organ that sat in his front room. He said he had to play it quietly, so as not to bother his frail, elderly mother, who rested a lot. Frances Billingsley lived with her parents and a sister just up the road from us. She expressed a need for transportation to church. These are the ones that started our church ministry. We picked up new passengers occasionally, and some of the originals got their own car or moved away.

All went well except for the occasional bus breakdown. God had prepared Bob to work on motors and vehicles. He had practically rebuilt his old truck. He kept busy on the bus replacing cables, belts, and such. It was fine if the bus was in our yard when it died, but it was frightening when we had to haul out and walk home in the dark, without a light. Faithful Bob always did his mechanic work free, and the church bought the parts. He had been told he would be the official driver when Clyde left for college.

Edward Cooper became a real inspiration to Bethel. He was always cheerful and excited about arriving at church early. The first one off the bus, he would run to get to the piano and practice. We loved to hear him play, and I had a selfish desire to play as like him!

I drew all the piano notes on our top doorstep at home and sat on the next step down facing the steps with my feet fitting between the plank steps. I had an old hymn book, and I had learned shape notes from Mr. Joe.

The Daniel and Cottingham families with the Bethel Church bus.

I accepted the task of helping Clyde get his graduation invitations in the mail. His baccalaureate service and commencement sermon was to be at the First Methodist Church. Mama admitted she couldn't make it to town twice. She chose to wait to see him walk and get his diploma. He would be the first offspring on either side of our family to do so. The graduation was to take place in two weeks. The entire family planned to go.

Milton took his family and four of us. We packed in his A-Model like sardines. Seatbelts were unheard of then. Our greatest problem was crowding in our full, ruffled skirts, without causing too many wrinkles. Even Daddy was dressed up in a suit and tie he had borrowed from Clyde.

The high school auditorium was standing room only. We all were fortunate enough to get seats in the same row, so we were proud to make a good showing for our boy.

The boys were chauffeured in grandeur by Bob and his truck. He wasn't about to be seen in a suit and tie, but at least got out of his overalls and put on khakis.

Clyde was the only one of us
to graduate high school.

The program was long and Mama was very tired of sitting up so long. As we were packing ourselves back in the car, she expressed her fatigue by telling Mary and me if we graduated, she would just get someone to take our picture. Daddy commented that girls didn't need to graduate—they would just get married and waste it. I was cut to the core by that statement, but I kept my mouth shut. I dreamed of being a teacher or a nurse.

Mary laughed out loud and said, "We'll be glad to quit school now, if that's what y'all want!"

She noticed I was frowning, so she asked loudly, "Why are you giving me a sour look?"

"You've got a sour look, alright, but I didn't give it to you," I retorted.

As we rode through town on our way home, Daddy said he would stop and get us some ice cream *if* only he had brought some change. Then he laughed and said, "That little word, *if*, is strong 'nuff to hold up a mount'n, ain't it?"

I didn't laugh.

✎✎

Shortly after graduation, Clyde received his license to preach, then he began to concentrate on getting into Ouachita Baptist College in Arkadelphia. Our pastor at that time, Bro. Zimmerman, was a teacher there, and was a big help in getting him registered for fall classes.

Clyde had saved enough money from his orchard jobs to pay for his first two semesters' tuition, but not room and board. He had counted on living in a dorm, but hadn't been told that cost extra. He then decided he would live at home and catch a bus to Arkadelphia. To make a long story not-so-long, he ended up trying to hitch-hike, much to Mama's chagrin. She cried every day when he left home. It was sometimes ten o'clock or after, when he caught a ride home.

He was about ready to give up on college, when he heard from a wonderful Christian lady, who had been raised at Boughton and had connections with the college. Mrs. Rosie Britt was a widow who heard Clyde was having to struggle to attend college. She didn't think he could ever make the grades he needed with all those distractions, so she had offered to help. She went to Ouachita and found out where he stood with the finances. She got it all rounded out for the first semester, with room and board and a college-directed job on campus. He became very fond of Mrs. Britt. They had so much in common, what with both of them striving to reach lost souls and being Boughtonites.

She, along with some acquaintances she had in Arkansas Baptist groups, arranged for him to start second semester at Southern Baptist College in Walnut Ridge, Arkansas. He was a full-time student with a major in Bible Studies. He managed to get both a job on campus and a part-time job at a radio station.

Clyde made many friends there and brought many of them home with him (a few at a time). He became close to another preacher, Don Chandler, and his fiancé, Polly. They played matchmaker and found a girlfriend for Clyde. Her name was Irene Gooch. They dated several months, and acted like they were stepping toward the aisle, when all at once the romance was over, at least for her.

37

Clyde and some of his preacher friends were thinking how good it would be to organize a tent revival. They requested the large tent that belonged to the college and were granted permission to use it. One weekend, they all came down and cleared persimmon saplings from the plot on which they planned to set up the tent. It was next to the road with off-road parking, about three hundred feet from our yard.

The tent went up prior to the set date with a huge red-letter sign across the front with all the information. They also posted some signs in town about it. It created quite a buzz, and because we had no phones then, many folks drove to our house to find out more. Several preachers and singers from college had been lined up, as well as some local musicians.

During the week after college was over for the summer, preachers began to roll in to find a place to sleep. We borrowed army surplus cots, and four of them slept on the unscreened front porch. The ladies boarded at Mrs. Era's house, while the married couple stayed at a deacon's house.

God blessed us all with a good number every night, except one stormy evening. The music was great, and well-heard with the speaker system the college provided. The community responded enthusiastically, with many coming to Jesus. The Holy Spirit was tugging me during that meeting, but I figured I was still too young. I wasn't needing revival. I was needing salvation.

Long after the tent was folded, and the men of God were scattered to other places to spread the gospel, good memories lingered about the Pleasant Hill tent revival.

I remember being very sad when the revival services ended, and all those fun college-folk had gone. However, Mary and I were tired of killing and dressing chickens. We had made chicken and dressing with giblet gravy one day, chicken and dumplings another day, and fried chicken more than once. I told her, "If this lasts another week, we'll be plum outta yard birds and eggs, too."

Mary helping prepare for the tent revival near our house in Pleasant Hill. Clyde and his friends from Southern Baptist College in Walnut Ridge organized and conducted the meetings in 1950.

Milton's family surprised us when they bought a new ice cream freezer and brought it over with all the other needed items to make a frozen feast. They were good at surprises. He wasn't as tight with his money as Daddy.

They had ice, salt, and sugar. We had milk, vanilla, and cream. Daddy had purchased an icebox recently. It was a large, wooden box with thick insulation inside and four compartments with doors. One part kept a block of ice, with a drip pan underneath to catch the melting.

The chipped ice and salt were packed around the ice cream freezer's inner can of mixed ingredients. I liked turning the crank that was connected to this cream can. In about thirty minutes, the crank would barely turn, which meant that, by some miracle, we had a gallon of ice cream.

Clyde was back home and had resumed the bus driving job. That freed Bob to drive his truck with his left hand and hug his gal with his right! They must have been getting serious, as they weren't taking on any extra passengers when they went to church now. I was glad to know Bob was right behind the bus in his truck. If the bus became ill, he could cure it.

I grew to love Bethel Baptist Church and everyone who entered her double doors, but I was becoming too disturbed about the decision I knew I needed to make, to concentrate. I clearly understood what the preacher meant when he concluded his sermon by telling us that he just might be giving the last invitation we would ever hear. I took in every word and tried, unsuccessfully, to breathe normally as he said we could be taken from this life on the way home, whether we are ready for heaven or hell.

I wasn't hungry when we sat down to the dinner table that day. Daddy had made biscuits and fried two chickens. Maybe I was just burned out on fried chicken. I should be really happy to have my brother back from college, and I was, but I had nagging worries.

When the dishes were dried and put away, I went outside to think. The men had been cutting firewood in the cool of the evenings. We burned big sticks in the heater that they set up in the front room each winter. There were several big piles of wood that hadn't been stacked yet. I sat on the ground in the shade of one of the woodpiles and was completely hidden by another pile behind me. It felt good to be hidden from everybody in the world. I thought…*They probably wouldn't miss me until another task was waiting on me. Nobody would care if I was missing, even gone.*

I guess I fell asleep on the ground with a thick clump of crimson clover for my pillow. When I awoke, the earth had revolved enough that the shade I enjoyed a little bit before, was gone, and the sun was shining right down on me. I don't know how long I dozed, but I was sure that nobody had looked for me. I was also sure I didn't want to go to church that night. My thirst was real, and so was my sweat. Why did my daddy not look for me?

He had always made me feel special when he and Dan broke up the soil for me to have a little garden. He was special to me in more ways than I could name. He would always be my hero! I slipped barefooted into the back door. Mama was sleeping, and Daddy was quietly leaned back against the wall in a straight chair, beside her bed in the front room. It appeared that everyone in the house was asleep.

I asked Daddy if anybody looked for me. He told me he didn't have to look for me—he saw my cotton head shining over the woodpile. He said he was just wondering what I was doing all that time. Then, he instructed me on where and how to stack that wood when Sunday was over.

I went to the cedar tree in the back yard, where there was a concrete tile to sit on, to read a book for the second time. I had barely turned a page, when I heard our cat, Ernest, meowing.

He had been missing for the past week. When I rubbed him, he felt so thin and scrawny. I heard another cry that sounded like a kitten. When I turned the other way, I saw six kittens walking toward me in a follow-the-leader line, each one with his tail standing straight up. They all attacked their mother, Ernest, for a round of feeding.

I ran inside and got Daddy and told him that we needed to change Ernest Tubb's name to Ernestine. When he saw the kittens, he explained that was why Ernestine had been missing. It takes nine days for the babies to get their eyes open, so they must be at least ten days old.

I made a good, soft bed on the front porch in a box for the new family. Everybody told me it was my job to feed and water them, because I found them. Dwayne, Jeannie, and Polly helped me take care of them, and provided much TLC.

38

In spite of my bouts of emotion, life was good at this place. We were living at our own place and were all eager to improve it any way we could. If we saw something that could be fixed our added to, we just all pitched in to make a perfect place better. Daddy wore his home-ownership proudly, and we, kids all supported him. He said often that he wouldn't allow his thoughts to dwell on the hardships of the past. His mind was set on doing everything he could to make a good future for all of us. The doctor had told him it would take a miracle for Mama's heart to be healed. He anticipated we would mainly be giving palliative care.

At this point, her chest pain had gradually increased to being relieved only by morphine injections every six hours. The doctor made a house call when other problems arose, such as respiratory distress, caused by the morphine. Her electric oscillating fan was at her bedside and stayed on twenty-four-seven.

Clyde, Mary, and I were taught by the doctor how to give her pain injections, and we taught Roy, later. Bob refused to learn. He was needle-shy but was good at keeping an eye on her. That was necessary all the time, in case she began to smother.

When she began the morphine regime, the doctor made us aware that it was addictive, but he wrongly assumed she couldn't live more than a couple of days. That was a few months ago.

All the men, except Clyde, had been employed in the log woods until the spring rains closed the roads in and out of the woods. Now, they were plowin' and plantin' again.

Clyde stopped by Mrs. Georgia's orchard, seeking a summer job to assist Mrs. Britt with his next year of college. She was delighted to see him, and said she knew all about his donor. I think they were kin—I can't remember. She hired him for the summer and said she wished his whole family could help her out again. He told her they were loggers now, but were laid off, but that he would tell them what she said.

When Monday morning came, we were up at Daddy's signal. He had hired Bonnie to take care of Mama, and a neighbor, Ruthie Mae Williams, to come when needed. We gave the old truck a push and managed to jump on before Bob floor-boarded it after it started.

The air blew across the old, flat-bed real cool that early in the morning, but we knew we would need cooling on the way home. Daddy was hired as straw-boss over the orchards. He told Mrs. Haynes I was just ten years old, but he would see that I earned my fifteen cents an hour. During heavy peach picking, Mary and I worked ten hours a day for $1.50. That was pretty much our life that summer. We were early to bed, and early to rise. It was a fruitful summer. We had all we wanted, to dry, can, and eat fresh. Bonnie was a big help, handling all the produce, and the children helped by eating all the peaches they could hold.

In all, there were more than thirty (mostly adults), picking the peaches. Not many over-ripes were showing up. Most were picked somewhat green, by request, to be shipped long distances. The big semi-trucks were lined up beside 67 Highway, waiting to be loaded with peaches, plums, watermelons, cantaloupes, apples, and other produce. Many folks worked at grading the peaches, watching them pass through rollers and quickly grabbing and removing the culls. They couldn't allow one rotten spot to be packed. As you may have heard, one bad peach spoils the whole basket. They were packed by experts in half-bushel and bushel baskets with a lid, then loaded and gone!

We all had work to do when we got home in the evenings. If it wasn't dark yet when he drove us through on the upper crossing of Cold Run Creek, Bob would stop and let us rinse off the peach fuzz that managed to seep around our bonnet and bandana. We left a tubful of clean water by the well in the mornings to be sun-warmed for nightly baths.

After our second week in the orchard, we went home on Friday evening to hear Mama tell Daddy that she got a letter from Uncle Ellis, her brother in Magnolia, saying that Granny had been with him and Aunt Mildred for a month, and was wanting to come to our house again. He said we would need to come in a truck, because she had a dresser, a trunk, and a rocker. Uncle said Saturday morning would be a good time to come.

Bob had to drive the truck. Daddy went out of respect, since Mama couldn't. He told me to go, so I could help Granny if she had to stop somewhere on the way back. It was a long, rough ride to Magnolia. Aunt Mildred had a good dinner fixed for us, but she called it lunch. She had chicken and dumplings, the best I ever ate. She said that was Granny's favorite, and I quickly said that "she was coming to the right place, 'cause we cook that a lot."

I also told them we eat hog pretty often, too.

Their house was small, but fancy, just like Auntie. She was shorter than me. I tried to see everything, because I knew Mama would have lots of questions, but Daddy was in a hurry to head back north to Prescott. He said it took about an hour and a half to get down there, and we had to get home before dark, in case the lights played out.

Uncle Ellis and I helped get Granny to the middle of the truck seat, after all of her belongings were secured on the back. They had removed the mirror from atop the dresser, wrapped it in a quilt, and told me to climb in the back of the truck, and hold it. Daddy gave me a newspaper to sit on. The mirror had much more cushioning that I did.

I didn't like riding in the back while going through a big town, but things got really rough and windy when he left the city and picked up speed. Wiggle room was scarce for me, and my bottom side was pressing on a rusted-out place in the truck bed. The wind was about to take my head off, as I was trying to scoot inch by inch to get off that piece of tin, that seemed to be boring a hole in my behind. My sister would have laughed her head off if she could have witnessed my misery. She and the others got to go pick peaches that day, to get some orders filled.

I was so thankful when we finally pulled in by the oak with the wedding ring. Home! Bonnie had saved my neck one more time, by cleaning our room, and moving our clothes to one side of the closet that the boys had built for us. She must have worked all day, making space for the dresser and the trunk. Granny stopped them in the front room with the rocking chair. It was the first rocker to enter our house. Mama made it through eight babies without rocking.

Granny said one of the girls could sleep with her. She had brought her own feather mattress, that had gone with her every time she moved. It fluffed up really high on top of our bed, and nobody could touch it until she was ready to go to bed.

She had us girls bring two straws from our broom. She made one of them shorter, then hid them behind her back to mix them up. Then, she told us to choose one. Whoever got the short straw can sleep on her bed.

Mary mumbled under her breath, "You're the one sleeping in our bed."

And Mary got the short straw. I slept rolled up in an old quilt beside my bed on the floor. Another item she moved in was a gray enamel pot with a lid. She called it her "slop jar". Mama had a white one, and we just called it a "pot". It was definitely not slop they put in them.

I found out the first time Granny got up to use her pot that my make-shift bed was gonna have to roll someplace else. There was no other spot for me in that room, so I took up my bed and walked to the front room.

About the time I was comfortable again, Mama needed a shot. It just dawned on me that I would probably become the designated shot person at night, since they would think it convenient that I was already in there. Oh, well.

❧❧

"I was glad when they said unto me, let us go into the house of the Lord" (Psalm 122:1). It was, indeed, good to be in the cool, quiet house of God, even though I continued to feel like I wasn't obedient to the Lord. I wanted to give my heart to Him, yet I still felt a need to obey my Daddy. I wished I could go home after Sunday School, because I didn't want to hear the invitation again, but I knew that wasn't going to happen. I also knew I couldn't hide in the woodpile every Sunday.

❧❧

Mary told me during the church bus ride home, that she wasn't sleeping with Granny Bradford any more, and she told me to ask no questions. Daddy and Granny made chicken and dressing while we were gone. He managed the coal oil stove, since Granny was afraid of it. She told him it might go "Boom!"

Our little ones next door fell in love with Granny immediately. She seemed to have an endless supply of bought cookies in her trunk. They loved her 'mater soup, and she would make it for them any time they asked. She called it 'loup'. Since we acquired an icebox, we could keep leftovers longer now. It was a good thing, because Granny believed in having more than two items beside bread and milk on the table for dinner and supper. We sisters thought we were doing good to have two when we were doing all the cooking. Daddy was still mastering breakfast with some help from his daughters. He wouldn't dare let anybody else make his coffee.

Before the next bedtime, I asked Granny if I could try out her feather bed, and she answered, "If your sister don't mind."

I liked it, but I was thinking that I sure hoped I didn't wet the bed. How would I ever dry Granny's feathers?

162

One of the boys had brought an old seat that had been taken out of an abandoned car to be used for seating on the front porch. Mary looked it over good and decided it would feel better sleeping on that than the floor, so we moved it inside, and padded it good with a comforter, made from our own cotton from a few years back. We placed it in a corner of the front room, so she could hear Mama when she needed a shot. Mary didn't want any part of that feather bed. She said she was afraid she would smother in it. I think she liked her Oldsmobile bed.

Granny had a hump on her upper back, which the doctors called a "dowager's hump". I never figured out why it was called that, because Mr. Webster said that a dowager is "an elderly, dignified woman of wealth". I loved her mightily, but she was forced to live from one welfare check to the next. She couldn't read or write, and her signature was an X.

Much of her little check was spent on postage stamps every month. I was her accountant. She kept her own money in one big, black purse, as well as every check stub, and every piece of mail she received. She depended on me to correspond with her other six living children. I was happy to do it, because she helped me a lot. When she received mail, it wasn't opened until I got home.

She thought the way Daddy did some things was funny. They didn't always agree. When she asked me to describe some of the things he did in the letters to Mama's siblings, I could write it in a little milder version than she told me and get by with it.

Granny brought in her trunk, all the scraps of fabric and supplies she needed for hand piecing quilts. She planned to piece one for each of her thirty-six grandchildren. At that time, she claimed to be over halfway through.

40

Granny could make a scrumptious chicken pot pie with a melt-in-your-mouth crust. She thickened the broth where she boiled a young frying chicken, then added six chopped, boiled eggs, and several canned vegetables. This was covered with a crust made from flour and homemade lard. Mary and I made it often after she showed us how. The only thing I didn't like about it was when Mama said, "You gals get out there and kill a chicken right quick!"

Milton and Bonnie took Granny to church in their car and allowed their children to ride the bus. She liked worshipping with us at our church, even though she had joined a Church of Christ one time. She never argued about church membership.

Our revival services had been planned for the last two weeks before school started, which was the last two weeks of August. Brother Wiggs G. Dove was coming as the evangelist to present the message of God. I can't remember all the details, but I think he was serving, or had served, as associational missionary for a nearby association. Bethel was in Red River Association.

When the revival services began, Clyde picked up a few extra passengers on the bus in and around Pleasant Hill. He had taken off these last two weeks at the orchard to attend church and get ready to go back to Walnut Ridge to school.

The adults met thirty minutes early for prayer meeting. Mrs. Era asked me if I would attend the children back in a Sunday School room, while the prayer service was conducted in the sanctuary. I felt honored that she asked me.

The first night, I was just baby-sitting the children, and they weren't easy to manage. I asked Mrs. Era if I could teach them some songs, and she joyfully said yes. The number of children increased the second night. Some of them came with parents who might not be there through the whole revival. I knew my nephew and two nieces would be there every night. I realized none of the children were old enough to read, so written words to the songs were only good for me. They would have to rely on their ability to memorize the songs. I found that repetition seemed to work well with children. I could just see their little minds beginning to learn the first stanza of *This Little Light of Mine*. Their eyes began to sparkle, and I'm thinking mine probably did, too. I was so excited to hear their voices making a joyful noise for the Lord. Time flew by too quickly, and the children begged to keep on singing.

Mrs. Era stepped in our room, and complimented the little singers, and told them to learn the songs well so they could sing for the folks in the big room, including their mommies and daddies. Then she prayed with us.

Bro. Dove preached directly to me every night—or so it seemed. Everything he said just fit my feelings. His voice was like I imagined God's would be, and his stature was fitting for a strong man of God.

We enjoyed listening to girl singers each night from Ouachita Baptist College. They seemed glad to have the opportunity to sing. I thought they would make excellent wives for some of the preachers I knew.

I asked my preacher brother if he would visit my class some night and tell my bigger kids the things he had taught me about reverence and respect for the house of God. I was hoping they could learn to be still and quiet when the Bible is being read or recited. I guess I've always thought that children should always bow their heads during prayer and know that God's house is a dedicated place of worship, and not a playhouse. Back then, the only food and drink allowed in the sanctuary was the Lord's Supper, which is formally served to church members. He spoke to my children the next night, and they tried to practice what he told us from then on.

I tried to concentrate on the three songs we were learning in our wee choir, day and night, to keep me from shaking when I thought about the invitation time. When Friday night came, the sweet little children had accomplished so much. They were serious about their songs, and they did their motions as well as children their age could possibly do. When our practice time was up, Mrs. Era appeared at our door and surprised us. She said she had been listening to us, and decided we were ready to present to the congregation. She said that she, Mrs. Rhea and Mrs. Alice had named our group "The Booster Band", because we were capable of boosting the spirits of Christians.

She also told us that from now on, we would have reserved seats on the front row by the piano. We entered the sanctuary in single file, all seven little ones and I. They stood by their chairs, and I stood facing them. We were introduced officially as The Booster Band.

The first song was *This Little Light of Mine* with all the motions. Then it was *Jesus Loves Me*, and finally, *The B-I-B-L-E*. After we finished the only three songs we knew, they tried to start over again.

The Holy Spirit didn't shake me up so much that night, but Satan surely tried to mess with me the next day. He put it in my head that things those church people were asking me to do was too hard. He almost convinced me to skip church for a while, and rest up, and take care of Mama.

My mind was in a turmoil all day. I wanted to stay home with my mama, but she told me to go on to church now, and I could tell her all about it tomorrow. I went on to church. I had heard plenty of times how Satan would try to buffet God's plans. He didn't want me to teach the songs to those babies. I had a feeling of freedom, having thwarted the devil's plans. I sincerely wanted to get my job done.

When it was the invitation time, to come down and repent and accept Jesus Christ as Savior, such a calmness came over me. It wasn't the same feeling I had been having. I knew my daddy had told me that I was too young to be saved, but I heard a greater voice, telling me to "step out of your place, and I will do the rest".

I was in the aisle before I knew it, shaking the pastor's hand, and telling him I wanted to be saved. He knelt with me in the altar, and I prayed the sinner's prayer. That was the first time I had truly prayed, and I felt sure He heard me. I stood up and said aloud "I am saved!"

I wasn't the only one converted that night. We all stood down front and received the right hand of Christian fellowship from the saved members in the congregation. Then I thought of Daddy, and asked God to help me deal with any consequences I might face. Again, He heard. My huge burden was finally lifted.

One of my brothers tried to help me out and broke the news to my parents before I could. Mama stretched her arms out toward me, and we hugged for a couple of minutes. All she said was that she was so sorry she couldn't be there for her baby. I told her I understood.

Daddy, who had held his head down, looked at me and said, he felt like I understood enough to know what I was doing, or I wouldn't have taken that step.

My insides were shouting, "Praise the Lord!"

I wished everybody I knew could feel like that. As I write this, I'm wondering how I failed to hold on to that joy one hundred percent of the time over the next seventy years. I still serve the one great God who saved me, and I praise His Holy, Precious Name. I'm faithful to read His

Word and praying to retain the joy that I had at ten years of age. I am looking to meet Him face to face, in all His glory, and also meet those dear loved ones whom I have written about, who have already passed into another realm.

Not long after the revival services had ended, we all went down to the Little Missouri River. The church authorized baptism for those converted in the recent series of meetings. The revival of God's people lasted much longer than the two weeks of meetings. I don't remember the names of all who were placed under the water and then lifted, representing the death, burial and resurrection of Jesus Christ, which is, and always has been, the gospel.

Mary was baptized in the river with me that day. Daddy and all the boys were there, yet I really missed my mama, who was suffering too much to get out in the summer heat.

41

I know school didn't change a whole lot over the summer, but I certainly did. I wanted to tell everybody about Jesus and my salvation, but soon realized most of the students didn't care to hear about it. I must have been nicer to the students I knew, and that made their attitudes toward me much better.

I heard no criticism about my apparel since I had earned enough in the orchard to buy fabric and sew several outfits, with help from Bonnie, and now had new shoes and plenty of underwear. I even heard a few compliments on my clothes.

Finally, I was getting off the school bus at the last stop. Eighth grade! All our classes were in the three-story high school building—but in the basement. We could see just a little bit of daylight through the high windows. My homeroom teacher was Mrs. Katie White, who had the word-of-mouth reputation of being tough. She didn't come across that way with me. I liked her very much, and she seemed to like me. She had taught all my siblings before me, and she commented that I wasn't like them. Whatever.

I wasn't nervous, like in my previous grades. I could get my assigned work done, and still have time to pull my library book from my desk and read, while waiting for my classmates to finish their papers. I could tell this was going to be a good school year.

It was easier to ride the bus now that there was no seat-saving, and no eyes rolling when we got on. I had made some good friends on there. Only two from the Daniel family needed a ride to school now. Mary wasn't at all happy at school. I met her for lunch break every day. We had open campus, so sometimes we walked up to the bakery in town with our friend and Bob's gal, Floy. We bought donuts or cinnamon rolls and ate them on the way back to school.

I also enjoyed spending time with some other girls in my class who rode our bus, Shelby Harris and Fern McLelland. They were both proven scholars, and I could trust them to always do the right thing. Shelby lived in the next house up our road toward Fairview. I didn't know then, that in the not-so-distant future, my marriage would allow us to become kin.

Prescott High School, circa 1952.

❧❧

Granny fast became a great asset around out house. I didn't want her to feel like we were taking advantage of her willingness to help out. When I pitched in to get the work done, she usually took over to show me how I could do it better. I was grateful for that since there were many skills I hadn't been taught. Granny was a great trainer. She had us doing household chores all through the week; it couldn't all wait till Saturday. It had to be done her way, which, typically was the right way.

I think the only complaint Granny ever shared was that the outhouse was too far from the back door. I agreed. She said she appreciated my promptness in writing her weekly bundle of letters. I loved cuddling next to her little, crooked back in that feather bed every night.

I didn't like to cook, but Granny insisted that Mary and I both watch when she was showing us how to cook something new. We had no cookbooks, so I began to write her recipes down. She often encouraged me: "You're gonna be smart."

Granny always appointed me to help her wash her hair. I brought in extra water and heated it. When I took her hairpins out and let her hair

169

down. It was very thin, but about three feet long, and just beginning to show some gray within the black. She couldn't bend her neck back, so I accommodated her stiffness in every way. When I rinsed and dried it, she balled it back on top of her head, and thanked me with tears in her eyes.

When I was home, Granny started asking me to walk out to the toilet with her when she had to go. She was beginning to feel tired and was afraid she would fall. I encouraged her to use her nighttime potty, but she refused.

I stood outside while she did what she came for, and was helping her steady her gait, when she looked between us and the house, and jumped and hollered, "What in the world!"

A creature I had never seen before was standing under the crepe myrtle tree at the end of the wood stack, about twenty feet from our back door. It was taller than a cow and had huge horns on each side of his head that stuck high in the air.

I screamed for help because he was just standing there looking at Granny and me. The whole family left the Sunday dinner table and came running out the back door. Then, the huge brown animal with about an eight-inch white tail, took off running right by us. We, as well as the others, got a good look at him, but none of us knew exactly what he was. He went straight south, just sauntering along until he was out of our sight.

Daddy said it might be a deer. He had heard that the government had turned some loose down in southwest Arkansas to multiply, but he hadn't seen one before.

Bob, the hunter in our family, had ordered a wildlife identification book through the mail. He immediately found a picture of a whitetail deer, and yep, that's what we had just seen. Granny was laughing so hard. I brought out a chair and got her to sit down. She was saying how glad she was that we encountered the deer on the way back from the outhouse, instead of before she used it. We all laughed with her. Bob further informed us it was called a buck deer, because it had horns. The female specimen would be a doe.

It was several years before the deer population increased enough to begin having hunting seasons on them. They, eventually, multiplied to the point of being over populated, and are considered by farmers and gardeners to be a nuisance by eating up their crops.

Deer hunting eventually, become the most popular of hunting sports, in the area. Some folks plan their vacation every year in deer season. They also count on getting their freezers stocked with venison, since many of them have acquired a hunger for the fat-free meat, that is deemed very healthy.

Our whole family liked coon hunting. The best time to go was right after dark. One night, Bob asked who wanted to go. Three of us jumped up, looking for boots to help deter snakes. It was too early in the autumn to worry about getting cold.

Bob said he wouldn't feed Ruff and Tuff until we got back, since they wouldn't hunt if they weren't hungry. I wasn't hungry, but I surely liked the excitement of being in familiar woods, and hearing the dogs howl a victory every once in a while. Sometimes, Roy and Bob would skin the coons in the woods and give the reward to the dogs, taking the skins home to sell.

If you have never tried coon hunting, don't knock it. I happened to be born into this type of lifestyle, so just forgive me for dwelling on it.

That night we ventured into a section of the woods that was new to us. The growth was so thick we couldn't manage to break through it. Then, Bubba Roy discovered it was something Daddy had been searching for—bamboo cane. We needed it to stick our pole beans in the spring and hadn't been able to find any since our last move.

Daddy had already taught us how to stick an eight-foot cane pole in the ground beside each of four adjoining running or viney bean plants. The four poles were tied at the top like a teepee. Bean vines would cling to the poles and climb to the top. That way, we could stand up and pick the beans all the way up.

That was a successful hunt! We cut the poles and hauled them in the wagon the next time the men had a rainy day off from cutting logs. It was most helpful to trim them and have them ready to poke in the dirt when spring came.

⚜

Mary and I didn't have much spare time after school. She had a heavy load of homework, including Algebra, which I knew very little about. I wished Clyde was home to help her with it. We took her textbook to our study nook, the old wooden homemade tool box on the porch. She sat on it, and I chose to sit nearby on a small stack of boards.

Mary found the page she was supposed to work on. We read it twice, then read three preceding pages to understand that page. As usual, she gave up and slammed the book shut. I got mad, opened it back up, and started on the first equation. She stuck with it and got the answer before I did. I clapped for her and told Mama how smart Mary was. Every time she got bogged down, I tried to convince her to not give up because she would threaten to quit school. I just didn't want to hear that.

The weather was beginning to get cooler, and that meant it was time to get all the outside jobs done. Fall cleaning to us, meant cleaning stables and hauling manure to the gardens and truck patches that needed fertilizer before they were turned under. Old Dan was on standby for that. He was a patient mule. I think he was still missing Ruby, who had been sold.

We had some nearly mature pigs, that would provide winter activity some real cold morning. I disliked feeding them in the cold, but I did like that larruping good, rusty-gravy from the ham. Granny was anxious to help us kill hogs. I was sure she would show us a better way to do it all. She liked to cook liver and lights and hogs' feet. We had always thrown those parts away, but she said as a widow with seven hungry kids to feed, she had learned not to throw anything away.

∽ଔଚ∾

When I got home from school one Friday, Daddy was pushing a wheelbarrow full of dry ears of corn toward the well. He motioned for me to come. I helped him shuck the corn, and then shell the dry kernels off the cob like we did to feed chickens and mules. We would do it again when we needed kernels to plant.

He explained that Granny had asked if he had any dry corn to make hominy. He said he told her that he had the corn if she had the know-how. We shelled out two gallons for that first trial run, then washed it good and placed it in the clean wash pot. The kernels of dry corn were covered with fresh water to soak overnight. Of course, we covered the wash pot with clean boards, just in case Ernestine and her kittens decided to do a taste test during the night.

The next morning, we dipped up the swollen corn from the pot, and filled it half full of water. Granny then added three tablespoons of Merry War lye that Daddy bought in town. He built a big fire under the pot, brought the water to a rolling boil, then threw in the swollen.

After forty-five minutes, the corn was lifted out with a strainer into a dishpan and rinsed to dilute the lye content. We removed the "eyes" from the kernels, then washed them again. The corn was covered with fresh water and simmered until tender.

We used the hominy seasoned like fresh corn or canned in a pressure cooker for later. That night, Mary cooked about two quarts of hominy for supper to go with some perch Roy had caught down below the spring.

Granny was tired from helping us cook outdoors, so we insisted she sit and explain to us, girls how to can the remaining hominy. We had about seven-quart jars of the beautiful corn, and Daddy told us there was more to shuck in the barn.

I meticulously wrote down Granny's method, because Mama liked the hominy. I made every effort to learn all I could from my Granny Bradford, while I had a chance.

She said when it snowed, she wanted to get the quilting frames hung so we could quilt together. I often told Mama how much I wished she felt like doing these fun things with all of us. She just replied, "You know I can't."

❧❧

Sunday rolled around again, and Daddy woke certain ones of us early (Mary and me), so we could kill, pluck, and butcher three young chickens before church. He thought the older lady in the house would be too tired to cook today, but she came on into the kitchen, tying on her apron to make us some tea cakes. She knew the little family next door was having dinner with us that day, and she really liked to please her great grandchildren. They had all been gone for several days, so we were anxious to see them. Milton had said they were going a little "norther" but didn't say where—just up 67.

I missed our little ones in The Booster Band, but some new kiddos showed up, and we learned a new song. It was all good, but I missed learning my class lessons. I needed Bible teaching, too!

When we were finished with our fried chicken, tater salad, cornbread, turnip greens, and cookies, Milton scooted his chair back a little, and announced that his family would be moving this week to Jones Mills, Arkansas. He had recently missed a lot of work in the log woods because of rain, and he knew more inclement weather was headed our way, with winter approaching.

He told us he got a job with Arkansas Power and Light Company. I don't remember what he said his starting salary would be. I just remember that Daddy said, "Go git it, Boy!"

That was when the elder son began to move up in the world. Mama cried and hugged her grands, and stated, "Money ain't everything."

She was right.

Not long after the move, Bonnie got a job at a huge General Motors plant, nearby where they lived in a housing project. All of us thought their visits back home weren't frequent enough. Life became pretty dull around the Daniel house, when we no longer heard those little feet pattering across the porch to holler, "Pappaw, 'et me in!"

42

In talking on the school bus with some of the Cottingham family, I learned there would be a really big coon hunt on the next Saturday night. Floy said she and Bob were making plans to take the dogs out on the cut-off road between Fairview road and Nubbin Hill road. We would be hunting behind what we called Buchanan Cemetery.

Floy said that all of our gang from their family and ours would be picked up about eight o'clock, and to tell our parents we might be late getting home.

She said, "Bobby will be the only person carrying a rifle, because it would be dangerous to have too many guns with that many folks along."

Four of our family members loaded onto the flatbed with the hounds, sausage and biscuits, and a good bucket of drinking water. We picked up four or five Cottinghams and that's when the boys discussed needing some more dogs. I heard the name "John L", and the words, "the more, the merrier".

When the discussion was over, we rode another mile or two and stopped at a house. There was a dog pen just a few yards from the house, with a couple of dogs jumping high on the fence and yelping as loud as they could.

Bob got out and talked with the boy, who I later learned was John L McWilliams. Bob asked if he would like to bring his dogs and coon hunt with us. I couldn't hear his reply, but he walked briskly into the house and came back wearing a jacket and cap. When he got his two dogs and started back to the truck, with both of them barking out of tune with Ruff and Tuff, the noise was deafening. It didn't help the situation when some of the girls were squeaking, also.

The long, thin boy climbed on the back of the truck, and held his two by the collar while Mary and I wrestled ours down to the floor and held them. I remembered seeing that boy somewhere.

When we had bounced about two more miles, Bob pulled into a horse and buggy lane. At a wide place, he stopped the truck. I was glad to change my position enough to get Tuff's weight off my leg. Tuff managed to jump off the truck pulling me to the ground right behind him. After we placed the snacks in the cab, we all took off walking to see which direction the sniffing dogs had taken.

It wasn't dark yet, and I was trying to watch for landmarks to find my way back to the truck. We were blessed with four coal oil lanterns this time and hopefully, enough trained hunters to keep us safe. I had always relied on my brothers to provide security in any situation, and they never let me down. I was so happy to get to follow the big crowd.

Ruff and Tuff showed their expertise that night, along with the other two dogs, Ranger and Scout. Bob allowed, "That was the best treeing and barking I've ever heard!"

The dogs worked so hard, they soon tired out and headed back to the truck, as did we. The men wagged half a dozen fat coons. I was anxious to get to the water bucket. We had eaten ham biscuits for supper, so I was suffering from extreme thirst. I kept wondering where I had encountered this guy they were calling John L.

Right then I heard faster steps directly behind me, and someone took my right hand. It was the guy! This was definitely my first male/female exchange. I said "hi" to him at the same time he said it to me. His smile was broad and seemed so real. I liked his gold-filled tooth in front. I still wondered where I had met him before. There wasn't much pondering time. We were both shocked when a rifle barrel pushed between our arms. I looked around, and in the dim lantern light, all I could make out was a pair of heavy boots. He was gone as fast as he came, and never uttered a word.

Roy and one other person had a small campfire going when all of us made it back to the truck. I drank two cups of water, then passed around sausages and biscuits, that were still slightly warm. I was also taking a good look at the men's boots. I saw at least three pairs just liked I saw on the trail. I didn't learn anything. But I was delighted to get that kind of attention for the first time. Maybe there was hope for me, yet.

Some of the men skinned the coons and stretched the hides on boards to dry. The canines were rewarded with the feast they had worked so hard for. Truly, a good time was had by all. I thought having the two extra dogs made it a good hunt.

Mary and I did a little whispering before we went our separate ways to bed that night. She told me she recognized the McWilliams boy as the one that sat with his feet across the bus seat, and then let Clyde sit with him. I remembered standing up all the way to town on the bus. All I could think of to say was, "I forgive him!"

43

Granny was ready for another letter to Aunt Georgia. She had been thinking about letting Mary have her bed back. I didn't want to hear this, but she told me exactly what to write, and I did just that. She didn't tell Mama until the letter had been mailed. I cried with both of them, although I knew it was too hard on Granny to live with so few modern conveniences, as she was becoming weaker. She had been a real trooper. I learned so much from her and would like to think I possessed some of her best traits. In spite of her hard life as a widow, she was very tender-hearted and forgiving.

I wished I could just snap my fingers, and a modern bathroom would appear for my granny so she could stay. I didn't believe in magic, but I did believe in miracles. They were brought about by God. I believed it is a miracle that our mama had been allowed to remain with us this long.

It always took a week for a letter to get to Emmet, and a reply get back. Meanwhile, Granny sent some money with Bob when he went to town, to get some cotton quilt batting and some domestic cloth for a quilt lining. She asked the boys to hang our quilting frame in the boys' room. It took up a lot of space, so she whipped the lining in wooden frames with long stitches, then spread the batting over it. Next, came the pretty patchwork she had gently sewn together by hand, as she rocked in her chair by the fire.

Granny gave us, girls our first class in hand quilting. When our shoulders and arms were too tired to do anymore, she showed us how to roll what was already quilted, and then roll the ropes up to the ceiling so the boys' heads could go under.

When we had time to quilt again, we just let the ropes down, and sewed to our hearts' content. I was amazed and grateful for the knowledge that little old woman had. She told us she thought we would be good wives if we found the right man. I had already been asking God to help me out there.

The letter came in the mail on Saturday. I read that Aunt Georgia and James, their son-in-law, would be there to pick Granny up on Sunday morning. She held up the letter and said, "'At's my ticket to Emmet."

I began getting her things ready for the road with tears sprinkling everywhere. I was thinking how much good Granny gives to others, yet like Jesus, she had no place of her own to lay her head. I told her bye before going to church, thinking she would be gone when I got back, and I was right. I missed Granny so bad! Mama just slept on.

I moped around, sadly, for a few days, not wanting to read or work on the quilt. I did manage to make a new flower bed. Daddy helped me put a board barrier around it to keep the dogs out. Ruff and Tuff gave me a funny look. I asked them if they would like to visit Ranger and Scout, and they both grinned.

The seeds were the ones I had gathered before we moved, and in a short time, we had a pretty assortment of blossoms. I walked Mama to the window and told her the flowers were for her.

∾∾

On the radio, we heard that there would be a live country music band coming to the old Pleasant Hill school house, now converted to a community building. The school had been closed and consolidated shortly before we bought our house.

The show was Johnny and Jack. Miss Kitty Wells was an added attraction. Among other hits, she had a number one song on the radio at that time called, It *Wasn't God Who Made Honky-Tonk Angels*.

Bob went to get Floy and her sisters in the truck, while we walked the quarter mile. There was a huge crowd. Pleasant Hill folks were starved for entertainment, and we were fortunate to get the best in country music. In the past, we had heard the Stamps Baxter Quartet, Red Sovine, the Wilburn Brothers and many others.

Bob and friends sat by us. He and Floy were a lovely couple, who were beginning to talk about marriage amongst our two families.

It could be that the reason for such an enormous turn out for the gatherings at that place was that many of them may have come to reminisce about their school days there. In the autumn, there was a mulligan stew supper there at the old school house. That was when most of the recent hunting successes were boiled in one big pot, and piles of fish were fried. Our community really liked the homemade desserts, too.

That part of the country was an active place at that time, with parties, showers and family reunions usually held at the old school before it began to be vandalized and was eventually torn down.

❧❧

Daddy, Roy, and Bob continued to work in the log woods. They worked hard but welcomed a rainy-day rest. Daddy did his paper work on pine boards. I saw a board between his bed and a wall with three names and columns of hours they had worked. He didn't want to be cheated on payday for such back-breaking work.

Clyde seemed to be doing well in Walnut Ridge. We got about two letters a week from him with lots of excitement in each one. He had met another young single minister about his age, who had a lot in common with him. Vernell Daugherty became a good friend, and Clyde brought him to our house many times. Vernell had a car and he loved driving home with Clyde.

We had to cook many chickens for two preachers. That gave Daddy an idea. He said our little bunch of hens didn't produce nearly enough young ones to last all year, so he thought he would order baby chickens from Sears and Roebuck. He told me to find their order blank and fill it out for him. I did all of it, then asked him what quantity he wanted. He looked at it, then wrote in 250 under "quantity" and placed a finger on his lips, telling me to keep it hush. I wrote a check for him to sign, sealed it, and off it went. We might get enough of fried chicken!

The rent house next door had remained empty since Milton and his family moved. We looked it over and Daddy decided to empty one room completely and prepare it with a lighted brooder to keep the baby chicks warm. We made plenty of feeders and waterers out of canning jars upside down in a pan or bowl. That room had sunny windows, which would be beneficial for the little peeps. The floor was covered with fresh sawdust from a nearby mill. The family would be surprised that it was possible to order live chicks, and they would be shocked again when they see how many we ordered.

The men used their Saturday off to go back to the woods, way down near the spring and cut fire wood for the heater in the front room. They had taken old Dan and the wagon for that. I stayed at the house and watched for the mail.

The mail carrier finally pulled up in our yard. Instead of stopping at the box, he got out and unloaded three big boxes, one at a time, and placed them at my feet on the front porch. I couldn't hear what he said for the loud "peeping". I just thanked him.

I told Mama and Mary I thought the chicks had arrived. Mary told me to go get Daddy. I ran all the way to the woodcutters and broke the news.

I told him "Hurry 'cause they're cold!"

We pulled the boxes into our front room until they warmed up. Mama's eyes opened wider than I had seen them lately. "My goodness" was all she could say.

Mary said, "Somebody must have miscounted."

It was quite a pile of hungry and thirsty day-old babies.

We hadn't had chicks in the house before. By the following day, they were a warm, satisfied bunch of biddies, scratching their way to the skillet in about eight weeks.

On Sunday after church, the Cottinghams came to see the chicks. Afterwards, we all played Monopoly under a tree in the back yard, while Mama slept. The game wasn't over, but we halted it for night church.

❧❧

I got up early enough to make sure there was enough mash and water for the babies, checked that the doors were dog-proof, and barely caught the bus. My friends had saved me a seat. Mary stayed home to take care of Mama and do the laundry. She still had her old car-seat bed in the front room.

I had plenty of busy work before and after school, trying to keep water and feed out for the chicks. They were growing rapidly, and frequently testing their little wings. Some of them could fly up off the floor already and flip the water jars over. Having about six inches of sawdust on the floor helped tremendously. I hoped it would last six more weeks.

The water jars had to be washed every other day. They all said that was my job, too, since my hands were the only ones small enough to fit in a jar top.

I asked Daddy how we could ever eat that many chickens, and learned that he planned to sell some, can some, and allow the rest to run on foot until we needed them to cook.

As they reached the age of accountability, I crafted an eye-catching sign on a board, and nailed it to the wedding ring tree. "Fryers for Sale - $1". I drew a chick running away from the words.

Before I got around the house to put the hammer up, a truck stopped, and the driver bought six. Of course, I had to catch them. I held six legs in each hand, all the way to the truck, with twelve wings flapping. I thought… *Maybe we would make enough to cover the cost of the chickens.*

44

Back at school, I hit the sidewalks with Floy and Mary for a lunch time sprint to the downtown bakery for cinnamon rolls. I gulped down two of them on the quick walk back. We barely made it before the bell called us to class. My side was hurting from walking too fast. An hour later, when we changed classes, I pressed my hand on my side to walk. I kept on having pains.

I sat real still at my desk through the last class of the day, but I started hurting again in my right side on the way to the bus. When I got home, I went to Mary's old car seat and flopped down in a fetal position. I told them about my pain, and Mama immediately said it was probably appendicitis. She had watched Roy suffer through a ruptured appendix when he was much younger, and said she was well aware of the symptoms.

The loggers got home on time. Daddy and Bob cleaned up some, then took me to town to find a doctor. The first office we found was Dr. L. Jack Harrell's, and he was still there. Dr. Jack immediately placed me on a table in a supine position.

I had a quick question... "How much does this cost?"

We had never heard anything about insurance, and I knew how hard my daddy worked, and how much he disliked spending.

Dr. Jack continued his exam as he told me we would talk about that later. He pressed his hand into my right side. It hurt so bad I bit my tongue, then screamed.

"She has a hot appendix, and it has to come out," he diagnosed.

Daddy breathed in long and hard, and I began to cry, telling him I didn't want to spend his money.

I think the doc could tell we weren't wealthy people. He told Daddy he would do the operation for a hundred dollars cash, or we could pay it off monthly, for two hundred.

Daddy took a hundred-dollar bill from his overalls bib pocket and paid him with a prideful look. He said, "We've already lost two kids, and can't afford to lose her."

I knew my daddy loved me.

"Who'll take care of the ch..........?"

When I awoke, it was hard to believe it was all over, but I wasn't hurting anymore. I had been moved to Cora Donnell Hospital for two days, they said. I wanted to go home to Mama. I surely didn't know it was morning already.

Daddy and Bob went home to eat and go to work. The next day, they returned to take me home. I felt fine, just sore for a few days. I didn't have to go to school or do chores for about a week. Then it was life again, just as I loved it.

Many of our young male friends had recently received letters from The Selective Service Agency in Nevada County. That wasn't a club anybody wanted to join. Healthy, young men in a certain age group didn't join, but were drafted into the U.S. Army. My mother had voiced her hopes, many times, that her boys wouldn't get one of those awful summonses, since Milton had already served our country.

When the letter came, I was the nurse of the day. I was tempted to hide it until the family was home, but it was the only mail we got that day, and she saw me get it out of the box.

Mama demanded to see the letter, so I complied. She was shaking all over. It was a request for Bobby Eugene Daniel to report to the local Selective Service Board to be examined and classified for entrance into the United States Army. Tears began to fall onto the letter. Then I started crying. All day long, we talked about Bob and what a good boy he was.

Mama asked for a shot to stop the chest pains. It helped her to nap the rest of the evening. When Mary got off the bus, I met her on the porch and told her about the letter. She suggested we take Mama's supper to her bed tonight. It would be too stressful at the table.

The loggers arrived for supper, and Mama passed the letter to my youngest brother, as she told Daddy what it was. I watched his face. I knew he was hurting just as much as Mama, but he had to be strong for her. He didn't cry.

Bob took the news well. He looked at the calendar and saw he had three days, yet. He thought about it, and after supper, he asked his parents what they thought about him and his girl getting married. He had asked her, and she said, "yes".

They both advised him to wait. Mama said, "Maybe you won't have to go."

But he did have to go! He received a 1-A classification, meaning he was mentally and physically able to serve. I told him he should have stayed in school. That old bully would have him still shakin' and stutterin' so bad, the army wouldn't have him.

Bob would have only two weeks before his life wouldn't be his own for a few years. Our parents told him it would have to be his decision about marriage or not. He went ahead and bought Floy a set of rings on Saturday. On Sunday evening he said she and her parents had made the decision that they should wait until he's home on leave to get married, when they could make better plans. Floy flashed her rings like she was really proud of them.

Words can't even begin to describe the sadness that prevailed on our place. Bob didn't cut any more logs. He was in the woods a lot, though, with his twin hounds. He fished nearby and picked some wild berries. I asked if I could use some sugar to make Bob a blackberry pie, and Daddy told me to go ahead. I made him some jelly, too.

Mary and I decided to throw a big home party for everyone who wanted to come. The little house was empty and clean, again. We sold a hundred chickens and took care of the others as instructed. There were still plenty for fresh eating.

We organized makeshift seats—even, wide stumps of wood. The walls were decorated with construction paper red hearts and pictures of roses. A big picture of Bob and Floy was posted after she left, so she would be surprised. There was an old-fashioned rose bush in full bloom by the entrance. Its fragrance filled the party room. The windows were all open and there wasn't a hint of chickie odor.

We still had no phones, so we just invited folks we saw, that we thought might come. Mary and Floy dared me to send a post card invitation to the guy who owned the good coon hounds. I didn't know what a dare was, but I sent the invitation, thinking he wouldn't come. I had heard he had a girlfriend. Mary sent a card to a fella she had met at town.

When the night rolled around for our shindig, we were amazed at how many people showed up. Several couples came, including the boy who hunted with us, and his girlfriend. Yes, he brought her, who I had never met. Yet, a few times, I caught him looking at me. The guy Mary

185

invited showed up alone, and he only had eyes for her. It was the beginning of a long-time relationship for them, but not marriage.

We built a bonfire, and roasted wieners and marshmallows. We also played a few competitive games between the boys and girls, until we were ready to go inside for quieter games.

One game we played was where the men were seated in a circle, and the ladies marched behind them until the music stopped. Then, the guy was to ask the lady a question, and she would give him an honest answer.

I had to stop behind the mysterious man, who held my hand for an instant on the coon hunt. He reached behind him and caught both my arms and pulled them around his neck!

His question was, "Did I go hunting with you?"

I was glad looks couldn't kill, because the stare his date gave us would have pierced like a dart.

The question she was asked was, "Did you come by yourself tonight?"

Next, was a game that paired off couples to go walking outside in the dark. I didn't play and stayed behind to clean and put the leftovers away. Some of the couples must have gotten lost. They were gone a long time. Luckily, John L McWilliams and his date left together. Lucky for her!

Bob and his steady, and Mary and Douglas left for town after the crowd was gone. I took care of Mama and fell into the Oldsmobile seat, conked out. I didn't know when the big kids got home.

⟡

Three of us took my brother to the bus station. They had given him a day, and time to claim his ticket and sign the roster. He didn't know where he was headed till he saw that the ticket said, "Little Rock". About a dozen young men boarded the Trailways Bus that morning. They didn't have to pack clothes, just personal hygiene products and pictures, if they wanted them. Bob was shaking badly when I got my last hug.

We stopped at a grocery store, and got a head of cabbage for Mama's craving, and a box of Mellorine, which was a frozen substitute for ice cream. Daddy didn't forget his snuff, either.

That cheered Mama for a while, then she thought about Bob, and cried herself to sleep. I boiled her cabbage for supper, and she ate well. That was our first time to buy a cabbage.

Our house was very quiet for a long time.

I started a letter before I even knew where to send it. It was sure to please Mama when she found out I was keeping a daily account of home activities for our soldier boy. We had been warned that it would be at least two weeks before we heard from him.

Roy learned to drive in the pasture, and the old Ford truck cooperated just fine. When he decided to try it on the road, though, he was as nervous as a mama cat on a porch full of rockers. He was finally able to get a license, but wouldn't drive in town—he just parked on this side, and walked on in. I didn't trust him for a long time.

Bob had relinquished the church bus, and left it parked at the church house. More folks had cars now, so it might be needed more in another direction.

Our little church of baptized believers grew in numbers, and in the Spirit of the Lord. The Booster Band continued to sing, and I gave God the glory.

I really wanted in Mrs. Era's class for Sunday School. I was old enough now, but the crowd really liked hearing the children sing, so we began practicing on Wednesday nights. They sang every Sunday morning, and never got enough of it.

When I made it to the teen class with Mrs. Era, it changed me for life. That's when I learned to read my new Bible that I bought with my orchard money, right after I was saved. I now had peace in my heart, that when I spoke to God, He heard me! All through each coming week, I recalled Mrs. Era's wisdom.

We liked to pose in front of John L's pretty car. It was a rare background for a picture.

45

I had so many pages in my daily diary for Bob when we finally got a letter from him, that I had to use two envelopes. He was training in Fort Hood, Texas for an unknown period of time. At least, we had an address. Mama was more at ease and required fewer shots.

Floy's brother brought her by on their way to town to tell us she had heard from him. She asked Mary and me to go with them to get a hamburger.

They chose to eat at Mrs. Escarre's small place behind Woosley's Five and Dime Store. I know I'm repeating, "That was our first time," often, but it truly was my first hamburger. We bought a bottle of drink called Dr. Pepper, but it wasn't hot like pepper.

I had only taken a bite or two when one in our group said John L McWilliams just passed on the sidewalk. I thought she was kidding me, so she pushed me out of my seat, then flung the door open. It was him, and he quickly turned around and smiled. He walked back and talked to us for a good little bit. My heart was beating at maximum speed, until I remembered his girlfriend.

I finished my hamburger and that Dr. Pepper, just when he looked straight at me and asked, "Would you go to the show with me tonight?"

I told him I would have to ask my parents, but it would have to be a double date.

Floy told us, "Don't look at me."

Her brother said he knew a feller that wanted a date with Mary. When he told her who it was, she said she would go if he asked her. We just happened to meet him in his truck before we left town, and he asked her.

I had mixed feelings when my parents said I could go if Mary was going. It was nervous city around there that evening. We washed and rolled our hair and primped every way we could with only one mirror in the whole house, and it was in the front room with Mama.

We were told we wouldn't have to kill any chickens that day. So, we would have ham and vegetables for Sunday dinner.

Daddy and Mama seemed to be pleased that the McWilliams boy was going to be my first date. Daddy said they knew his parents, and they were good people. He warned Mary that she was to keep an eye on me at all times, though.

Mary's date came in his International pickup, so we all went in John L's 1940 Ford sedan. He had it shining like a mirror inside and out. The boys were nice enough to go to the door and make themselves known to our parents.

Yes, it was my first time to go to a drive-in movie, but it wasn't the last time. We all four proved that Christians could have a good time yet be separate from the world. We had a very good time and got home pretty early. We felt good chemistry among us. It got to be a usual Saturday night thing, and soon became an all-day Sunday event, as well. Often, Floy joined us and fit right in. We included her for Bob's sake, as well as hers.

Just playing under a shade tree in the summer was an ideal place we all enjoyed. Country folks are not hard to please. Sometimes we rode around to nearby towns on Sunday evening, or to some lakes. Several times we challenged each other to climb the forestry tower, that happened to be in walking distance from our house. Mr. Willie Treas, who was John L's neighbor and friend, sat a hundred feet in the air on that tower to watch for fires in the woods. He used some type of radio to the forestry commission, when he spotted a fire. We climbed the steps to the top, but coming back down, our legs were shaky. The soreness didn't set in until the next day.

Some of my friends discovered I was dating John L, and really teased me at school, because he was seven years my senior. At that time, he got a job helping his uncle, John McWilliams, deliver Coca Cola to Prescott and several other towns in the surrounding southwest Arkansas area. All cokes were in glass bottles then and rattled loudly when the truck was moving. They delivered their drinks to our school every Wednesday. It just so happened I was in Mrs. Overstreet's algebra class when the bottles rattled to a stop below the third story windows. My class members pointed and laughed at me. The teacher was puzzled as to why freshmen were so thrilled to hear a coke truck, that they had to rise from their seats to see it. When she found out why they were doing it, she just laughed too.

She even suggested I go to the window and acknowledge him. I only waved once. She told me, in private, that she was happy for me. She had heard he was a gentleman. Beside his picture in his senior year annual (1949) is the comment, "Slow and easy going, but dependable."

My whole family liked it when he spent time just hanging around with us on weekend days. He worked in denim overalls, but when he came to visit me, he always wore dress pants or khakis and nice shirts. He didn't own a big wardrobe, but his mother kept his clothes clean and pressed. He was an only child, but with primitive laundry appliances like rub boards, tubs and clotheslines, it was never an easy task.

He was always clean-shaven. His pretty, blonde, wavy hair was always combed down smoothly, and smelled like *Brylcreem* (a little dab'll do ya!).

After dating frequently about six months, I was admiring his class ring, and he pulled it off and asked me to honor him by wearing it. I had to wrap adhesive tape around the band to make it fit, so I wouldn't lose it.

I did a lot of thinking about my future, and eventually gave his ring back. I liked him a lot, but my goal was to be a teacher or a nurse. I was afraid he was more serious than I.

It wasn't uncommon for girls to marry young with parental consent then, but my heart was set on finishing an education. Prescott school didn't allow married men or women to attend. I asked John L not to come any more. We were both very sad. When he drove away toward his home, I sat on the old wooden tool box on the front porch and cried for a long time. Nobody bothered me.

When we sat down at the eatin' table, my family looked sad, too. They didn't ask me any questions. In fact, they didn't talk at all.

It was two days before normal conversations resumed at our house. I told them that we broke up because he was talking about building a house, and things I wasn't ready for. Daddy asked if I really cared for him. My answer was that I liked him, but I wanted to finish school.

Shortly after that, I was sitting in my favorite spot on my box, reading, when my daddy brought a chair out and joined me. He told me he had been trying to think of a way for me to go on to school, but it looked like I would have to pay my own way for the last two years. He said he was running out of money, and the doctor said Mama would have to have her heart medicine to live, and it was costing a lot.

I told him I was sorry I had appendicitis, and I would try to find a job and give him a hundred dollars back.

46

Daddy and Roy had found a better job making wooden crates and pallets at the box factory in town. Their pay was supposedly better, and I had no idea he was still so worried about his finances. Mary was no longer in school, which suited her just fine. Daddy was paying her five dollars a week to take care of Mama.

I had worked extra hard most all my life at home, in the fields, in church, and in school, trying my very best to make my daddy proud of me. That is what I still intended to do. I loved him above anything earthly.

Roy took Daddy to town to get necessary groceries on their day off from the factory. I was allowed to go with them. I carried some of my own money I had been saving, but I didn't spend a red penny. I marched down that busy sidewalk to Sterling's Five and Dime Store and went straight to the office. Upon entering, I introduced myself in a very determined manner, to the manager.

He invited me to sit, and I explained that I was there seeking a job as a clerk. When he asked my age and I told him the truth, he slightly shook his head, and excused himself to go out in the store. I couldn't see who he talked to. When he came back, he handed me some papers to sign, and told me I could begin next Saturday. I would start off working eight hours one day a week, and as I grew older, he would allow more days for me.

I thanked him twice, and headed to the alley, where our old truck was parked. Roy was afraid to park on the street. They were already in the truck, waiting for me.

I was nearly bursting with pride, when I told Daddy I got a job, and I would start next Saturday at eight o'clock at Sterling's. I told him some of my friends at school had weekend jobs there, and they said it was a really good place to work.

When they finally managed to get the old, flatbed truck started, Roy was gunning the gas to it, so it wouldn't die on him, right there in town. The noise was deafening. When we were out of city limits, he let off on the gas a little. That's when Daddy spoke again. He asked me how I would get to town to work, and I immediately replied, "I ain't 'shamed of this old truck!"

He let me know that, "This ol' truck ain't taking you there and picking you up. That'd be two trips ta town in a day. Hit'd take a heap of gas ta do that, and gas costs money."

I wrote a nice letter to the manager of Sterling's as I was lying across our bed, crying. Mama was asleep again. She might never know I got a job. I wrote Bob, too. He would understand my feelings, and so would Clyde, if he knew. I read as much as I could, out on my box.

⋞⋟

Sometimes, John L took the long way home from work, just to wave at me on the front porch. He had a better-paying job now, mowing grass around the mill and offices for Ozan Lumber Company. Most of it was done with a nearly-new 1950 Ford tractor. I learned that from Mary's boyfriend.

I hated to admit it, but every time he drove by, I wanted him to stop. I later learned that was what he wanted, too. Several more weeks went by, and I found myself losing interest in quilting, sewing, writing to my brothers, and just about everything else. I did only the chores I had to do and didn't try to create jobs just to stay busy, as I had in the past. One of the hardest things to accept, was that my mama didn't pay much attention to us anymore. I missed her love.

I finished my work, took a bath, shampooed and rolled my hair all over my head, then took my place on the porch with a book. It was the same routine every Saturday evening. I'm a firm believer that entering God's presence in His house deserves our best efforts.

It was a hot, humid day in Pleasant Hill. Sweat came naturally, and the menacing summer flies were buzzing as if rain might be eminent. Frogs were ribbeting, which was a sure sign of rain. It was pleasant and restful enough to cause me to close my good book and listen, until I dozed.

I heard an unusual sound and opened my eyes to see a blue Chevy turning in our yard. It was John L. He had traded cars, and I guessed he was just coming to show it to me. My heart was churning.

192

He was clean and casually dressed. Every hair was combed into place. I invited him into my space. He chose to remain standing and quickly asked me to go with him to the show that night.

I pondered whether to tell him "no", or to tell him that I had been wanting to see him ever since I broke up with him.

I decided not to tell him what I was really wanting to say, so I simply said, "Yes. I would like to go to the show with you."

He had to run back home two miles away but was back in no time. He was so kind to me, and good looking, too.

We went to Nevada Theater and saw a Ronald Reagan and Jane Wyman early movie. When we spotted Mary and Douglas, they motioned for us to sit with them. After the movie, we went to Arkady Café, just a mile south on 67. Mr. and Mrs. Steele, the owners, had come from northern United States to retire here. They loved to make new friends, so they claimed us right off the bat.

They always started cooking our cheeseburgers when we entered their place and brought us a Dr. Pepper. They knew what we were there after, and we usually had such a nice visit getting to know them, until later when they got so busy, they had to hire help. Prescott loved them, and they continued their business until age and poor health forced them to close.

John L took me home and asked if he could take me to church in the morning. It was easy for me to say, "Yes."

I didn't know when Mary got home. I guess I went sound asleep, thinking about tomorrow.

I went to Mrs. Era's class because that was to be John L's class too. She said she would get a girl in The Booster Band to lead them.

It was easy to absorb everything Mrs. Era said, even though I was so proud to be sitting by John L. He took me back to Bethel that night, and from then on, it was a routine I really liked. We went to my church twice on Sundays, and also to prayer meeting on Wednesday nights. My folks seemed pleased as punch. Roy always rode to church with us, as did Mary, if Douglas didn't come.

Our recent letter from Bob informed us that he would get to come home on leave soon, before transferring to El Paso. He stated, "As of yet, date unknown. Please hug Mama for me."

I did. That was all I had on my mind, till I heard from him again. Clyde and Milton were put on notice that brother Bob would be coming home, so that they could come on a moment's notice. Clyde was working through the summer for a mortuary in Walnut Ridge, and he was preaching at various Baptist churches, to save money to finish up college.

God bless him, he was determined to be able to put God's Word out there in the best way possible, with an education.

∽ઈે∂

Daddy shocked us all. He bought an electric icebox, called a refrigerator. I didn't understand all about it, so I studied the accompanying booklet. The others wouldn't even read it and expected me to answer all their questions.

We no longer bought ice. It made plenty—if I could keep the removable aluminum trays filled with water. When they froze solid, I emptied the trays of cubed ice, just about an inch and a half square. This was so convenient for keeping cool water for Mama to drink, and I dropped cubes in her pan to cool her face, without having to chip ice with an ice pick.

We had always had to churn our soured milk. Now it stayed fresh longer, and we drank more. Our family had few broken bones throughout the years, and I believe the reason to be because of the excessive milk drinking we all did.

All of us were grown before we went to a dentist, and we all had healthy teeth. Daddy was prepared for us to have a toothache, but I don't think we ever did. His locked trunk held a pair of tooth pullers that had belonged to his father before him. They were heavy metal, and resembled wire plyers. He did use them to relieve us of our baby teeth, when he got tired of seeing us wiggle them. Lots of kids! Lots of teeth!

Daddy had no cavities, but he said he had the same problem his mother, Icy Monk Daniel. His teeth wore down into his gums, and he had to get the dentist to cut the remnants out. Eventually, he obtained dentures that he wore mostly at mealtime. He said they didn't give him room for his snuff. He had paid more than a hundred dollars for them.

As far as I know, Mama never went to a dentist, nor had a cavity, and she had pretty, straight teeth. My granny Bradford still had her own teeth when she passed away at eighty-five.

47

Cold weather made it to Pleasant Hill before Bob did. He was still waiting for a leave. The family was becoming more eager every time we got a letter from him.

Clyde and Milton came for a weekend at the same time. It was a pretty rowdy farm house, with all of them joining us. We had moved some extra beds into our party room in the little house. Clyde brought another preacher friend, Alvin Wiles. He played guitar and sang at church for us, and Clyde preached. Bonnie and the kids went to church with John L and me. This allowed Milton to get in some quality time with Mama and Daddy.

We girls had prepared the chickens as always, but now had them refrigerated. We chose some late fall vegetables from the garden for sides, since frost would claim it all soon. All we could can had been canned. We surely missed Bonnie and our granny helping with that. The barn loft held a good supply of Irish potatoes and sweet ones, too. They would have to be covered with old quilts soon, to prevent them from freezing. The food cycle continues, thanks to God for providing the seasons.

John L ate Sunday dinner with us. I think he was hoping he wouldn't be noticed in all that crowd. He was very shy and didn't like to mingle. As soon as I helped with kitchen clean-up, he asked me to ride around with him, so we went to town and he bought me a double-dip ice cream. It calmed us both. I think this was our first time to be out alone in his car. He took my hand and asked me to move closer, so I scooted toward him maybe three inches. There were no bucket seats or middle dividers in cars or trucks then, just one long seat. I could hardly move over with an ice cream cone in my hand!

Our company had all left for home when we got back, and the church goers had gone on ahead of us. It paid for us to be a little slow. We rode to Bethel and then all the way home alone. We liked being with the gang, but that night we found out how sweet it was to be alone. I told my sis that night that I liked him a lot, but I didn't tell him, yet.

Time was flying by. Winter was coming too soon, and I was back in school too soon this time. My sophomore year was going well, and I liked my teachers.

Somehow, we didn't get the wood pile high enough before we installed the heater in the front room, as we were accustomed to doing. Daddy set aside the next Saturday for woodcutting. He had us up early, and we had a full belly by daylight.

Mary agreed to stay and play house. I was glad to get to the woods. It was hard work, but maybe we would warm up a little. I had on gloves and my hands were ice cold. Daddy and Roy were on opposite sides of a big hickory tree, starting to cut it down with a crosscut saw. Their effort was completely manual, no motors involved. One man pulled the five-foot-long saw all the way to his side, then allowed the other sawyer to pull it all the way to him, as the teeth of the saw sank deeper and deeper into the tree, until it reached a notch that had been cut on the unsawed side. I screamed, "Timber!", as the tree slightly leaned, then fell to the ground.

Daddy pulled the ear flaps loose on his winter cap, and threw it to the ground, then started removing his denim jumper. He couldn't manage to get his left arm out. I helped him, and he began to unbutton his shirt. I asked why he was doing that, as cold as it was. Then, I knew something was wrong. He was sweating profusely, and his face was turning blue, as well as his hands. He could barely speak.

Thank goodness we took the truck that day, instead of the wagon and mule. I told Roy to help get him in the truck and drive home fast. He couldn't walk, so I got pillows and quilts, and tried to make him comfortable, stretched out on the truck seat. Roy had parked the old truck at the wood stack in back, so we wouldn't alarm Mama.

I flagged down a neighbor who was driving by and asked him to stop at the nearest house where there was a phone and call Dr. Hairston. I told him about my daddy, and he spun gravel to go get us some help.

When I returned to the truck, he had pushed up his shirt sleeve, and was rubbing his upper left arm. I could see an egg-sized lump on the inner side of his arm. He was writhing in pain, and tears rolled down his cheeks. Mary came out and offered to help, but all we could do was wait.

I prayed that God would work out all problems and send us a doctor in a hurry. I definitely felt like he heard me. He let me know that my daddy would be alright.

I was learning to depend on the Lord more and more. He could do anything but fail! He already knew our every need but wanted us to ask: "And whatsoever ye shall ask in my name, that will I do, that the Father may be glorified in the Son."

Our neighbor returned very soon and told us the doctor was on his way. The patient became calmer, and told our neighbor, "Much obliged."

Dr. Hairston arrived and began his evaluation, telling Daddy, "I've been here many times to check your wife, but never for you."

When he felt the lump in his left upper arm, he told us it was coronary thrombosis, a big name for heart attack. He gave him a shot for the pain, and medicine to dissolve the blood clot. He told us he would have to take things easy for a month or so, to allow his heart to heal. The doctor said he should stay in bed for a week, except to go to the bathroom. I laughed inside—he didn't know how far it was to our bathroom. I would have to retrieve Granny's makeshift toilet for him.

We got Daddy into the house and put him in a bed in the boys' room where it would be quiet. His natural color returned, and his breathing was better. He seemed to be asleep.

Dr. Hairston checked Mama briefly and told her all she needed to know about Daddy. He told her what we all wanted to hear… "With proper care and rest, he will be alright."

Even though I was the youngest sibling, it felt like Mary and Roy had non-verbally elected me the decision maker all at once. So, I turned to the One who had all the answers!

I prayed, "Dear Lord, I am more than willing to see that my parents get the tender loving care they deserve. I will try my best to do my part, with your help. But, Dear God, you know I can't pull a crosscut saw! We are short on wood for the first time I can remember. I know you are aware of all my predicaments, but you told us to ask, in the name of your Son, and I'm asking."

I glanced at him in the boys' room, lying so still with eyes closed, and respiration so slow. My hero, my rock of stability, my safety net, my earthly advisor and counselor… *Lord, help us!*

❦❦

Daddy didn't awaken till midnight. He called for help to the potty, and said he was thirsty enough to drink a lot of water and some milk. I took that as a good sign. I brought his alarm clock and set it by his bed. He said the ticking helped him to sleep.

Mary was up several times during the night with Mama. She was worrying about him. We both elected to miss church, but Roy went. I don't know if they understood his speech, but he said he told the church about Daddy.

Mrs. Era showed up after dinner. I knew she would. As a registered nurse, she skillfully checked their blood pressures and listened to their hearts. I can't even begin to describe the feeling of comfort and security she brought to me that day. My inside secret description was that it was like Jesus came to our house, in person.

I missed getting to be with John L. He came to take me to church, and I told him about Daddy, so he went back home. He was very understanding, when I told him I needed to stay home today and would miss school tomorrow.

❦❦

I felt sure Milton and Clyde would drop down to see about Daddy by the weekend. Bob couldn't make his own decisions, so who knew when we would see him.

It was sad to have to wave my school bus on that next morning. I had to put forth an effort not to cry. I had done my share of that lately, but I didn't like to miss school. I got busy picking up pieces of scrap wood around the place. Most of what I found was pine, and it wouldn't produce much heat, but I could mix it in the heater with some of the few oak sticks we had left on the wood stack. I tried hard to keep some fire going, day and night in the heater. That was easier than having to restart a fire from the beginning. The outside temp had risen considerably, and that helped a lot with the wood shortage.

I remember taking the wheelbarrow down in the pasture where I knew there were some pieces of an old board fence that would burn hot. I loaded the one-wheeler and rolled it back to the stack. I knew Mary was holding down the fort inside. That was what she preferred, and I liked it better outside.

Just as I laid the first chunks of wood on the pile, someone behind me tapped me on the shoulder and asked, "You need some help?"

I turned around, and we hugged, and I cried, and Bob cried. His army khaki shirt was soaked with tears, but oh, how good was that release!

I knew he didn't get the letter about Daddy, because I had just mailed it that morning. He got his furlough and said he had to report to Ft. Bliss in El Paso in three weeks.

He had been in and seen Daddy, and he tried to get out of bed, but Mary stopped him. Bob told us he just had his first taxi ride from town with the well-known driver, Mr. C. J. Childers.

Mary fixed him something to eat, and he pulled a chair up to Mama's bed and gave her a bite or two, then he ate. He said the conversation and the food was good.

He held her hand till she went to sleep. Then he got up and went to Floy's house to surprise her when she got off the school bus. This was her senior year.

He brought her home with him for supper. It was so good to see them together again, although they seemed a little strained. That was just my inner thoughts, and I didn't speak about it.

You can't keep a good man down. Daddy was up and outside one week after the heart attack.

48

When the week of bedrest was over, Bob dressed Daddy in his chambray shirt and overalls, and took him to sit on the back porch in the sun.

All the while, daddy was repeating "Hand me my snuff… right there in that fruit shelf…"

We all knew where his snuff was, but he had been too sick to ask for it, till now. Bob managed to load Daddy's bottom lip with snuff, then got a big dip for himself, and they sat and talked, and spat, and sometimes, they just sat. Bob said, "This is home!"

It was coming up on hog-killing time, but wasn't quite cold enough, yet. We decided to go ahead and cook the pork that was left in the smoke house. In case the other brothers came in for the weekend, we would have enough without killing more chickens. We had enough to do already and were hoping Bonnie would come. We knew she would help us catch up again.

I was back in school, but my mind was back on Rural Route #5 with my dear folks. John L came on Wednesday night, and I was so ready to go to church. Bob wanted to go in the truck with his girl, so that gave us another ride alone. I don't think anybody noticed. He asked me to take charge of the radio, so it was country music with our faves, like Hank Williams, Hank Snow, Patsy Cline, Loretta Lynn, Johnny Cash, and the Carter Family with Mother Maybelle.

Our prayer service was awesome and uplifting. I prayed out loud when it was my turn, for all my family, and for firewood, and I asked for God to supply someone to help us kill hogs. Afterwards, we went to Arkady for our usual cheeseburger, DP, and fellowship with Pa and Ma Steele. They were expecting us, so our food was ready in a minute.

It was relaxing to be with John L, and he said he really enjoyed spending time with me, and then he asked if he could come on Friday night, as well as the usual dates. He drove slowly taking me home, waiting for an answer to his question. I finally told him, "Okay, come on, but I'll have to ask if I can leave home or not." So, he walked me to the door, kissed me goodnight, and left happy.

I was reminded of the parable of the prodigal son, in the fifteenth chapter of Luke. Daddy ordered Bob to get ten pounds of sugar when he went to town, so we could make him plenty of cakes and pies while he was here, and Mama wanted to try some sweet iced tea.

Daddy was feeling much better, but now and then we could see he had a bad day. Bob hadn't told either parent that Ft. Bliss would just be a stopover, where he would train to be deployed overseas, destination unannounced yet.

He told me, and nobody else, that he thought he and Floy would get married on his leave, even though she kept putting him off. He thought she wanted to wait until he was a civilian again, and that would be a long time. Bob kept that quiet, and they continued to date and have fun, apparently.

Our house was full by bedtime on Friday. We were glad they had all had supper before they got there. We bedded some down in the little house, and some rolled in quilts, which we called Baptist pallets, on the floor.

We planned an early breakfast to show sympathy for those wallowing in the floor. We didn't expect Daddy to cook, and I really missed him. Some of them complained that I didn't make the coffee strong enough, and I simply told them to stop by the fruit shelves and fill their lower lip with snuff, and they probably wouldn't even think any more about coffee.

Dwayne, Jeannie, and Polly were growing so fast. Their grandparents commented on how smart they were. They enjoyed re-exploring the place every time they visited and were naturally delighted to see we had a refrigerator.

Clyde, Bob and Roy slept in. They tucked themselves to bed in the little house, where there was no noise to wake them. It was so comforting to have the whole family home. I was doubly elated because it was Saturday. This was my day to primp some and be looking good when my fella arrived late in the day. John L came earlier each time. He had also bought some fine men's cologne. Perfume hadn't come my way yet, but I had bought myself a big bottle of Jergen's lotion.

I didn't get all of my jobs done that day. I played with the kids and visited with my three brothers and Bonnie. I got Mama cleaned up and dressed, while Mary assisted Daddy.

It seemed like a whole new world had opened its doors and let me in. The menial tasks didn't seem so demanding any more. I felt more carefree. It crossed my mind that Daddy still might go carefree with his paddle, too, if I shirked my duties. I ironed the men's shirts and khakis for Sunday and helped with dinner. We had enough leftovers for supper, and I knew at least three of us would go out to eat.

Mary and her friend went with John L and me to an inside movie. It was a Bing Crosby movie. The boys were glad it was short. We went to our usual hangout, and it was crowded. We had told too many people how much we liked the food and the owners.

It was getting late when we gave up on the wooden puzzle at our table and called it a night. Time went by rapidly, when I was with John L. I so looked forward to his set-in-stone dates that he said he wouldn't dare miss. He always held my hand all the way home and drove with the left.

When he told me goodnight at the door, his hug was a little tighter. Mary got out after I went in. I hoped nobody was mad that we left our company. Going with John L felt necessary, and I smiled just knowing there would be a next time.

∼∂∂∽

Mary and I fixed a big breakfast of everything we could find: biscuits, sausage, bacon, gravy, eggs, blackberry jelly, butter, and a bowl of mixed canned fruit. I put two extra spoons of Maxwell House in the percolator, and they all said it was better than snuff.

It wasn't an easy task to clean up after breakfast with so many people in the house, much less clean up ourselves in a four-room house with no bathroom or sinks, and no locks on any door.

I felt like dancing around with an umbrella with balloons on it, until it took me up, up and away! I felt cloud-light, and my heart rate always went up when that '49 blue Chevy turned in the yard by the wedding ring tree. We would be going to church, so I would be next to him for a while, and nothing else mattered!

We drove off and left them all to find their own ride to Bethel. He and I were together. When the service began after Sunday School, Mrs. Era asked if the Daniel Quartet could sing. We chose *Never Alone* and announced, "Although he's singing with us, this is for Bob, who'll be deployed overseas soon."

I didn't have a Kodak, but I snapped a permanent picture in my mind in church that day. My four brothers sat next to John L and me, then Floy, Mary and Douglas.

Bonnie stayed at our house and cooked. She used her kitchen talents well, as usual. It was cold outside, but we jacketed up, and played Monopoly all evening under the tree. Such good company gave me a giddy feeling—or maybe it was his new cologne. I behaved quite well when he was there.

⊰⊱

I went back to school with more determination than ever that I was going to keep my grades up and make Daddy proud of me. I was eager to show him that graduation was as good for girls, as it was for boys.

I would be dating for two more years while I finished, if John L was willing. I was definitely in "like" with him, and wanted to share our whole lives together, but finishing what I started eleven years ago was important to me. I learned easily and had trained myself to retain it. There was certainly no help at home, or encouragement.

No lunch for me at school anymore. I went to the library and caught up with all my homework, so I would have more time for chores, and caring for both sick parents. Daddy was better and getting around the house and yard, and even to the barn. He would have to go to the doctor before being released to go back to work, and Bob was there to take him soon. His furlough was fast coming to an end. He and his girl had come to a mutual understanding about the wedding date. They were together most of the time, trying to make the most of their precious love.

He preferred to wait and tell our parents when he was ready to be deployed overseas. He couldn't stand for them to worry about it, as he knew they would. I hurt for him and prayed protection for him and all soldiers who faced the same dilemma.

49

My brothers had taken care of the woodcutting while they were there. There was enough wood stacked for the rest of the winter, and next year, too!

They offered to put an electric pump in the well, and build a bathroom, but Daddy refused. He said when you start putting all that stuff in the house, it just creates problems with pipes and stuff. His philosophy was, "The fewer desires, the more peace."

Daddy had gone for a checkup with Dr. Hairston and was released to go back to the box factory, Mondays through Fridays, if he would rest on Saturdays and Sundays. That request didn't help us, girls any.

When he got back to work, they told him they allowed he wouldn't be able to work anymore, so they had replaced him. What a blow!

He asked Roy to take him to Ozan Lumber Company to look for a new job. They both were hired on the spot with better wages, and Daddy's work wasn't nearly as strenuous as the old job. Roy was delighted to change jobs, and they both worked the same hours. The Lord works in mysterious ways.

※◈※

We soon got our first letter from Ft. Bliss. I opened and read it at the mailbox to get my cry out so I could read it to Mama without crying. She got upset, but not too badly. She went right back to sleep. I missed Bob so much!

I could quickly turn my thoughts to the guy I planned to marry sooner or later. I thought just two years from now, all will be well. I was in the final quarter of my sophomore year. I had a few friends at school, and some at church, but my best friend was John L. We confided everything to each other.

On Sundays, when it wasn't my turn to care for Mama, we visited his folks. I liked them a lot, and the feeling seemed mutual. John L's mother, Annie, fixed dinner for us occasionally. She was a wonderful cook, but I got so nervous every time.

John L said his parents and cousins were inquiring if our relationship was serious. He said he told them we were really struck on each other. Not long after that, the whole county knew we were serious when he took me to McLelland's jewelry store in Prescott and bought me a set of engagement and wedding rings.

❧❧

It was in March of 1953, when Daddy let me know he couldn't support me in school any more. He told me if I continued, somebody else would have to take over the expenses.

I silently tried to count how much I had cost him this last year... Not a dime! I still had money in my dresser drawer that I saved from my orchard work. I hadn't bought any new clothes or shoes since my appendectomy, although I did receive some hand-me-downs. Clothes weren't as important to me as cleanliness, and we kept ours clean without the support of anyone. There had been no time for sewing this year.

In April 1953, our group of young people had a wiener roast and picnic on Grassy Lake, between the church and Highway 19, north of Pleasant Hill. The lake was hidden on a back road we had never traveled.

It was my Saturday to put Mama to bed and make her comfortable enough to sleep, so Mary and her new boyfriend, Junior Adams, had gone on earlier with Roy and his new-found friend, Laverne. I told Daddy we would be back before she needed another shot, and he okayed it.

John L and I listened to the *Grand Ol' Opry* on WSM Radio. Minnie Pearl and Roy Acuff were on. We hugged each other and laughed nearly the whole ride. We saw headlights coming toward us, and the road was so narrow two cars couldn't meet easily. There was green grass growing in the middle of the road to prove it wasn't traveled much. John L pulled over beside the road, because there was no ditch there, to let the car pass on by.

He didn't move the car when the other one was well out of sight. Instead, he took both my hands in his, and said, "Let's get married."

I was stunned for a minute, and I didn't answer "yes" or "no". Finally, I said, "When?"

We went on to the church party and joined right in the fun. I kept the secret until we were home, then I told my sister.

That's how we made it to the point of buying rings in May. I wore my beautiful engagement ring to school, and I wasn't ashamed to tell everybody I would marry John L McWilliams in June.

I wanted Mary to see my ring first. She was almost as excited as I was. She screamed. I caught Mama when she was wide awake and ready for supper. Daddy was with her when I showed them my ring. Mama hugged me with what little strength she could muster and cried. Daddy smiled big. I knew I was doing exactly what he wanted me to do.

John L waited while I did what I needed to do in the kitchen, then he helped me draw water and bring in enough for the night. Mary stayed there to strain the milk when Roy finished milking.

Then we went to show his parents my ring. They said it was real pretty, then Mr. Mc asked if we got Cracker Jacks with it. Ha-Ha! They both told me they were pleased that they would finally have a daughter. (I will say right here, that as long as they lived, they treated me like a daughter, and I loved both of them dearly).

We went to a drive-in movie that night, but I can't remember what it was about. We were busy discussing wedding plans all through the show.

We decided to marry the week before the Fourth of July, because the traffic might be bad on a holiday. We certainly didn't want to wait a week after the Fourth. When we looked at a calendar, we decided on June 26, 1953. I wanted to marry in Bethel Church, but I knew Mama couldn't make it, so we concluded it would be at my house with families and a few friends.

We knew we wanted a honeymoon, to get away and see some scenic places, but we would think about that a little longer. He had gained my trust, and I would be willing to follow him anywhere.

I had learned to use bought dress patterns in home economics class at school. With Mrs. Adam's help, I made a brown, corduroy, fitted skirt with a kick pleat and matching weskit, which was very popular at that time. I also became familiar with the use of interfacing in the wide lapels of the weskit, and I learned how to make buttonholes by hand.

The next time our old truck had to go to town, I hitched a ride and went to Sterling's. I planted myself on a high stool beside the pattern book counter. Daddy gave me an hour to look for a dress pattern for Mama. I had told him I wanted to try making her a dress for my wedding.

I looked at the page for women's plus dresses. Wow, I hadn't expected to see so many. I only turned one page and found a group of "easy-to-make" dress patterns. The one that caught my eye did look easy. There were four buttonholes and a side zipper. An all-around sash that tied, wouldn't be a problem. With God's help, I could make this dress! I pulled open the drawer and found it in stock.

I kept thumbing through the catalog and found "Misses Special Occasion" patterns. I had contemplated buying a nice Sunday dress with the last of my dresser drawer money, but I might not have to spend all of it, if I could sew my own. I found one with a sweetheart neckline, cap sleeves, and gathered skirt and scallops that went all around the skirt near the bottom and around the neckline. The picture showed it made in frosted organdy, but I could make do with a cheaper fabric. I would have to buy new undergarments if I used that sheer organdy.

I was holding both patterns in hand, when Daddy came back to get me. He asked me what I was scared of. I didn't realize it showed. I paid for the patterns and asked if we could go where fabric was sold. He told me he would pay for Mama's material, and he would buy some for my wedding dress, too!

I had decided I wanted puckered nylon, which was a new fabric just out. I found it at the second store we visited. I chose navy blue for Mama, and sparkly navy buttons. I got two yards of navy broadcloth to make her a princess slip to go under the nylon. We bought her some new nylon stockings, too.

This store also had new patterns of the frosted organdy. I showed the picture to Daddy and asked what he thought about that with a white-on-white piece for my dress. I then showed him a cheaper fabric. He told me to get the better one if that was what I wanted.

When the clerk got through cutting it, he told her to get me all the underworks I needed, and a pair of shoes. I was holding back tears. He couldn't afford school, but he could afford to give me away.

To keep from crying, I allowed my thoughts to go back to the Sunday evening when John L asked my parents if we could get married. We went riding down the lake roads after dinner. He wanted me to help him to decide how to ask my parents if we could get married. This was after the proposal, but before he bought the rings.

He told me what he was going to say, then he drove back to the house, full of determination. Roy and Mary knew his plans, so when we stepped in the front door, they went out the back. John L lost his nerve to ask, so we followed out the door. We talked a little, then went back in to carry out his plans. He just turned to me and asked if I would like to go to Bessie Pearl's for ice cream. On the way to town, we lost our taste for ice cream.

On the ride home, I just mentioned that maybe I wasn't worth such a hard request, so just forget it. He was shaking when he barely entered the front door. He grabbed my hand, looked at Daddy, and sharply said, "Can we get married?"

Daddy replied, "If you think you can take care of her."

Mama said, "I want you to be good to her."

He nodded his head in the affirmative and muttered, "Yeah."

We were pretty much oblivious to our surroundings at Grassy Lake the evening after he proposed marriage to me.

50

When I showed Mama the fabric and patterns, she was real pleased. I wished school was out, so I could sew. Bonnie showed up just in time to help me with the buttonholes on the navy dress. She thought it was very appropriate.

Next was my white dress. All went well until I tried to make the scallops even. After a lot of ripping out, I soon got the hang of it. My friends at school couldn't believe I was making my own wedding dress.

I learned to do embroidery on my own, and I had numerous, pretty dresser scarves, dish towels, and pot holders made from bleached feed sacks in my "hope chest"—a large paper bag. I also had a quilt that Granny helped me make, and a dish collection consisting of two cups and two small bowls that John L won at the fair carnival.

I dreamed one night that we were having a church wedding under an arch of red roses and ferns. Then we cut a tall, beautiful wedding cake, with a little bride and groom on top. I awoke with a thankful heart that I didn't have to prepare for all of that. I had all the work I could do.

My pastor, Brother Sam Cathy, and Mrs. Era attempted to talk me out of getting married, because I was too young. They thought it wouldn't last (I still think it might).

We had no wedding shower from my church friends until a year after our wedding, when another couple got married, and they gave us a shower at the same time.

Mary had been in Malvern, babysitting for Milton and Bonnie for a few weeks, as the date got closer. When school was over and done for me, I concentrated on routine jobs like picking, shelling, and canning, like every other summer of my life. Mama wasn't able to participate, but Daddy and Roy helped a lot after work every day.

Clyde was trying to graduate from college, and had plans to move to Charleston, Missouri, where he had been called to pastor Aniston Baptist Church. He wouldn't be coming anytime soon. Daddy's sister, my Aunt Ellen Finney, and my cousin, Agnes, were planning to see us marry. They would come from Nashville, Arkansas. Bob wanted to come, but he said he wouldn't even think of asking us to wait. He had word from headquarters that their group was being deployed to somewhere in Germany.

We didn't invite many folks, mostly family, along with Shelby and Carolyn from up the road. They snapped the only photographic memories we had of that precious time. They divided them with us later.

When June 26 rolled around, I set my mind on all I intended to do that day and made a list. I picked a big bucket of pinto beans and cooked them all so there would be leftovers for the next day. I also made fresh cabbage and cornbread.

The floors had to be swept and mopped. Dusting was next. After Mama and I ate dinner, I got the kitchen cleaned up, then packed enough clothes for a week. I only had a few of what most folks called essentials, so packing was quick. I hadn't missed what I didn't know anything about.

I gave Mama a shot, then started on her sponge bath. Eventually, we got her new clothes on and her hair fixed. She didn't like jewelry or makeup, but she surely did like her new dress and slip. She told me she was proud of me for many reasons, but mostly, because I chose to honor my father and mother. I had supper on the table, as usual, for the men after work. They ate hurriedly and cleaned up, dressing in church clothes.

The kitchen cleaning got a lick and a promise from me, just as I saw a car parking out front. When I realized I was still in cut-off boy jeans and a faded red t-shirt that was too small, I ran to my room, while it was still mine, to change. I was glad I had bathed and curled my hair earlier. There was no mirror in our room, so I would have to finish in the front room.

When I went in, there was a knock on the door and the preacher, Brother John Baker and his wife, Mrs. Annie, walked in. We hadn't seen them since the DeLaughter farm days when they were our neighbors. He had officiated at Milton and Bonnie's wedding.

I got Mama up to sit in a padded chair and hoped she could last there through the "I do's".

I finished my primping in front of the preacher.

Looking out the window, I caught a glimpse of my sweetheart's car pulling up, shining brightly in the setting sun. His parents were right behind in their 1941 Chevy pickup. I wondered if they were sad.

My man looked suave and handsome in his three-piece suit and tie. I know they were proud of him. We both were nervous when we said, "Hi."

When all were seated, we took our place in the open door to the boys' room, facing the way the planks ran on the floor. Old folks warned us to not get crosswise with the planks, or we would often be crossed.

We told Brother Baker to go ahead, even though it was ten minutes till time. It was a short, simple ceremony. He pronounced us husband and wife, then, we kissed in front of God and everybody. Shelby and Carolyn took some pictures outside.

Milton's family and Mary got there in time to decorate our car, much to the owners' dismay. Milton was showing off a brand-new 1953 Pontiac. He had left in a Model A Ford, so his last job change must have been very profitable.

Aunt Ellen and Agnes drove up just as we were leaving. We told them all bye and that we were going to Petit Jean State Park to see all the sights and spend two nights there in Mather Lodge. John L had been there on his Senior trip in 1949, and he wanted to share it with me.

Just married!

I had mixed feelings about leaving home. That was something that hadn't happened often in my life. When we passed Mrs. Maude DeLaughter's house on 67, I felt a wave of reminiscence, like I hadn't felt before. I prayed silently, "Lord, thank you for my parents and my past, and all my family, and my home, and this wonderful man that you have given me for keeps the rest of my life. Please keep us safe and happy."

❧

Highway 67 was still the main thoroughfare through Arkansas and some other states. John L drove through Arkadelphia and then on to Caddo Valley. We spotted a flashing marquis for Caddo Valley Motel. He stopped in front of it, pulled me closer to him, and asked, "Do you want to spend the night here?"

My first thought was to tell him I would like to drive on to Timbuktoo tonight, but I didn't want to hurt his feelings, so I went with him inside while he registered us for room seven. The clerk handed him a key and said, "Have a good night, Mr. and Mrs. McWilliams."

That was truly a hot night in June! The humidity was at its worst. We had the car windows open as we traveled, but out clothes were wet with perspiration.

We experienced a pleasure that night that we hadn't had before. We had a window fan that pulled a breeze directly through our room. It was like the wind over Cold Run Creek in the early spring. Before we left the next morning, John L found a water hose near where his (our) car was parked. He washed it, except for the words, "Just Married", which were rolled on with white shoe polish. That would just have to wear off. A short while after that night, we drove by the motel again, and it had burned to the ground. Huh!

As we continued on our way to our honeymoon destination, the weather was perfect and the ride was beautiful, but I had something pressing on my mind.

I asked my husband, "Did I miss something? What does 'killing chickens and making biscuits have to do with getting married?" I fell asleep with his right arm around me, as we rode off into the mountains.

We stopped in Morrilton for gas. He asked if I packed a bathing suit, to which I answered, "No, I didn't have one."

He wanted to swim atop Petit Jean Mountain, so he stopped at a department store to buy one. At the cash register, he discovered they couldn't cash his check that he had received on Friday, so he asked if I had any money on me. I paid for the five-dollar bathing suit. He said he would pay me back when he cashed his check. Well, it has accrued some sixty-six years of interest now.

The drive on up the winding path to the top of the mountain was very frightening to me, because I hadn't ever been high enough for my ears to feel like they were bursting—not to mention the aggravating dizziness and nausea that came later. I trusted his driving completely, but I did scoot over to my side of the seat, to allow him to drive with both hands.

The view took my breath away when we parked. I stepped from the car and all my queasiness left. What a beautiful place! I kissed him out of sheer delight to be touching the earth again. My thoughts were a mixture of bitter and sweet. I knew that everything that goes up, must come down. Again, my trust was in him to get me down from there.

Honeymooning at
Petit Jean State Park.

The whole park was a respite from the sweltering heat and humidity in Daddy's garden in Pleasant Hill. A wave of guilt swept over me as I wondered who was picking the green beans and pintos today. It was time to pull the onions and get them turned upside down in a cool, dark place. The beets were ready to be canned. The potatoes needed to be dug and stored. The tomatoes were just about to reach their peak. I hoped my in-laws had a lot of good stuff in their garden to cook. I guess I married into a garden, too.

There were adequate breezes in every shade. We visited the grave of little petite Jean, a young French girl who, as legend has it, fell from a certain cliff to her death.

We hiked some fantastic, secluded trails, and encountered many splashing, refreshing waterfalls. I'm sure when he suggested this place, he was thinking of how it would fascinate me. Most of my life had been confined to farms in Nevada County, with one trip to Magnolia and Malvern, a couple of trips to Nashville, Arkansas, and I must not forget when Mr. Hignight took us to Hot Springs.

It was a full day of sheer enjoyment for us, and we didn't think of food until late afternoon. That's when we decided to drive on back down the mountain, instead of spending the night up there. For once, it was our decision. We could change our plans any time, and we were the only ones affected.

Driving back through Little Rock, we saw some billboards advertising Tommy Trent's Hillbilly Park. We both liked the same music. He found the park and also a nice cafe and motel, so we ate and registered. I carried my paper sack luggage in, and his fancy bag. We had time for a relaxing nap before we went to the show.

This show featured Lonzo and Oscar most weekends, plus special guests each time. The music was extraordinary, and the comedian kept us laughing throughout the show. Even after that night, whenever we would think about his antics, we'd start cackling. We were so thrilled that we had found that place!

I had so much to tell Mary, but it would just have to wait.

I didn't awaken early on Sunday morning, but when I did open my eyes, I was glad I was where I was—with my love, my lifetime partner.

We wouldn't make it to Bethel today. It would be a nice, restful morning in an air-conditioned room. As I've said before, there is a first time for everything, and we were making the most of it.

There was no work to be done in all those places we visited. I enjoyed more leisure time that I could recall. I don't remember ever being able to just lie back down and take a nap.

When check-out time arrived, all I had to do was tote our luggage back to the car and ride. We went to a quick-food place and got a really good cheeseburger and Dr. Pepper. It was hard to believe I was a lady of leisure in Little Rock on a Sunday morning.

John L drove fifty mph or less, down 67 South, as we talked and made plans for our immediate future. We had already made plans with his parents to stay with them a couple of weeks, then maybe move into his uncle's house, a short distance up the road from them. It was vacated when Uncle Hop moved his family to California. We would be willing to accept any household items that anybody wanted to give us.

When we finally crossed the Little Missouri River, I realized it was the same river my family played in nearly every Sunday, and the same one I was baptized in.

Then we reached Haynes' Orchards and Five-Way Market, where I had walked to school at Boughton. Sweet, wet memories rolled down my cheeks. I wanted to go see Mama and Daddy first, and so we did.

Daddy and Roy hugged me on the porch. When I went to Mama's bed, she held up her arms and hugged me and cried, which made me cry. Mary just smiled and straightened Mama's bed sheets. She had packed a few more of my things she had found. Now, she had the room to herself.

Daddy had some garden stuff boxed up for me, just in case I needed it. He told me it was my garden, too, since I had put in so much work on it. He told me to get vegetables any time I wanted something, if John L's parents didn't have it.

It was too late to go to church that night, but we didn't let it become a habit to miss. We faithfully attended every service, continuing to go to my church. When I told John L it felt spiritual there for me, he agreed that he felt good there, too.

His parents had hugs for us, too, when we got to their house. They welcomed me and tried to make me feel at home. Mrs. McWilliams had food for a feast, ready to be warmed for our supper. I ate way too much. She had many questions about our trip, but we were both a bit embarrassed to talk about anything, except the beautiful mountain scenery, and the cool rooms we enjoyed.

I think John L felt strange taking me to his tiny room to sleep. He only had a twin bed, which turned out to be plenty spacious for us. There was a tiny fan, too. After two lazy days and three awesome nights, it was back to Ozan Lumber for him, and a long, nervous day for me.

51

I was accustomed to working steadily every day, to try to stay caught up with my jobs. There was no garden produce to work up at this time, and the McWilliams house was already spotless, so all I had to do was make up our little bed. John L had gone to work in our car, and his dad, Leon, went to work on an Ozan Lumber forestry truck with several other men.

My mother-in-law persuaded me to see if I could drive their old, black truck. My only driving lessons had been with John L driving and me steering. I got the truck started and backed it around before she got in it. We went half a mile up the gravel road and visited her sister, Mamie, who lived in her parents' house since they passed. There were many antiques and interesting, large pictures on the walls. It helped to pass the day away, but I was anxious for my husband to come home from work.

When he got home, he told me to grab a towel and put my bathing suit on. We went to Wilson Wash Hole on upper Cold Run Creek. He kept a bar of soap in the car. He had been used to going there for a bath and a swim late in the evenings. His parents, like mine, lacked running water in the house. They had a tin bathtub in a little building near the back door, where they stored potatoes. We had to stay half-bent in there, since the ceiling wasn't high enough to stand up in it. I loved the creek bath, but it was definitely, seasonal.

I was surprised when wash day arrived. Mrs. McWilliams had an electric, wringer washer. She still heated the water by building a fire under the big, black pot, to pour into the washer. The agitator in the washer took the place of a rub board. Then, they were run between the two rollers to wring them. The rinsing in a tub I knew well and hanging on clotheslines was the norm for me. We were finished in much less time than I was used to. Spare time came in abundance.

Mrs. McWilliams had never learned to drive, so I offered to teach her. She said she would rather let me do her driving. She was glad to be able to visit her circle of brothers and sisters without having to walk every time. We visited at least one of them every day. We also went to the empty house that John L and I were going to make our love nest in. I would soon have it ready to move in.

We stopped to see my folks on our way to Bethel, and I offered to stay with Mama so Mary and Roy could go. Mary asked if I could stay one night on the weekend instead of tonight, so she could have a date with Junior, so I agreed. From then on, I helped out whenever I was needed. That eased the guilty feeling I had for leaving Mary with so much to do.

I got the feeling that Mary and Junior knew that they, too, had found their lifetime partners. I was surely hoping they could live with Mama and Daddy. I prayed for them and trusted that God could work out the toughest problems.

❧❦

The first time I used my new name and address was the return address on letters to Bob and Clyde. They must've snickered a little when they read "Mrs. John L McWilliams, Route 4, Prescott, Arkansas". I was super-proud to bear that name then, and I still am to this day.

Bob had warned us he wouldn't be able to get any mail to us for several weeks while in Germany, but I kept on writing him. He got a stack of mail when they finally delivered it.

I asked Clyde to just write Mama, and I would keep up by reading her letters. He had moved to Missouri and was a very busy pastor now. I prayed for him regularly. I had read a medical column in the *Picayune* that said the job of being a Baptist pastor ranked higher than most other jobs for causing heart attacks. He told me he was described as 'obese' on his life insurance evaluation, but still got the policy.

I gave Bob the offer to just write letters to Mama, if he was tired of writing so many, but he said he could write stuff to me he didn't want to worry her with. I was intrigued with opening every one of those air-mail red, white and blue-trimmed envelopes.

John L dropped me off at Mama and Daddy's house on his way to work early one morning, so I could help Mary with the major green bean processing day of the year. That meant picking, snapping, washing and canning.

217

Daddy had told Mary she needn't can so much this year, since the family was smaller, but we had been raised to not let good food go to waste. There were fifty-one quarts that day.

We removed the last cooker full of green beans from the coal-oil stove to allow the pressure to go down, so we could take the jars out. I stepped out the back door to pour the rinse water in the hog trough, and heard a woman screaming. I could see across the pasture, which was thickly grown up in sedge grass almost waist high. Billows of smoke and flames were coming our way pretty fast.

Mama was asleep. It would be too difficult to try to evacuate her, so we just took off running through our garden, heisted ourselves over a netting fence and immediately had to get through a barb-wire fence. We each broke a big, green pine limb off a tree to fight off the fire. The fire started gaining ground on us.

The neighbor who let the fire get out of control was burning trash in her back yard. She just stood there, screaming and flinging her arms. We decided to go around and get behind the fire, where it wasn't as dangerous for us. Mary ran to another neighbor's house, where there was a telephone. She asked Mrs. Trevillion to call the mill and have them send Daddy and Roy home.

She was back in a minute, grabbing her weapon and yelling to me, "We are NOT gonna let this fire burn our house down with our Mama in it!"

"Please, dear God," I prayed, "hear our prayers and help us get this fire put out now!"

We both picked up speed wielding our branches against the fire. We couldn't speak above the crackling sedge, but I was still uttering praises to God every time I saw the flames diminish. We could see more and more blackened ground, and less and less roaring flames.

That beautiful old Daniel Ford truck came rolling through the pasture with Daddy and Roy bouncing to the roof, as they hit the terraces. They jumped out and broke new limbs and fought with us to our garden fence, where we finally beat down the last flames.

Mama was awake and grunting with chest pain when we got inside. I washed up first, then gave her a shot and a hug. I silently said a prayer of thanks for her and the house. God was, and is, good!

I told Mama how many jars of beans we canned. She never knew how close the fire burned.

Mrs. McWilliams had asked us to bring Mama to visit when she found out some of us were going to celebrate the Fourth of July at the river, below Nubbin Hill.

Milton got Mama into the front seat of his new car, right beside him, and propped her up with pillows. She rode well for the two miles. It took three of us to get her into the house. She got nervous about whether she would get her shot on time, so Clyde stayed with her. He was only home for two days.

The whole family floated a good distance down the river on inner tubes, with only two blowouts. Then, we walked back upstream beside the river to where we left our food. Mary and I both pranced around in new bathing suits, and our skin was blistered by nighttime. We hadn't been introduced to sunscreen.

None of us got an ear infection or swimmer's ear, though. Daddy had taught us to lean sideways and hold a hot rock to our ear to draw the river water out of our ears.

❧❧

John L and I had bought some new furniture at Prescott Hardware. They were happy to allow us to buy it on credit when they learned who our parents were. I was so proud to come from a good, honest family, and also to marry into one.

We bought a beautiful, red brocade living room suite, consisting of a sofa bed, rocking chair, and club chair. We also purchased a stained walnut coffee table with a glass top, which became my prized possession. Next, was a three-piece blonde, oak bedroom suite with a vanity dresser and stool.

Our kitchen had pretty, ivory-colored, built-in cabinets, with doors trimmed in green. We got a brand-new butane Hardwick range and a new Philco refrigerator for ninety-nine dollars each. I think we chose wisely, and our clerk, Mrs. Vuel Chamberlain, accommodated us every way she could.

John L's parents gave us a homemade eatin' table. They bought six strong, oak chairs, that have been in use over sixty years.

We did accept two more wedding showers. John L's cousin, Ruby Collins gave one, and a distant relative, Alene Cornelius honored us with another. I had more household utensils than I had ever seen, for which I was humbly grateful.

Unfortunately, the water well was dry at our new place. Mr. McWilliams hired an elderly man to dig a well for us. He had done this for years. He dug by hand about twenty feet deep and struck a water vein that produced enough water for us for a short while, then dried up again.

We had no running water in the house, so we didn't use much. I carried a gallon jug of water under each arm from his parents' well every day. I liked to spend the day with Mrs. McWilliams often. Our bathroom was a stall in the old barn that still stood near our back yard. We called ourselves the "squatters".

I enjoyed shopping with the same peddler we had before our marriage. He knew to bring plenty of boxes of Kraft Macaroni and Cheese dinners for me. We had just discovered it and liked it so well I cooked it almost every night for supper.

The taste of our food changed, dramatically, when I started cooking with butane gas. I didn't miss the odor and taste of coal oil. The gas tank was outside with pipes to the stove.

I bought a piece of cloth, thinking Daddy would let me have the sewing machine, since I was the only one who used it. I asked him next time I went there, and he sold it to me for thirty-five dollars. It was a blessing in disguise. I have pretty much always had thin ankles, and I attributed that to peddling that old, treadle-powered Singer. I used it until my only daughter was about three, then traded it for an ultra-modern Pfaff electric, that sewed like a dream. I learned to appreciate my own sewing room in later years. It was equipped with the newest sewing appliances in a private setting with a perfect view.

We frequently had visitors in our humble abode. Our pastor from Bethel, Sam Cathy, who was one of those who tried to talk me out of being a child bride, came almost every Sunday to have dinner with us. He seemed to be glad we married now. Roy came often, to tell me how pretty my house was. He would look at everything I had, and brag on it.

Our young, twin friends, Pat and Patsy Parks, who lived a couple of miles through the woods, would often come to visit. They were Bethel girls, and a lot of fun.

I helped my in-laws with their garden and got all the vegetables I needed. Mrs. McWilliams taught me some new ways to cook them. She was very patient in teaching me many things, not only in the kitchen, but with needlework. I wanted to be a good wife for her only son. He seemed to be pleased and told me often how happy he was that we were married.

I hadn't thought about how I would feel when everybody except me started back to school. I heard a familiar-sounding vehicle approaching my house, and just as quickly, it passed on by. I ran to the window and got a glimpse of the yellow bus, my bus, going right on up the road. I sat on my beautiful, red couch and cried, because I wasn't finishing what I started.

I dried my tears, and I thanked God for all the ways I was blessed, vowing I wouldn't cry for that reason any more. I opened the lid of my very own sewing machine, and sewed the first seam of my new, red dress. My sewing now took place in our spare bedroom. It was to have space to leave everything when I got tired.

Mary and Junior Adams had reached an agreement to be married, they just didn't know how soon. I believe they were counting on having more financial stability. They had known each other for a long time—since our families were Delaughter sharecroppers. We were excited when he gave her a ring. They weren't planning on a big wedding. Mary said it would be similar to ours.

Roy was taking his girl to the show on weekends, and that was the extent of his courting. They let me know ahead of time when I needed to be on duty with Mama. I looked forward to my visits with her, and John L didn't seem mind.

Around that time, I got some sad news from Bob. He had received a "Dear John" letter from his girl. Floy was to marry someone else. There was a popular song on the radio at that time called *Dear John*. Appropriately, it was about lost love and a badly hurt soldier.

He asked me not to worry our poor Mama about it, so I didn't tell her. I did tell all the other family members. It wasn't easy to see the girl, or worship with her and her family, but we managed. For a long time, we acted like we didn't know. It was slow coming, but forgiveness arrived for me, at least. Bob's letters were so sad. I tried to write comforting letters often, but it was hard to come up with funny musings.

❦

Daddy didn't want a big celebration for Christmas. He bought his usual stash of candies and fruit so the little kids wouldn't be disappointed. We decorated a small pine for Mama. She liked the fragrance of a fresh tree. She chose the decorations as I placed them on the tree, as well as at other vantage points in the front room. I loved our old ways of Christmas with the focus on Jesus Christ.

I bought Mama a small, living poinsettia. As I set it on her bedside table, I told her that was the closest I had ever been to one of those. I asked if she knew why the poinsettia had become so much a part of Christmas. She guessed that it was because of its brilliant, red beauty. She admired it, repeatedly running her fingers along its soft leaves. I later bought a single plastic poinsettia blossom for my new coffee table, so I could be reminded every Christmas of my mama and her poinsettias.

All of us were home for Christmas Eve, except Bob. I placed an 8 x 10 of him in uniform under the tree and prayed for him to feel peace instead of loneliness.

The grandchildren's joy was contagious. It allowed us to eat plenty and laugh heartily. We didn't know then, that this gathering of family at Christmas would never be the same again, but we did know that we would celebrate the birth of our Savior at Christmas time.

The Pleasant Hill place, 1956.

52

My new refrigerator was giving me an offensive odor every time I opened the door. I removed every item that could possibly smell bad, but the stench was still there. John L couldn't smell anything. The next complaint I had was stinking grease when I cooked his fried eggs for breakfast. The scent stayed in my kitchen all day.

Then the final straw. I woke up nauseous three mornings in a row. John L persuaded me to go to see Dr. Hairston at his office. He took the day off from work to go with me.

The doctor was surprised to know I was married, and we were both surprised when he told me I was expecting a baby in about seven months.

I told John L when we got back in the car. His face turned white as snow, as he tried to think of what to say. He replied with a big smile that showed his gold-filled tooth.

Back then, there was very little known about postponing the births of children until a more convenient time. Most women expected to be expecting shortly after marriage, or whenever it was God's timing.

We were elated and kept the news to ourselves for a week or so. When we revealed it to our parents, they were all overjoyed. Mama patted the other pillow on her bed and told me it could lay right there. I was more careful with what I ate, and the nausea subsided.

✍✍

We had planned to go to Victoria, Texas with John L's Uncle John, who drove the Coke truck that used to disrupt my Algebra class. The plan was to visit his daughter, Jo. I hadn't been to Texas before and wasn't too thrilled about going.

The day before we were to leave, I went down to the McWilliams' to do our weekly ironing, because I wasn't equipped to do that at our house. When I was almost done with the ironing, a cramp hit my lower abdomen. I made several trips to the outhouse, before I realized something bad was going on. The cramps got more painful and more frequent. When I told Mrs. McWilliams what was going on, she made me lie down.

By then, it was time for John L to come home. His mother met him at the door and told him to go up to the tower and call the doctor. The doctor arrived quickly and diagnosed a miscarriage.

He ordered an ambulance and hospital admission. I cried with the severe pain until I was given an injection. The physical pain left, but my heart felt like it would break. I had lost a part of us.

I was glad when Mrs. Era came to visit me and told me that my little child was safe in God's arms and would greet me when I get to Heaven. I have greatly anticipated that moment!

After five days in the hospital I was home. Mrs. McWilliams had received a letter from my mother who was anxious to hear exactly what my problem was, and if I would be alright. She admitted that she would have to rely on Mrs. McWilliams to take care of me, and that she was turning me over to her, because she knew Mrs. Mac would be a good mother.

⤞⤝

I wore my new dress to church for Mother's Day, along with the white pumps Daddy bought for my wedding. Hats and gloves were very stylish then, so of course, I had bought some. When we stopped by to see my parents on our way, Daddy told me I would probably be the prettiest girl in church that day. I was shocked and over-the-top pleased. Compliments from Daddy were rare. I have remembered that one since 1954.

We ate dinner with them, and we all rested afterward. When Mama woke, she asked if John L and I could take her for a ride. Everybody was stunned at her request. Most days now, she refused to get out of bed.

I dressed her in the navy dress I made for her to wear at my wedding, and rebraided her hair. I couldn't get shoes on her, because her feet were so swollen and discolored. Her respirations were labored as we got her into the car. I motioned for Daddy to come along. I visited with Mama in the back seat and made her smile some after she was breathing better.

John L asked where she wanted to go. She mentioned Sweet Home Cemetery. She had two children buried there at different times, when each was two years old. Mama couldn't walk the distance to their graves, so we walked out there and pointed to them. She was satisfied, and on the way back, talked about Lois and Charles more than I had heard before.

When we got back, Mama barely had enough breath to speak, but she managed to thank John L for the ride. I positioned her faithful fan to blow on her, while Mary gave her a shot and a cool cloth for her head. She, gradually, breathed easier. None of us ever imagined that was our last Mother's Day with the one we celebrated.

I helped my in-laws dig potatoes early the next morning, and then helped Daddy dig his after work that same day. It was difficult to see he had suffered heart damage, the way he worked. He had intended to sell Ol' Dan but was glad he hadn't, after watching him perform on the potato job. Good Ol' Dan!

Laundry was necessary, even when the garden was demanding our time. We preserved food any way we could and provided fresh veggies to neighbors who weren't as blessed. Eventually, we bought a deep freezer which brought about a whole revolution in our food preservation.

I had a much smaller pile of laundry now, but John L only had a week's supply of overalls for work, so I had to wash on time. We did his parents' laundry and ours together.

I was ironing on Thursday, when I heard a vehicle stop out front. It was Roy running up to the door crying.

"Mama died!"

I unplugged the iron and ran to the truck with him, thinking if we could get there in a hurry, maybe somehow, she wouldn't really be dead. That didn't happen. The doctor was there, but he was too late.

Mary said Mama had started frothing at the mouth and smothering. She worked with her a minute, then she quit breathing. Mary had run to the neighbors and called the doctor and the mill.

She said it seemed like an hour, then the doc arrived followed by the old truck. Dr. Hairston immediately told them that Mama was gone. He repeated it when I came in.

Was his word so final? Can't doctors do something to keep people from dying? She wasn't old enough to leave all of us kids behind. What about Daddy? I fell to my knees beside her bed, and asked God, "Why?"

I felt a hand on my shoulder, and heard the doctor say he was sorry I had to face this, after all I had just been through with losing the baby.

He told me I could have plenty of children, yet. I wanted to tell him I couldn't get another mother, but I just kept on sobbing.

When I saw tears running down the cheeks of my daddy, I dried my eyes and went to him. I wanted to help him be strong, and to get through losing the love of his life.

Dr. Hairston asked for Bob's address overseas. I found a letter and tore off the address. He told us he knew the Red Cross advocate who was responsible for getting boys home in a case like ours. We were informed the next day when that person came to our house, that she had learned it wasn't possible to get him home.

She told us that because Bob wasn't the oldest child, nor the only son, the army said there were others who could manage the funeral. I thought, "Cruel army regulations!"

We made a list of phone numbers of relatives we needed to notify. John L drove Mary and me to a phone booth in town with a pocket full of change. It was so hard to tell our brothers the news on the phone. When I called Aunt Georgia, she broke down on the phone. I know it was hard for her to tell Granny that her firstborn child was gone. She said she would let the rest of the sisters and brothers know.

I called Daddy's sister, Aunt Ellen, and she was there soon with Agnes, who could always cheer him up. Mrs. Era was my next call. I cried as soon as she answered, then just blurted out, "Mama died!" She told me she would be right there.

Mary said she hadn't cooked all day. On our way home, we tried to figure what to throw together for a meal. There was plenty of food there, and we no longer had to wait for a woodstove to heat up. We would just look in the fruit shelves and pick something.

We didn't expect what we found at the house. The yard was filled with cars and people. They offered sympathy as we made our way inside. So many of them had brought food. The tables in the kitchen were loaded with food already prepared for a meal. Mama had been taken to Cornish Mortuary in Prescott.

I couldn't imagine how word got around so fast. Most of the people here had no phones. I surely didn't know our family had so many friends. I told Daddy the boys would soon be on their way home, and that Clyde had asked if we could hold the funeral till Sunday. He wanted some of his friends to come and sing.

The next day when Clyde got there, he took Daddy and the other boys to the mortuary to plan the funeral. Mary and I continued to manage everything at home. Bonnie helped us clean the whole house. We didn't need to cook, and I was so glad the food would keep well in the new refrigerator.

John L stayed by my side. Neither of us had completely healed from our recent loss, but it was comforting just to hold hands. I had lost twenty pounds during my ordeal. My skirt was so loose I had to hold it up at the waist. I wondered if John L's boss was okay with his missing work.

The grandkids wanted to see their granny. I sent them to Uncle Clyde for an explanation. Consoling them was quite difficult. They were convinced that if they hadn't moved off, Granny would still be living.

Junior came to see Mary as soon as he heard about our loss. He was worried because she was alone with Mama when she passed. She perked up quickly after she talked with him.

My thoughts kept going to Bob, being so far away. The Red Cross advocate told us that he received the message. There was no one to console him, but the real Comforter, the Holy Spirit. I prayed for that.

On Saturday, the mortuary staff brought Mama back home, as Daddy had requested. That was very common in those days. She looked so restful in a pink chiffon gown, with a jeweled brooch. The inside of the casket was ruffled, with white satin and silk lace. Her lips and fingers weren't blue anymore. Her skin looked pinkish. I asked if she needed her fan on, and they assured me she didn't.

Mama's casket was placed on a stand in the same corner where her bed had always been, and there she would lie until time for the funeral on Sunday.

Before long, the flower shop van came, and many pretty flower arrangements were brought inside to be placed around my sweet mama. Even more came later.

Some cousins and friends sat with different family members that night, as was customary. There was no official visitation time. We made plenty of coffee to stay awake. This was our last night to be near our precious mama.

Clyde's long-time friends, Don and Polly Cooper got there Sunday morning. Not many of us chose to eat before the two o'clock service. It was at Sweet Home Church. Brother Don Cooper officiated, and his wife, Polly, sang the most touching rendition of *Sunrise Tomorrow*. Clyde did the eulogy for a crowd of folks.

I visited, briefly, with Granny Bradford and most of Mama's siblings after the funeral. We invited Granny to come and spend some time at our house. She told me she liked my husband, but she didn't want to move any more. I was glad my in-laws were there, too. They were pleased to meet my granny and some of my aunts, uncles, and cousins. I was proud to introduce my husband and his parents to all of them, as well.

Mama was laid to rest beside her two, little children who made it to Jesus before she did. She's been waiting for all her family members to come there, and as I write about this, I believe they are all there, except me. I am the only one from my family still living, but, "I'm coming, y'all!"

53

I think Mama and Jesus had already had a talk before she asked to go to Sweet Home Cemetery on Mother's Day. It was annual homecoming day there on that day. I believe she felt *her* homecoming was near.

On our ride that day Mama had told me, privately, in the back seat, that she knew how bad it hurt to lose a child. She said when her little ones passed away, it helped reduce the sadness, both times, when she found out she was having another baby.

With tears brimming for both of us, she said she hoped I would have more children soon. I patted her out-stretched hand, and told her that was our hope, too. She said she believed John L would be a good daddy, and she knew I would take extra good care of my children. Her words meant the world to me!

Just about six months later, Dr. Hairston told us it looked like we were trying again. He said we could expect this one to be a May baby. We were almost afraid to tell anyone. I suffered nausea more than before, and it lasted until after Christmas. I missed church so much, most of them guessed why I was sick.

❧❧

Mary and Junior were married in December and lived with his folks in Laneburg. It was as simple as a wedding could get, at the preacher's house with his wife as a witness. Either they were both too shy to want guests at their wedding, or they thought everybody would be busy shopping—it was December 23, 1954.

In a month or two, they went north to Pennsylvania. Junior's sister, Adell East, and her husband, Clint, lived there and helped Junior get pipeline work. After they had been there several months, Mary came down with morning sickness. I missed her so bad—I knew how she felt!

Her letters to me were mostly about all the things that stunk in Pennsylvania. She couldn't even stand to smell the newspaper in the mornings. She wanted to come home, but it was too hard to save money, even though the wages were good.

John L and I had moved to a duplex apartment in town. When I kept being sick nearly all the time, we decided to make the move, closer to his work, so he could come home and check on me at lunch every day.

It worked out well. Ernest and Marie Lambert lived in the other side of the duplex. They had three children, and the whole family helped us so much. Marie taught me a lot about having babies.

I was lonely in town, though. On Saturdays, I sat by my bedroom window and watched as Daddy and Roy passed right by my apartment in Daddy's car. He had sold the truck, and bought a shiny, black Plymouth. It was used, but new to him. He still wouldn't try to drive.

I wanted them to stop and visit me, but they chose to visit Daddy's woman friend, Zelda. He saw her every Saturday and married her ten months after Mama died. They came to see her sister, Ether, every week, but not me.

John L worked every day but Sundays at the mill, and because he was a member of the National Guard, he had to go to drill two weekends a month. In addition to that, he had to satisfy them with two solid weeks of camp away from home in the summers.

I tried to like Daddy's new wife, but it wasn't easy. The first time I went to his house was a month or so after they got married. I hadn't met her, and we weren't invited to their wedding. Roy was the only one who was, since he was the driver.

I was shocked when I saw Zelda. She had the same build as Mama and was her size. When I arrived at the house, she was swinging in the porch swing, wearing the navy, puckered nylon dress I had made my mother for my wedding. She also had on Mama's new house shoes she never got to wear.

My first thought was to back my car up into the road, and take off, but I didn't. I had brought pictures that were taken at the funeral to show Daddy, but I left them in the car and went on in.

I learned that she was a sweet Christian woman, who was good to my daddy and to me. In spite of my determination not to accept her, I learned to love her. She made the best applesauce cakes, nearly every Saturday. We liked to go by on Sunday and have a slice.

54

John L and I made an early trip to Cora Donnell Hospital on Wednesday, and our Johnny boy was born twenty-four hours later, on Thursday, May 12, 1955. Our firstborn child was a son, John Daniel McWilliams. At eight pounds, twelve ounces, with a lot of black hair, everybody agreed he was beautiful. I couldn't argue with them! He squeezed my finger with love that day, and we both feel that love to this day.

I was a seventeen-year-old mama, who was eager to learn all I could about early childhood development. Johnny and I had a nice two-block stroller ride to the library, weekly. He was born liking books, and now, has written some.

When Johnny was three months old, in August 1955, I decided to move my church membership to my husband's church. John L had attended Missionary Grove Baptist Church, near his home in the Nubbin Hill community, all his life. He was saved and baptized in August 1947, in the same river I was baptized in the same month, and maybe, even the same day. He was downstream from me.

I was hesitant to leave my beloved Bethel, but I now know it was a wise move. My intent was to keep serving the Lord, and there was plenty of room for me to do that there. I'm very thankful for my experiences at Bethel and Missionary Grove.

Mary and Junior were back in Arkansas for their first anniversary. His leg was in a cast from a work accident. I remember asking her if she broke it just to get back home.

When Mary's time for delivery got close, they stayed with us in town. She loved holding Johnny, and that allowed me to get caught up with some jobs that had been neglected. It was wonderful to have my sister close again.

What a cold morning it was when she announced she was ready to go! Their windshield was frosted over so badly, Junior had to open his car door and stick his head out to see how to drive to Cora Donnell. Thomas Wesley Adams was eager to see us. Mary had a short labor. He was a precious big boy, too. Of course, there were no indications of the gender of our babies until we laid our eyes on them. Whenever we gave a shower gift for an expectant mother, it was often in white, pastel green or yellow, which suited girl or boy.

In fourteen months, Mary had James Franklin Adams, then in fourteen more months, twin girls, Marilyn and Carolyn. Mary and Junior had four in diapers and bottles! Then later came Paul Glen. She named him after the doctor, just because someone told her that would stop her from having any more. It was just a myth because little Connie Janine came later. She was the one who couldn't wait to get to the hospital to be born. Junior gave Mary roses and promised that was the last one, and it was.

We finally got a television and enjoyed staying at home with our little boy. We watched a good show every evening about a family with a teenage daughter. It was called *My Little Margie*. She was an adorable little blue-eyed blonde. If we could be blessed with a baby girl, we decided her name would be Margie.

Margie Faye McWilliams was born after only twelve hours of labor, not long before the old Cora Donnell was closed. She tried to come by way of breech and was manually turned in utero at a crucial moment. This was on Wednesday, December 4, 1957. She tipped the scales at nine pounds, two ounces, and she had plenty of dark hair, but when she rubbed it all off in her bassinet, it came back blonde, like her daddy.

Margie's first pretty smile lit up her eyes. She was jaundiced off and on for several weeks. The doctor suggested that I treat that through my diet, and it worked.

I loved playing with her long, blonde hair, and gave her a Tonette perm for little girls at eighteen months of age. Her hair was in rollers every Saturday, as long as I could hold her down. She became a beautiful adult, inside and out.

We wondered if we would have more children for years. When Margie was nine, we were surprised to find out that my gastro complaints would go away after a while. I discovered I would bear another child. When Johnny was twelve and Margie ten, the Lord sent Gary Damon McWilliams, thus named by his brother. He was ten pounds, two ounces, and was born fifteen days late on Wednesday, January 17, 1968. His size was quite noticeable when he was placed beside a five-pound girl in the nursery. He was a gift for our whole family.

His siblings love him as much as humanly possible. They spent their allowances on presents for him for two or three years, and he loved them still, even after they stopped. Much happiness comes from knowing that all three of our children, their spouses, and their children, are faithfully serving God. Our sons are ministers, and our daughter is a church pianist.

I am looking forward to spending eternity in Heaven with (at this point) our four children, eleven grandchildren, thirteen great grandchildren, and my Sugar-Daddy, John L.

❧❧

Helping our children get an education was highly important to us. We didn't just fork over the whole amount for college. They all worked real jobs and showed independence, while obtaining their degrees. Their daddy and I worked hard through those years, also.

I wrote these memoirs because my adult children wanted to know all about life when they were just a sparkle in their daddy's eye. I taught them early on, that happiness is not about getting all you want, it's about enjoying all you have. I love my life and my family, and if I could do life over again, I would want it to be exactly the same.

My dream of being a nurse finally did come true, after receiving my GED diploma on our twentieth anniversary. I decided to do something big for our thirtieth. That's when I became a nurse!

God is so good, and His mercy is everlasting. I know one book can't contain all that has happened since my children were born. Actually, that's when my life really started! Praise the Lord! To God be the glory!

Epilogue

Clyde was found deceased in his car beside the road on October 22, 1960, from an apparent heart attack at thirty years old. He was near Charleston, Missouri, where he pastored a church.

Daddy died in the old kitchen on November 6, 1965. He had just returned from his morning trip to the old outhouse which he refused to give up for indoor plumbing. This was his third heart attack.

Granny Bradford passed away in 1955, in a hospital in Malvern where she lived with Aunt Georgia and her family. She was in her mid-eighties.

Bob died in a nursing home in Bedford, Indiana, where he had lived and worked for years. After several heart surgeries and a lengthy bout with diabetes, he succumbed on March 31, 2008.

Milton and Bonnie divorced when their youngest child, Ruth Ann, was about eight. He remarried shortly after to a sweet woman, Mary Joyce, who had a two-year-old daughter, Phyllis Joy. She was a good mother to his children, and he loved his new daughter as his own. Mary Joyce enjoyed their life together until her sudden death in 2002.

Lonely and brokenhearted, Milton reunited with Bonnie after forty-six years apart. She developed Alzheimer's and they lived together in Hillcrest Nursing Home. Milton passed away suddenly with heart failure in while walking to the dining room for supper.

Mary married Junior Adams. They raised six kids together. The youngest one, Connie was born in a pickup truck on the way to Nevada County Hospital from Bodcaw, some 25 miles away. At the age of 58 Junior had a stroke, and Mary took care of him at home for fourteen years until he passed away there. He and his faithful dog died on the same day. Mary was burying the dog in their back yard when Junior suddenly took worse and died.

My dear sister Mary left this life on December 28, 2013 in Hillcrest with her six faithful and loving children close by. She had suffered horribly the last few days with pancreatic cancer. Mary had worked at Hillcrest many years prior, doing what she did best—caring for others.

Roy married late in life, after Mama died, to a very sweet, soft-spoken lady who was about eight years his senior. Edna Zavanna Loe resembled our mama so much it was unbelievable. My brother Roy, who was born a preemie, survived ninety-two years! His weak heart gave up on May 15, 2017 at Hillcrest. Roy was never bed-fast and loved entertaining the residents with his funny antics.

Among those waiting for me with Jesus...

John Wesley Daniel, 1895-1965 (Father)
Priscilla Odessa Daniel, 1902-1954 (Mother)
Milton Daniel, 1922-2012 (Brother)
Roy Daniel, 1925-2017 (Brother)
Lois Marie Daniel, 1926-1928 (Sister)
Clyde Daniel, 1930-1960 (Brother)
Bob Daniel, 1932-2008 (Brother)
Mary Daniel, 1933-2013 (Sister)
Charles Lee Daniel, 1935-1937 (Brother)
Leon McWilliams, 1901-1971 (Father-in-Law)
Annie McWilliams, 1901-1985 (Mother-in-Law)
Sarah Ross Bradford, 1870-1955 (Grandmother)
Baby McWilliams, 1954

Made in the USA
Coppell, TX
03 December 2020

42977189R00142